THE MANUSCRIPT HUNTER

The American Exploration and Travel Series

CHARLES ÉTIENNE BRASSEUR DE BOURBOURG
Undated photograph by Nicolas Claude Persus, Bibliothèque nationale de France, département Société de Géographie, SG PORTRAIT-1278.

THE MANUSCRIPT HUNTER

Brasseur de Bourbourg's Travels through Central America and Mexico, 1854–1859

CHARLES ÉTIENNE BRASSEUR DE BOURBOURG

Translated and edited by
KATIA SAINSON

UNIVERSITY OF OKLAHOMA PRESS : NORMAN

Library of Congress Cataloging-in-Publication Data

Names: Brasseur de Bourbourg, abbé, 1814–1874 author. | Sainson, Katia, translator editor.
Title: THe manuscript hunter : Brasseur de Bourbourg's travels through Central America and Mexico, 1854–1859 / Charles Étienne Brasseur de Bourbourg ; translated and edited by Katia Sainson.
Description: Norman : University of Oklahoma Press, 2017. | Series: THe American exploration and travel series ; volume 84 | Includes bibliographical references and index.
Identifiers: LCCN 2016054033 | ISBN 978-0-8061-5502-9 (hardcover) ISBN 978-0-8061- 9416-5 (paper) Subjects: LCSH: Central America—Description and travel. |
  Mexico—Description and travel. | Brasseur de Bourbourg, abbé, 1814–1874—Travel—Central America. | Brasseur de Bourbourg, abbé, 1814–1874—Travel—Mexico.
Classification: LCC F1432 .B83 2017 | DDC 917.2804—dc23
LC record available at https://lccn.loc.gov/2016054033

The Manuscript Hunter: Brasseur de Bourbourg's Travels through Central America and Mexico, 1854–1859 is Volume 84 in The American Exploration and Travel Series.

The paper in this book meets the guidelines for permanence and durability of the Committee on Production Guidelines for Book Longevity of the Council on Library Resources, Inc. ∞

Copyright © 2017 by the University of Oklahoma Press, Norman, Publishing Division of the University. Paperback published 2024. Manufactured in the U.S.A.

All rights reserved. No part of this publication may be reproduced, stored in a retrieval system, or transmitted, in any form or by any means, electronic, mechanical, photocopying, recording, or otherwise—except as permitted under Section 107 or 108 of the United States Copyright Act—without the prior written permission of the University of Oklahoma Press. To request permis-sion to reproduce selections from this book, write to Permissions, University of Oklahoma Press, 2800 Venture Drive, Norman, OK 73069, or email rights.oupress@ou.edu.

He belonged to the old Leonardo da Vinci and Michael Angelo type—the Herculean mold.... No advance can be made in any branch of the study [of Maya inscriptions] but he supplied all the preliminary stepping-stones.

J. T. GOODMAN, "The Archaic Maya Inscriptions"

CONTENTS

List of Illustrations
ix

Acknowledgments
xi

Translator and Editor's Note
xiii

INTRODUCTION
3

NOTES FROM A VOYAGE IN CENTRAL AMERICA:
LETTERS TO ALFRED MAURY
29

FROM GUATEMALA CITY TO RABINAL:
AN EPISODE DURING MY STAY IN CENTRAL AMERICA
DURING THE YEARS 1855 AND 1856
51

VOYAGE ACROSS THE ISTHMUS OF TEHUANTEPEC
IN THE STATE OF CHIAPAS AND THE REPUBLIC
OF GUATEMALA IN 1859 AND 1860
109

Notes
239

*Selected Works by
Charles Étienne Brasseur de Bourbourg*
269

Bibliography
271

General Index
277

Geographical Index
281

ILLUSTRATIONS

FIGURE

Charles Étienne Brasseur de Bourbourg
frontispiece

MAPS

Brasseur's route through Nicaragua
30–31

Brasseur's route from Guatemala City to Rabinal
53

Brasseur's route across the Isthmus of Tehuantepec
111

ACKNOWLEDGMENTS

I would like to thank the family of Jorge Skinner Klee for their hospitality, which brought Brasseur and me together for the first time. Thanks to the staff of the Département des Manuscrits of the Bibliothèque nationale de France in Paris and especially Laurent Héricher, Conservateur en chef du service des manuscrits orientaux, for their help locating Brasseur's letters, manuscripts, and collections. My deepest gratitude to Allen J. Christenson, Associate Professor of Humanities, Classics, and Comparative Literature at Brigham Young University, for his generosity in providing comments on this manuscript. I am also grateful for the support of Terry Cooney, Dean of the College of Liberal Arts, and Lea Ramsdell, Chair of the Department of Foreign Languages, at Towson University. Thanks also to Paporn Thebpanya, Associate Professor in the Department of Geography and Environmental Planning at Towson University, for her quick, thorough, and artistic renderings of Brasseur's travels. Thanks to Edith Pirio at the Archives nationales de France for her help in acquiring documents and navigating the system and to Nadia Prévost Urkidi for so graciously sharing her unpublished thesis on Brasseur de Bourbourg and the French Américainistes. And finally, thanks to John Hessler, Curator of the Jay I. Kislak Collection of the Archeology and History of the Early Americas and Specialist in the Geography and Map Division of the Library of Congress, for his help with more than just the cartographic aspects of this project.

TRANSLATOR AND EDITOR'S NOTE

The reader will find two sets of notes throughout this book. Brasseur's original notes are found at the bottom of the page in the form of footnotes and are referenced with a "B" preceding the note number. In some cases, I have added my own comments in brackets to those notes. All other notes in the introduction and in the translated texts appear as endnotes at the back of this volume and are my own. All translations are my own unless otherwise credited. My approach regarding the spelling of place names varied, but my goal was to reflect the historical context in which the texts were written. In the translations, I have generally adopted the most widely used spelling of a place name in English-language sources from Brasseur's time. If there seemed to be no consensus based on maps or written sources that were contemporary to Brasseur's time, I kept his spelling and added a note indicating alternative spellings. In some cases in which modern spelling includes an accent mark that was not to be found in nineteenth-century sources, I have added the accents. Similarly, I have added accent marks that were not found in the original versions in the case of proper names of people and have in some cases changed Brasseur's spelling in the case of historical figures whose names I could verify. I have altered Brasseur's sometimes-French-inspired spelling of Spanish words that are found in the texts to reflect contemporary spelling. I have also adopted the contemporary spelling of nomenclature like K'iche' and Kaqchikel that Brasseur spelled Quiché and Cakchiquel. I have, however, kept Brasseur's spelling of Maya proper names. Finally, unless noted, the uses of italic type in the text are those of the author and not the translator; most often Brasseur used italic type to indicate his use of a foreign word.

THE MANUSCRIPT HUNTER

INTRODUCTION

When I came across the name Charles Étienne Brasseur de Bourbourg for the first time, it was a chance encounter. I was perusing the shelves of an extraordinary collection of books on Mesoamerica in the private library of Jorge Skinner Klee[1] in Guatemala City, where Brasseur's name kept appearing engraved on the spines of weighty tomes. Who was this Frenchman who wrote so extensively on the New World while all his compatriots with a taste for ancient civilizations seemed to be turned toward the east? The resounding responses to my first inquiries could not have been clearer. If twenty-first-century scholars of Mesoamerican studies know Brasseur, it is because his name is attached in some way with the discovery and dissemination of an astonishing number of the foundational texts in the field—texts such as *The Popol Vuh*, *The Annals of the Cakchiquels*, *Rabinal Achi*, *The Codex Chimalpopoca*, *The Codex Troana*, and his Rosetta Stone–like discovery of Diego de Landa's *Relación de la cosas de Yucatán*. By the end of his collecting life, this French priest had spent two decades traveling throughout Mexico, Central America, and Europe scouring libraries, archives, and monasteries to amass hundreds of manuscripts and printed books, including grammars and vocabularies that brought to light languages and cultures that were little known at the time. If scholars know anything else about Brasseur it is this—the father of modern Maya studies was a crackpot. Already at the time of his death, he was sneered at and ostracized because of his theories that suggested that Maya writings had double meanings that revealed, among other things, their civilization's association with the survivors of Atlantis. By the twentieth century, the contempt for the theoretical turn that Brasseur's work took in the final decade of his life had all but obliterated his contributions to the field. Even in the most sympathetic descriptions he was portrayed as a lax and "sloppy scholar,"[2] who by the time of his death in 1874 had gone "off the deep end."[3]

And yet, when I started reading Brasseur's travelogues I found a striking alternative to this distorted caricature. These were captivating works by a great manuscript hunter and protoethnologist. Written in the 1850s, these texts, which have never before been translated into English, can easily stand next to classics such as John Lloyd Stephens's *Incidents of Travel in Central America, Chiapas and Yucatan* and Anne and Alfred Maudslay's *A Glimpse at Guatemala*. Brasseur's exceedingly approachable and engaging works provide an unrivaled source on the birth of Mesoamerican studies in the nineteenth century. Unlike his predecessors or contemporaries—John Lloyd Stephens, Désiré Charnay, and Alfred Maudslay, who focused on the area's archaeological ruins—Brasseur was not looking for great stone monuments. Rather, he sought the more ephemeral remains of a pre-Columbian culture, whose traces could only be found on paper or in the spoken words of indigenous languages.

This great storyteller's narratives provide vivid geographical descriptions, as well as keen social and political analysis, steeped in his vast knowledge of the region's history as well as his abiding interest in indigenous culture. He was a witness to a period of great turmoil, when civil wars raged throughout Mexico and Central America and foreign interests sought every means to gain access to the area's rich resources and strategic territories. While almost all the other foreigners with whom he crossed paths pursued wealth and power, Brasseur's focus was on uncovering Mesoamerica's past, which had been veiled in mystery, by examining the Maya culture's fragile remnants in ancient manuscripts and living oral traditions.

Brasseur was born in 1814 in the town of Bourbourg, located twelve kilometers from Dunkirk. He recalled that as a young child in that town of northern France, one of his first tantalizing brushes with the New World was in the pages of the *Gazette de France*. The story described a newly discovered tomb in Brazil, purportedly containing vestiges of Macedonian origin with objects upon which Greek inscriptions could be made out. Thus, from the start he felt the pull of several questions that vexed the nineteenth century: what were the origins of the population living in the Americas, and what was the possibility of their having had preconquest contact with—depending on the source—the Phoenicians, Greeks, Egyptians, Chaldeans, Vikings, or Chinese?

In his twenties, after several years struggling to survive as a writer in Paris, Brasseur entered a seminary in Ghent. A young American who met Brasseur at the end of the Frenchman's life, quotes him as saying, "I am an abbé in the Church but my ecclesiastical duties have always rested very lightly upon me."[4] The Church, it seems, was less a calling than a passport, which allowed him to pursue his intellectual passions. As his biographer Pedro Escalante Arce has written, "Brasseur was a pastor of myths and legends, much more interested in probing the past than in preaching the Gospel."[5]

From the moment he left the seminary in the early 1840s, Brasseur's traveling life began. First there was Europe—Rome, Germany, and Sicily—and then in 1845 he set out on his first trip to the New World to take an appointment teaching in Canada, thereby allowing him to visit parts of Quebec and the northeastern United States.

By the time he returned to France in 1846, Brasseur had made his first contacts with North American clergy as well as collectors and antiquarians with interests in indigenous American culture and history. In Boston he came upon William Prescott's *History of the Conquest of Mexico*, a book that had come out three years earlier and persuaded him that his vocation was in the Americas. After less than two years back in Europe, mostly in Rome immersed in the Vatican Library, he left a continent in the throes of the revolutions of 1848, where Louis Napoleon—whose eyes, like Brasseur's, would be drawn toward Mexico—was rising to power.

At the age of thirty-four, having traveled from New York to Ohio and down the Mississippi, Brasseur left New Orleans by boat for Mexico. On board the steamer, bound for Veracruz, he made a chance acquaintance of enormous consequence with the new minister plenipotentiary of France to Mexico, André Nicolas Le Vasseur, a staunch republican eager to make his diplomatic mark in his new post.[6] The diplomat invited Brasseur to become the chaplain for the French Legation in Mexico City—an appointment that opened the doors to the libraries, archives, and monasteries where Brasseur spent his time seeking out unknown manuscripts and learning Nahuatl. After two years, he took an extensive trip from Mexico to San Francisco by way of the states of Querétaro, Guanajuato, Jalisco, and Sonora, and through the ports of Mazatlán and Acapulco, thanks to the support of the American businessman L. S. Hargous.[7]

By 1851, he was back in Europe having begun to amass his collection of rare books and manuscripts and having published his first work on Mesoamerica.[8] Thus began the preparations for his first trip to Central America.

Unlike so many of his contemporary antiquarians, Brasseur had neither a personal fortune nor a diplomatic appointment to help defray the costs of his predilection for travel and collecting. Financially strapped upon his return to France in 1851, Brasseur, who had been supplementing his income since the 1840s by publishing religious histories and novels aimed at a popular audience, interrupted his "serious studies in order to write lesser works which nevertheless provided a little bit of money to fill [his] purse."[9] However, churning out trite but extremely popular narratives, often set in the exotic Orient,[10] telling tales in which faith and morality are tested but always prevail, would not be enough. He was daunted by expenses for this trip and his limited resources compelled him to part with cherished pieces of his fledgling collection—a missionary's portable chapel and a Mayan vocabulary.[11]

Along with these "painful sacrifices"[12] Brasseur also solicited funds from the French government. In the end his petition was unsuccessful, however it generated a positive report by the great novelist and cultural preservationist, archaeologist, and one-time inspector of historic monuments of France, Prosper Mérimée, who declared the need to act immediately:

Since the discovery of the New World several American languages have completely disappeared along with the nations who spoke them. This situation, these challenges, must not discourage research. This is yet another reason to collect as carefully as possible the precious documents that otherwise might escape us.[13]

NOTES FROM A VOYAGE IN CENTRAL AMERICA: LETTERS TO ALFRED MAURY

In 1854, Brasseur left for Nicaragua, with the intention of traveling on to San Salvador and Guatemala. Although this trip did not receive funding from the French government, it serves as a milestone in the advancement of knowledge of ancient Mesoamerican cultures, as Brasseur tried to fulfill the mandate articulated by Mérimée to collect and preserve cultural remnants on the verge of extinction.

The earliest travelogue in this collection, "Notes from a Voyage in Central America: Letters to Alfred Maury," takes the form of two letters dated 1855 that describe the first leg of this trip as Brasseur traveled through Nicaragua. Having come from the United States, he landed in San Juan de Nicaragua (also known at the time as Greytown), via a route established by Cornelius Vanderbilt to convey passengers between the Atlantic and the Pacific coasts. This region was the site of speculation, the likes of which was equaled only by what Brasseur would see later when he crossed the Isthmus of Tehuantepec. Nicaragua in 1854 was a country devastated by civil war and earthquakes as well as attacks from American warships and the disruptive presence of William Walker and his supporters. Brasseur traveled down the wide San Juan River to Lake Nicaragua, making stops to explore the surrounding area. Despite the constant presence of raggedly dressed and unpredictable soldiers, who at one point took him into custody and then freed him, Brasseur managed to continue on to the capital, León, passing through the towns of Masaya, with its deep volcanic lake, and a much-damaged Managua.

Brasseur's "Notes from a Voyage," which focused mostly on oral traditions, sparked a dialogue with the American archaeologist, ethnologist, and collector, Ephraim George Squier, who had preceded Brasseur first as a chargé d'affaires to Central America and then in exploration related to constructing an interoceanic route in Nicaragua. During his stay, Squier took an interest in the region's deep past. In "Notes from a Voyage," Brasseur offered his earliest speculations on the origins of the region's indigenous languages, with the nascent signs of the theories that would later lead to his undoing—when he suggested that these languages may have Scandinavian origins.

Squier, who responded immediately and forcefully, bristled at Brasseur's tendency towards free-wheeling theorizing: "I have failed to discover a single fact . . . which would necessarily indicate an extra-American and least of all a Scandinavian origin for the aboriginal inhabitants of [Nicaragua]."[14] And yet Squier saw "many resemblances in some cases perhaps amounting to absolute identities that exist between the aboriginal families of America, and those of the continent which we are accustomed to distinguish as the 'Old World.'"[15]

FROM GUATEMALA CITY TO RABINAL

After Nicaragua and the state of San Salvador Brasseur made his way to Guatemala City, in another state ravaged by a civil war that threatened the region's cultural patrimony:

> My three months in the capital were spent visiting its monuments but also its libraries. These precious depositories, where clergymen from different orders collected treasures related to the history and philology of the indigenous people of this region, unfortunately no longer contain within their walls more than mere scraps of their past glory. The dire effects of the revolution are everywhere. . . . The country's archives and books . . . were piled into manure carts and brought to the University in complete disarray only to be tossed on the floor in a dark, humid room. There they stayed for ten years until their legitimate owners returned to the country. Meanwhile, anyone was free to pillage and

plunder.... When the current president Rafael Carrera came to power his first concern was to recall the clergy.... Their monasteries, libraries and documents were all returned to them—but in what condition! Most of the works from the libraries were returned with pages missing or riddled with wormholes. Sullied manuscripts were falling to pieces covered in a pungent dust."[16]

Brasseur spent three months, searching through these monasteries and libraries, and in 1855, with some of the most important manuscripts he had discovered tucked in his knapsack. Brasseur set out from Guatemala City to the town of Rabinal, where he had been entrusted with an ecclesiastical position and where he hoped to become conversant in the population's indigenous language. In "From Guatemala City to Rabinal," first published in French in 1859, he describes a journey, during which he rereads the historical geography of the country through the lens of his newly unearthed ancient texts, such as the *Popol Vuh*, transcribed in the seventeenth century by the Spanish priest, Francisco Ximénez, thereby reconnecting the landscape to its pre-Columbian past. As he rode along the Guatemalan mountain passes, Brasseur muses: "I never grow tired of these isolated places in which I spend my life as a traveler. They seem fully inhabited and I have never for one moment felt alone." He arrived in Rabinal, where Ximénez, himself had once been a parish priest. While there, the Frenchman played an instrumental role in bringing to light what Mérimée had called "those precious documents that otherwise might escape us." It was here that he encountered the dance-drama, or *baile*, which had been forbidden under Spanish rule. Known as *Rabinal Achi*, it is the only such work in the Mesoamerican corpus to survive from the preconquest era.

Shortly after arriving in Rabinal and recording his first baptism on May 18, 1855,[17] Brasseur sent a letter to his friend and collector José Mariano Padilla[18] in Guatemala City on May 23, 1855. At first he was a bit disappointed; the native inhabitants of Rabinal were good, gentle people but "almost all of them speak Spanish, and I haven't found anything interesting in their archives." A few weeks later he sent off another letter in which he discussed nearby ruins and requested that his friend send him seeds, in particular onion seeds for his garden, because of the difficulty in finding vegetables—apparently in this domain the Frenchman had come to the conclusion that Rabinal "is not Paris or Guatemala City." He also wrote something that unbeknownst to him would come back to haunt his reputation as a scholar long after his death:

> I have discovered another manuscript here in the possession of the uncle of one of my young servants; it is the text of the dialogue and story of the ancient Rabinal Achi, the heroes of Rabinal, and from the little I have been able to establish, it also refers to the same figures found in the Ximénez, Padilla, and other manuscripts [I have with me].[19]

He adds a line in French at the end, which expresses that thrill known to all collectors when they have stumbled upon a jewel: *C'est une bonne trouvaille.* "What a find!"

A few months later, in August of 1855, Brasseur sent out another letter, this time to E. G. Squier. No doubt because there were few who could appreciate the nature of his discoveries or perhaps to impress a rival collector, Brasseur's letter is full of details about his finds since arriving in Central America in 1854.[20]

> Nicaragua and Salvador had offered but little to my curiosity concerning antiquities [and] I was only able to obtain a few words belonging to their languages and four or five *airs* of their *bayles*.[21] I can say that I was as poor as when I left New York. I hoped very much that Guatemala would satisfy my curiosity and so it did in reality.... I have still been able to make the finest collection of Central American MS that exists in the world. Some originals were given to me as presents, some others copied for my sake, and some I copied and the remainder I bought. The archives of the cabildo still contain very valuable materials for the history of this country since the conquest and of the conquest itself; many original letters of Alvarado and companions and of Las Casas; there I have seen also the original manuscript of Bernal Dias del Castillo which differs in many things from the printed copies.

Introduction

Brasseur then mentions that he "had discovered" the "original manuscript of Ximénez," which includes the *Popol Vuh*, and that

> Dr. Carl Scherzer, a German gentleman who was here but a few months before me, had been able to look into the book. But in place of taking a copy he transcribed but a few passages quite useless in their way. After all Dr. S did not remain long enough in the country to find out what was to be found and learn the languages without which it is impossible to [derive][22] any advantage.[23]

Brasseur continues with the following list:

> I possess five or six dictionaries of [native] languages, also manuscripts more or less complete. Besides some other papers on Guatemala and Vera Paz I have come into possession of a MS history of Guatemala very good in Spanish with great details on the astronomy and religion of the people, of a MS history of San Salvador, another of Vera Paz, another of the Tzendal rebellion etc, etc.

At the end of this inventory, the abbé recounts the story at the center of his "From Guatemala City to Rabinal":

> Some six weeks ago I gave to one of [the Indians of Rabinal] a remedy that cured him of a pretty severe illness. From gratitude, he came afterwards to me and told me that he was a lineal descendant of some great family: that by the order of his fathers he had learned by memory the whole of one of their *bayles*. *Bayles* or dramatic dances in which he [was][24] one of the principal parts in the time they still danced and played. Knowing that I had vainly asked for that bayle from the other Indians, he proposed me [*sic*] write it under his dictation. I accepted in spite of the difficulty for it was to be said in the Quiche dialect of Rabinal. But *improbus labor omnia vincit*[25] after twelve days of the most arduous dictation I ever did, even when I was at school, I got the whole of the *bayle*. With the aid of my grammars and dictionaries I corrected the orthography, and now I can boast of possessing the only old original

11

American drama that exists in the world. For it is a very real drama, comparable for the style, poetry and choice of the subject to the best of the old German poems of the Middle Ages to which it bears great resemblance. It is most curious. The scene is here in Rabinal and the personnages [*sic*] are the first heroes of the Quiche and Rabinal nations, the time being about the beginning, I suppose, of the 12th century.

These two letters, the first to Padilla in May and the second to Squier in August, are the first published mention of the baile that has since come to be known as *Rabinal Achi*. This sole surviving preconquest indigenous drama has been called "a unique jewel"[26] that is "undeniably one of the major works of Mesoamerican literature."[27] Today two copies of Brasseur's 1862 edition of *Rabinal Achi* have taken on a sacred nature to those involved in performing the dance drama, and when René Acuña first set eyes on the 1862 edition, which had been passed down in Rabinal from one generation to another since the nineteenth century, he was told: "This book contains all our stories."[28]

The bailes were a ritual form of worship, where performers with "masks and costumes, recite memorized dialogue, and during musical interludes do dances related to the plot."[29] Brasseur had knowledge of sources on native practices in Mexico written at the time of first contact that provided "irrefutable proof" of the existence of poetry and music—a claim that might counter any notion that these were not "advanced" civilizations—and could cite references to dances witnessed by such chroniclers as Diego Durán (c. 1537–88), Diego de Landa (1524–79), and Diego López de Cogolludo (1613–65) as well as the appearance of dance in a work such as the *Popol Vuh*.[30] But he also knew that the Spanish clergy had driven this central ritual of indigenous culture underground after the conquest. In "From Guatemala City to Rabinal" he explains:

> Before the conquest of America, we know that dance played an integral role in the religious rites of all the nations on the continent. . . . When the missionaries, charged by Spain with their conversion, got to know the indigenous people of these

lands, they were horrified to learn the idolatrous nature of these theatrical performances. They were so deeply rooted in the customs and mores of the culture that it would have been impractical to suddenly forbid them. Any attempt to do so, would have been not only futile but would have jeopardized the fragile peace. In their anxious attempts to resolve this situation, they proposed alternatives with Christian themes that would be performed in accordance with the festivals of the Christian calendar. As a result, there are indigenous towns and villages that perform something called *Bayle de la Sierpe*, the "Ballet of the Serpent," drawn from the legend of Saint George and the dragon or others with dances that tell of the Moors' defeat in Grenada or Cortés's conquest of Mexico. However, these efforts to wipe their historical and religious ballets from the memories of the natives were completely unsuccessful.[31]

In areas in which hard-line clergy considered such dramas as "sacrilege against the divine faith"[32] the practice was driven underground. Given that an act of human sacrifice is performed at the end of the drama that "would have been offensive to the Spaniards"[33] it is not surprising that upon his arrival, Brasseur, an outsider, was told that *Rabinal Achi* "had long been relegated to the past, a memory that was now all but forgotten."[34]

Brasseur recounts that he countered this claim with an appeal to cultural authenticity and ethnic pride:

> As far as I was concerned, seeing *Rabinal Achi*, which was based on actual events from their national history, was much more compelling than watching a performance based on the story of Cortés and Montezuma, which was a degrading reminder of the humiliation to which their race had been subjected.[35]

Brasseur had clearly understood that this drama had deep roots in the history of this people. *Rabinal Achi* is a work fully rooted in the history and geography of the Guatemalan highlands: it is the story of the staged trial of a K'iche' warrior, called Queché Achi[36] in

Brasseur's translation, who has been captured by Rabinal Achi, the son of the king of Rabinal, and brought to the royal court. It speaks of the pre-Hispanic capitals of Kajyup, the seat of royal power for the people of Rabinal, and Utatlán (or Q'umarkaj), the center of K'iche' power.[37] The people of Rabinal and the K'iche' had formed an alliance but these former enemies, turned ally, became enemies once more when Rabinal Achi captured Queché Achi, who had turned "renegade."[38] The drama has three main speaking parts: Ahua Hobtoh or Goptoh,[39] King of the Rabinal people; Rabinal Achi,[40] the king's son; and Queché Achi, a K'iche' warrior.[41] One more small speaking role and three nonspeaking parts bring the total number of actors to seven, although Brasseur also cites the presence of twelve Eagles and Tigers on stage.[42] The three main characters reconstruct past events in dialogues that lead to the accusations against Queché Achi for having committed wrongs against the people of Rabinal. The captured enemy admits his guilt and makes a series of requests of the king, which are granted him, before his execution. The play ends with the enemy's ritual execution acted out by the dancers on the stage.

This story of a cultural artifact "unsurpassed in value among sources relating to the pre-Hispanic Quiché"[43] preserved through oral tradition and finally transcribed upon Brasseur's arrival to Rabinal should be counted as one of Brasseur's great contributions to his field. And yet, little more than a century after Brasseur published his first account of his discovery of *Rabinal Achi*, scholarly storms brewed. The abbé's jubilant theorizing in the last decade of his life caused an unshakable distrust among some scholars, who questioned every aspect of his work, even this one in which neither Atlantis nor Scandinavians or hidden double meanings ever enter into play.

We can set aside those who accused Brasseur of having penned *Rabinal Achi* himself, since it is now overwhelmingly accepted that the drama is written in "authentic old Quiché, therefore it is by no means that of a French priest who was just learning [the language]."[44]

The question that has caused scholarly headaches revolves

around the previously cited letter to Padilla in which Brasseur writes "I have discovered another manuscript here in the possession of an uncle of one of my young servants." Much ink has been spilled over this sentence. How can Brasseur have mentioned a manuscript in June 1855 and by August 1855, and later in 1859 and 1862, only spoken of a dictated text?

The eminent specialist on *Rabinal Achi* and dance-dramas of the Guatemala highlands, Carroll Edward Mace, who is also the author of the most thorough English-language appraisal of Brasseur and his work, accuses Brasseur of being "deliberately inaccurate" in his description of *Rabinal Achi* and goes as far as to warn that "Brasseur's novelistic imagination seemingly makes his 1862 version undependable."[45]

Time and again Mace reminds his readers that Brasseur had a stint as a hack novelist and clearly questioned whether a priest who at times turned to writing novels had the ability to tell truth from fiction. In fact, Mace's response to Brasseur's account of Bartolo Sis, the Indian who offers to dictate the drama to Brasseur—mentioned in the previously cited Squier letter, in "From Guatemala City to Rabinal," and again in the 1862 version of *Rabinal Achi*—is that "the whole episode might have been a chapter from one of Brasseur's earlier novels."[46]

For Mace, the fact that in one letter Brasseur mentions a manuscript and in all other accounts speaks only of a dictated text is irreconcilable and a sign of the Frenchman's untrustworthiness. He suggests that the "answer may lie in two conflicting aspects of the man's personality, a devotion to truth and a love of romantic fiction."[47] Mace continues: "it becomes clear that the dictation story was only an unfortunate attempt to aggrandize his own role in the episode."[48] Mace, who didn't hesitate to accuse Brasseur of taking novelistic flights of fancy, seems to have indulged in at least one of his own; with no actual evidence he surmises:

> After arriving in Rabinal, [Brasseur] must have heard about *Rabinal Achi*, made the acquaintance of the Indian who had written it down and obtained permission to copy it. Brasseur translated it—probably with the help of the Indians—and

published it in Paris in 1862. It is not at all unusual that Bartolo Ziz should have decide to write down the baile in order to preserve it.... This explains how Brasseur obtained the drama, but an even greater problem remains. Since he copied it from a manuscript, where is that manuscript today? Brasseur had an extraordinary gift for obtaining them and it is difficult to imagine that he would let this one slip through his fingers. He would also be anxious to conceal it—perhaps to destroy it?—to keep his story from being discovered. He could have obtained it by offering Ziz some money and a copy of his book, but after his death it was not found among his paper and books; nor is it in Rabinal.[49]

In his bibliographies, Brasseur often noted when he had copied original manuscripts or had copies made, and in fact, today there are many texts that have survived only through those transcriptions. Brasseur's previously cited letter to Squier mentioned the various ways he obtained his texts: "Some originals were given to me as presents, some others copied for my sake, and some I copied and the remainder I bought." Brasseur's published texts are certainly consistent. He may have "imprudently bragged"[50] of having found a manuscript in a private letter without thinking it was necessary to publish a retraction, but it seems quite a stretch to accuse this avid collector, this preservationist who decried the pillage and plunder of documents at the hands of warring armies, of having destroyed an original manuscript.

Without going so far as accusing Brasseur of an act of cultural vandalism, many scholars have assumed that a manuscript may have predated Brasseur's arrival in Rabinal. These scholars point to Brasseur's own text. In his 1862 edition Brasseur included a prologue in K'iche' and French attributed to Bartolo Sis, which reads:

> On the twenty-eighth day of the month of October of the year 1850, I transcribed the *original* of this Ballet of the Tun, the property of our town of *Saint Paul* of Rabinal, to leave as a remembrance to my children and so that it remains forever after with them.[51]

Thus this prologue implies that *Rabinal Achi* had been committed to writing before Brasseur's arrival in Rabinal, in 1855, since the text with Sis's name mentions the date October 28, 1850. Dennis Tedlock takes the mention of the 1850 date in the prologue as incontrovertible evidence that Bartolo Sis "made a copy of a previous version that has long since been lost" and, according to Tedlock's scenario, when Brasseur arrived in Rabinal he "did not succeed in gaining direct access to the Sis manuscript or its predecessors, but he did persuade Sis to read the text aloud to him while he made his own copy."[52] Of course, all of this is based on speculation, since we have no evidence that there was a manuscript, nor that Brasseur was read to from the manuscript.[53]

Brasseur's own texts hint that there might have been a transcription before his. Alain Breton points out that when Brasseur tells the story of Bartolo Sis's offer to dictate the text, he stated that Sis suggested the Brasseur should "*in turn* transcribe it" which implies that the text had already been written down.[54] Brasseur actually tells us as much when he explains that his informant had been putting this work together—in French he describes Sis's intention as *le recueillir en entier* (to collect the whole thing)—in order to pass it on to his children, which might indicate that he had undertaken a transcription. Moreover, Brasseur's title page for *Rabinal Achi* reads as follows:

> *Rabinal Achi* or *The Dance Drama of the Tun*, A Drama from the City of Rabinal, *Transcribed for the first time by Bartolo Ziz*, an elder of that Town, as a remembrance to his children, The elders of Rabinal performed this drama on the days of the festival of the Conversion of Saint Paul on January 25th, in the year of 1856, in honor of their priest, administrator and elder, Brasseur de Bourbourg, who translated it completely from the K'iche' language into French.[55]

This also seems to reinforce the theory of a preexisting manuscript, which Brasseur may never have seen, and a transcription that should be credited solely to Bartolo Sis. These inconsistencies troubled those who have followed in Brasseur's footsteps to study

Rabinal Achi. Those who might accuse him of being an unsystematic ethnographer certainly have a case, but of course in 1855 as he made his way through Guatemala he did not do so with the knowledge that would come to later ethnographers, namely that oral and written transmission sometimes go hand-in-hand. Each one of the scholars mentioned here—Breton, Carmack, Mace, and Tedlock—have written about their own struggles in gaining access to tightly guarded manuscripts. Breton maintains that

> Brasseur should not be so harshly criticized for having announced *the discovery of a manuscript* rather than *the discovery of the existence of a manuscript* as was most probably the case. It is plausible, moreover, that some of his hosts ... in fact had informed him in that direction, whereas others might have refused to show him the manuscript, going so far as to deny its existence. One can understand Bartolo Sis's reluctance to share his manuscript with a foreigner (a priest, moreover) who barely settled, inquired with such insistence about a text that Sis knew was condemned by the Church. By asserting that he knew it by heart, Sis thus protected himself from any possibility of someone taking the document or from any risk of losing it.[56]

And Carmack insists that all these scholarly disputes over a preexisting manuscript should not keep us from remembering to evaluate Brasseur "in the context of the times in which he wrote":

> If we do this, we realize that he was ahead of his contemporaries. He recognized the scientific importance of Indian culture and history; he placed importance on the study of native documents; he dedicated himself to learning native languages in order to study native culture; he recognized the utility of living in the Indian villages in order to learn of their culture firsthand in order to be able to interpret the documents.[57]

These disputes over whether Brasseur had access to a manuscript or actually was the first to commit a previously orally transmitted text to writing while obviously a worthy avenue of scholarship should not overshadow the enormous value of Brasseur's contribution. Whether Brasseur's text is or is not the first to fix *Rabinal Achi* on the page, his printed text from 1862 was the vehicle by which the world beyond Rabinal learned of this cultural treasure. While most of his contemporaries interested in Mesoamerica saw only ruins of a great civilization, Brasseur was equally receptive to the indigenous culture present before him, even while rummaging around dusty libraries and archives for its vestiges. The residents of Rabinal, whom he portrays in his travelogue, namely Bartolo Sis, Nicolás López, or Mateo Coloche, were never distant "others," and Brasseur valued the oral tradition they guarded as much as the documents he collected.

When Brasseur published his 1862 bilingual edition of *Rabinal Achi*, he sent two copies back to Rabinal. It is striking that those texts have in a sense become sacred in Rabinal. Dennis Tedlock remarks that one of the two editions that Brasseur sent back is "handled with circumspection in the same way a manuscript would have been, and it became stained with candle dripping and the smoke of incense."[58] Mace was witness to the same sort of reverence for Brasseur's book: "Before I was allowed to touch it, I had to make the sign of the cross, offer *guaro*[59] to the four directions and to the book itself. The owner offers it candles and *guaro* frequently and wants it to be buried with him."[60] He recounts the story of an Indian whose hand was said to have become paralyzed after having taken up the book without having asked first of the "permission of the book."[61] This seems an apt legacy for a great collector with his own reverence for the prized text and a Mayanist with an abiding respect for indigenous culture.

After Brasseur left Rabinal, he continued traveling, collecting, and writing in Guatemala. He had short stints as an ecclesiastical administrator in San Juan Sacatepéquez (where he went to improve his Kaqchikel) and Gualán, and then he was named pastor of Escuintla for two months, where the indigenous natives spoke Pipil-Nawat. This first and highly productive Central American venture ended in 1857 when, accompanied by his young servant

Colash López, Brasseur made his way from Guatemala City to Izabal, where they said their good-byes and Brasseur departed towards Belize.[62]

VOYAGE ACROSS THE ISTHMUS OF TEHUANTEPEC

Brasseur chronicles his return to the region in his most developed piece of travel writing, *Voyage across the Isthmus of Tehuantepec in 1859 and 1860*. In a letter to Léonce Angrand, a French diplomat and collector who served throughout South America starting in the 1840s, Brasseur wrote of Mexico in 1860: "I have never seen a country so painfully troubled. These upheavals, the destruction and horrors that I saw lead me to believe that the country is headed towards dissolution."[63] Brasseur arrived in Mexico at a time when its future hung in the balance. Its land faced steady encroachment by its northern neighbor, a devastating civil war tore it apart, and yet it was still seen as a land of milk and honey, thereby attracting both public and private interest not only from the United States but from major European powers, including France, which hoped to gain access to its riches.

In this travelogue, with its novelistic flares, Brasseur recounts his trip from New Orleans to Tehuantepec and across the isthmus of that name along a route still under construction—a route that would never be completed by the North American Louisiana Tehuantepec Company. This was a time when:

> The imaginations of all people . . . were fired by ideas and predictions and statements about railways, which soon were proved to be utterly fanciful and unwarranted. . . . Men of intelligence spoke of a railway across the almost unknown, unsurveyed wilds of Vera Cruz and Oaxaca as if they expected to make a journey on it next week.[64]

The pursuit of an interoceanic route in this time before the construction of the Panama Canal held out extraordinary promise. One of the founding stakeholders in the Louisiana Tehuantepec Company, Judah Benjamin, a senator from Louisiana who would later become the secretary of state for the Confederacy, saw this stretch of land as a gateway to untapped wealth:

> When we cross this Isthmus, the Isthmus of Tehuantepec—what have we before us? The Eastern World! Its commerce has been the bone of many a bloody contest. Its commerce makes empires of the countries to which it flows, and when they are deprived of it they are as empty bags, useless, valueless.[65]

Brasseur tells the history of the land grant acquired by Benjamin's Louisiana Company, which had first been awarded to the Mexican engineer José de Garay in 1850 and was eventually bought up by North American interests. During his travels Brasseur turns a penetrating eye towards the American representatives of the Louisiana Tehuantepec Company scrambling to control this coveted stretch of land that promised easy access to the Pacific coast from the United States.

Brasseur offers a discerning assessment of the political situation in Mexico, during this period of the War of the Reform with portraits of Benito Juárez and Porfirio Díaz, whom he meets in Tehuantepec. But along with these powerful figures who shaped the fate of their country, Brasseur also offers sketches of the people he meets along his way—from American hotelkeepers on the promised Tehuantepec route to a Zapotec woman named Didjaza, who was purported to have magical powers.

Looking beyond the contemporary landscape, where, as he says, everyone was looking to get a piece of the pie, his true interest lies in the ancient history of Mexico and its vibrant indigenous culture. What drew Brasseur to this region was his interest in Nagualism. Referencing historical sources such as those of the sixteenth- and seventeenth-century Spanish priests Francisco Burgoa and Bernardino de Sahagún, who had discussed these folk beliefs on shape-shifting, Brasseur is irresistibly drawn to the magical forces his precursors had described.

> Was it true, as the most reliable and sincere Spanish authors had claimed, that Indians were capable of transforming themselves into all sorts of animals? Was it possible that

they could be transported instantaneously from one place to another, so as to be an invisible presence at their enemies' council meetings? Can we give any credence to Sahagún when he says that before the eyes of spectators they could make rivers, springs, forests, or palaces appear where just minutes before there had been nothing, and then could make them disappear a moment later. Can we believe him when he says that they could slit open their stomachs, cut off the arm or leg of a neighbor or even kill him, and then heal or resuscitate him immediately afterwards without any trace of a wound? And all this, in front of a crowd of people assembled to witness this fantastical spectacle! These things are scrupulously reported, and perhaps what makes them all the more astonishing is that they are reported by serious-minded men writing in a time that is not so distant from our own. Were these all just the result of strange hallucinations, produced by unknown causes?[66]

Brasseur's examination of indigenous spiritual beliefs puts the accounts of native informants at the forefront, and he returns to a theme that is central to all his work during this period: how ancient indigenous beliefs and culture had been driven underground as a result of conquest and colonization. There is no question that Brasseur made the link between these beliefs and political resistance. He recounts the story of King Cocijopij, the last Zapotec king, who "ostensibly obeyed the new laws that were imposed"[67] upon his people and yet continued the traditional practices of his people as a counterbalance to the Church and colonial domination.

Much later, in his *Bibliothèque mexico-guatémalienne*, Brasseur returned to Sahagún, when laying out his theory of "amphibology"—namely that there was more than one way to interpret Maya hieroglyphic writing. According to Brasseur, Sahagún had understood that since the conquest, the indigenous people of Mexico had learned to hide their "idolatrous beliefs" and in a sense "taken refuge" in "a language of double-meaning." Brasseur returned to a quotation from Sahagún:

> It is obvious that the dark way in which our enemies escape us, is through the songs and ballads, to which they alone hold the secret key. They sing them, and with the exception of the few indigenous people who know their language, no one is able to understand. Thus they sing whatever they please, undaunted either by war or peace, or praise or contempt for Christ, and no one can understand them at all.[68]

Although by this time Brasseur was using these words by Sahagún to justify his misguided readings of ancient texts, this quotation sheds just as much light on Brasseur's focus both in "From Guatemala City to Rabinal" and *Voyage*. Keenly aware that there was an entire civilization hidden below the surface, Brasseur, not unlike the archaeologists who were beginning to dig up and uncover the lost past of the ancient civilizations of Mesoamerica, was trying to excavate a much more ephemeral culture: the culture of song, language, myth, and drama, the culture of the written and spoken word.

Brasseur's *Voyage* was to be the first of a two-part series. However, he never published a first-person account of the rest of his trip, nor for that matter did he ever publish anything about of his subsequent travels. Through a letter sent to Léonce Angrand, written from Guatemala City and dated January 1860, Brasseur recounts the rest of his journey after leaving Tehuantepec. He never made it to his intended destination, Mexico City "for fear of being caught in the crossfire" and abandoned plans to travel through Oaxaca because he "didn't want to take the chance of falling into the hands of brigands or the warring parties (which comes down more or less to the same)," and he therefore set course for the state of Chiapas where he "was able to collect some unique and extremely precious manuscripts related to the languages and history of the area."[69] While traveling through this region Brasseur met the young French Mesoamericanist Désiré Charnay on his way back from Yucatán, via Chiapas where Charnay had spent several months taking photographs of the ruins of Uxmal, Chichén Itzá, and Palenque.[70] Brasseur ended this trip in 1860 with a return to Rabinal and then, accompanied by "the two young Indians who had served him in the past" he reached the last leg of his journey at Lake Izabal.[71]

After Brasseur's trip across the Isthmus of Tehuantepec and back through Guatemala, he never produced another travelogue, although he continued traveling until his death in 1874. He returned to Central America in 1863 to visit Quiriguá and Copán and then Mexico again in 1864 when he was asked to serve on Napoleon III's Mexican Commission, at which time he also traveled to Honduras and the state of San Salvador. He made a last trip back to Mexico where he was finally able to reach Palenque in 1871. The only trace of these travels is found in the few letters remaining in archives written in Brasseur's hand and in fleeting mentions in his books.

It could be argued that after 1860 Brasseur had his greatest successes. He published works that are now recognized as major references in the field—the texts that we have previously discussed, namely the *Popol Vuh* (1861) and *Rabinal Achi* (1862), but also two volumes that this supreme manuscript hunter discovered not in Mexico or Central America, but in Spain: Diego de Landa's *Relación de las cosas del Yucatán* (1864) and the *Manuscript Troano* (1869).

While searching through archives at the Royal Academy of History in Madrid, Brasseur found a copy of Landa's long-lost work that had been made after the Spanish cleric's death in 1579. The book, which is "a gold mine of information"[72] regarding the practices and customs of the Maya population in Yucatán, also contained "Landa's A, B, C of the Maya script."[73] Brasseur hoped that this text, which is often compared to the Rosetta Stone, would provide the "key to those mysterious inscriptions that exist in such great number today in the Yucatán, Palenque, and Copán."[74] In fact, the secret of Maya hieroglyphs would not be penetrated until the mid-twentieth century, although Brasseur was able to decipher some signs related to the calendar.[75] Several years later, once more in Spain, Brasseur discovered a Maya codex, which he christened the Codex Troano.[76] This was yet another triumphant find, given that only a precious few preconquest Maya books, written in hieroglyphic script, had survived the destruction wrought by conquering Spaniards such as Landa.

Introduction

The 1860s were also a decade of gratifying institutional recognition for Brasseur. The Emperor Louis Napoleon, who had had his eye on Central America for quite some time,[77] launched a French intervention on Mexican soil and installed the young Austrian archduke Maximilian as Emperor in 1861 in the hopes of establishing some sort of French foothold in the region that might stem the North American advance. In this same year, Brasseur published his bilingual edition of the *Popol Vuh*.

Three years after the start of Louis Napoleon's military venture, Brasseur wrote Léonce Angrand from Madrid. His most pressing news was that he was enclosing a photograph of Landa's A, B, C from the manuscript he had just discovered in the library of the Royal Academy. He added, almost as an afterthought, his lukewarm reaction to an offer he had just received from Paris:

> Three days ago, I received a letter from Mr. de Quatrefages[78] about a scientific expedition they are planning to Mexico ... under the auspices of the emperor.... I will have to give it some thought before accepting anything.... I am closer to 50 years old than I am to being 40, and then, of course there is Spain with its increasingly tantalizing archives.[79]

In the end Brasseur accepted a position to compile a report on the archaeology, history, and linguistics of Mexico. However, the expedition proved unfulfilling, and Brasseur was frustrated at every turn. Travel was impeded by the unstable political and military situation, and local officials showed little enthusiasm for France's quest for either power or knowledge. He had planned to document the region's archaeological sites, however his photographer Henri Bourgeois was taken ill. Moreover, even with his Landa in hand he was not able to decipher the ancient glyphs, nor had he been able to undertake excavations in the hopes of uncovering codices that he believed might be buried in the tombs of Maya priests. Brasseur returned from Mexico diminished, "with less brio."[80]

Despite the triumphs in the archives and the imperial stamp of approval, in the end the 1860s was the period during which he also published the texts that brought down on him "the opprobrium ...

of a century of Mayanists."[81] These were the years of the great unraveling. During this last decade of his life, his theories often on display in the introductory material to his most important publications grew increasingly eccentric. The essay preceding his text of the *Popol Vuh* is entitled "On the Myths of Ancient America, On the Probability of Communication Between the Continents in the Ancient Past, and On the Migration of Indigenous Peoples of America," and as part of the prefatory material accompanying Landa's *Relación* is an essay with the title "On the Sources of Mexico and Central America's Primitive History As Found in the Monuments of Egypt and On the Primitive History of Egypt Found in the Monuments of America . . . ." Of course, Brasseur was far from the only scholar to entertain such ideas in an era when ethnography and comparative linguistics were sciences in their infancy and at a time when there was an explosion of discovery, inquiry, and theorizing about the common threads that might tie together disparate cultures in Europe, Egypt, Mesopotamia, and the Americas.[82] Seen from this perspective, Brasseur's speculation shares a great deal with his contemporaries in the fields of ethnography, archaeology, linguistics, and natural history, who sought a unifying theory of origins. This having been said, by the time he published his last major work, the great bibliography of his collection *Bibliothèque mexico-guatémalienne* (1871) he used the preface to explain how he had come to understand through his work on the *Traono* and the *Chimalpopoca Codices* that a single line contained two meanings, which were "not contradictory but completely different" nonetheless.[83]

These fanciful theories have too often shaped the way Brasseur is remembered, despite his insightful observations, his dogged research, and the efforts he made to safeguard ancient as well as living indigenous culture. Although after *Voyage across the Isthmus of Tehuantepec*, Brasseur never published another piece of travel writing, that final work, his *Bibliothèque*, is in a sense an extraordinary travelogue through a life of collecting. The bibliography includes documents in more than forty indigenous languages from Achi to Zapotec, with annotations that tell the tales of these vestiges pulled from the archives. There is the manuscript about which he writes: "This document is the only monument known today of the language of Chiapas"[84] or the one given to Brasseur by the priest of Taktic, near Cobán, "where the Poqomchi' language is spoken."[85] These pages tell the story of the lands he traversed from Mexico to Guatemala, and within the pages of this detailed bibliography he is at his most meticulous.

After Brasseur died in the Mediterranean city of Nice, while on his way back to Paris from working in the libraries of Rome, his entire collection was bought by Alphonse Pinart, a Mesoamericanist, who put it all up for sale a decade later in 1884. The collection scattered; a majority of it was purchased by Hubert Howe Bancroft, the *Popol Vuh* and *Memorial* were sold to the American Edward Ayer, and other titles were acquired by the Bibliothèque nationale in Paris. In the end, the great manuscript hunter's collection was dispersed, but his legacy to his field is found in those hundreds of titles preserved for future scholars.

In the decades after Brasseur's death, the Englishman Alfred Maudslay journeyed down many of the same paths that Brasseur had once explored during his travels. After years of meticulously photographing some of the most important Maya sites of Mexico and Central America, Maudslay published his findings between 1889 and 1902 in *Archaeology*, his five-volume contribution to that encyclopedic illustrated catalog of flora and fauna of Central America, the *Biologia Centrali-Americana*.[86] The systematic documentation in Maudslay's magnum opus, which was devoid of speculation or flights of fancy, can be seen as a sort of pendant to Brasseur's life's work. Maudslay's goal was to make a precise record of the ancient monuments of Mesoamerica by reproducing exact copies of their carved hieroglyphic inscriptions—using photography as well as molds from which replicas could be made—so that scholars who could not travel to those sites might be able to decipher these inscriptions and unlock the secrets of the region's deep past. In the appendix to Maudslay's *Archaeology*, entitled "The Archaic Maya Inscriptions," Joseph T. Goodman makes the association between these two early Mayanists—one who was trying to safeguard paper vestiges and the other who was hoping to preserve ones of stone. For those dedicated to the study of the Maya past, Goodman wrote, Brasseur "was to its bibliography what Maudslay is to its archaeology."[87]

Whereas Maudslay's work was immediately recognized as ushering in a new era of scientific archaeology, by the time of his death Brasseur had already been dismissed as a relic of a less rigorous scholarly past. In "Archaic Maya Inscriptions" Goodman makes an impassioned plea against such a thoughtless dismissal:

> It has become fashionable with the school of dilettanti that has succeeded him to speak lightly of Brasseur; but he was the grandest of them all—the only one to whom I uncover. He belonged to the old Leonardo da Vinci and Michael Angelo type—the Herculean mold—men who achieve in a dozen different lines what we incompetents are incapable of accomplishing in a single one. No advance can be made in any branch of the study but he supplied all the preliminary stepping-stones.[88]

Goodman stridently defends Brasseur against those who follow along the path that the Frenchman helped lay and yet spurn his work:

> What if he went astray at times? He was delving single-handed, but with a zeal that will never be equaled, in the vague of an unexplored past. What if he mistook the meaning of some of the treasures he exhumed? No one else would ever have dragged them from their crypts to turn the glare of even a misfocused searchlight upon them. If he could only live today in the fuller light he was chiefly instrumental in creating![89]

With the travelogues in the present volume, we follow Brasseur along the roads of Mexico and Central America with the hopes of shedding some "fuller light" on this neglected scholar who was laying the early foundations—those preliminary stepping-stones—for the study of the history of the indigenous peoples of America.

NOTES FROM A VOYAGE
IN CENTRAL AMERICA

Letters to Alfred Maury[1]

GUATEMALA MARCH 28, 1855

Sir,

Less than eight months ago, you and I were together in Paris chatting in the Institute's library[2] about Mexico, Aubin's[3] steady and essential work on Mexico's ancient languages, and writing systems. We talked of Central America, where every day new cities and monuments are discovered that have been buried in their dark forests for centuries. And now, here I am in Guatemala, where for the past three months I have been exploring the vestiges of this region's lost civilization and gathering the documents necessary to reconstruct its history.

At the end of October 1854, after a few weeks visiting libraries in New York and Washington with precious manuscripts related to the history of America before the conquest, I embarked for Greytown, which is also known as San Juan de Nicaragua, a city which recently came to international attention when this British protectorate that had been ceded to the King of the Moskitos was bombarded by a United States' warship.[4] I will save some very curious stories on this subject that I heard while on my way there on an American steamship for some other time. The port of San Juan is located at the mouth of the river of the same name and is shaped by a strip of land called Punta Arenas, which stretches from east to west. The American company[5] that provides transportation across the isthmus to California has its operations at one end. The city, built on low sandy ground, is across from this strip, on the coast that is attached to the rest of the Nicaraguan landmass. This means that

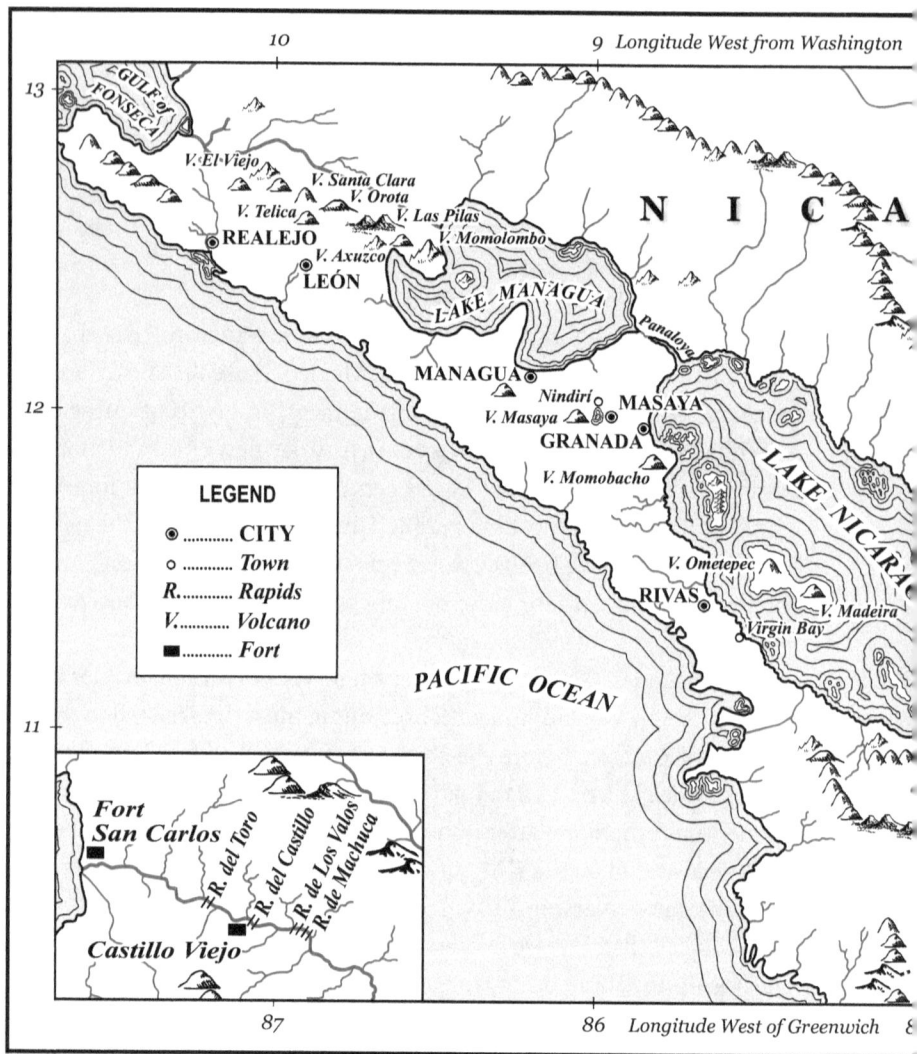

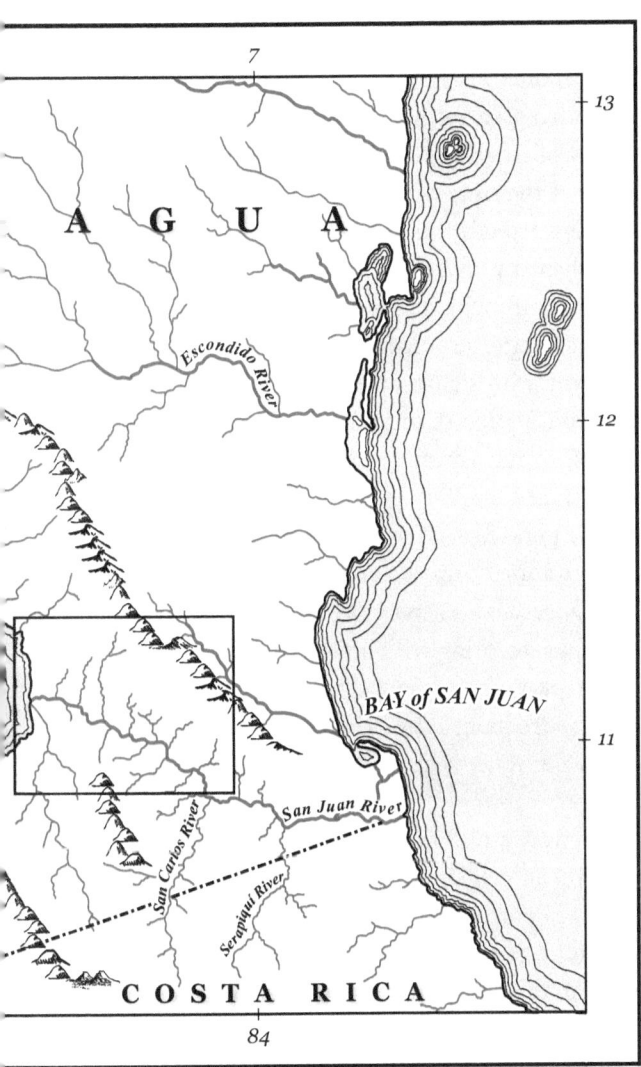

MAP OF NICARAGUA Based on Ephraim George Squier's Map of Nicaragua, 1851. Sarony & Major. *Map of Nicaragua showing its departmental divisions and projected routes of interoceanic communication.* (New York: s.n., 1851). Accessed at Geography and Map Division of the Library of Congress. Map by Paporn Thebpanya. Copyright © 2017, University of Oklahoma Press.

the conditions there are generally much healthier than is sometimes said in Europe. Beyond the city are salt marshes that could easily be drained, and further on, there are stretches of cool, lush woodlands, with an enchanting diversity of flora. Greytown's port—the busiest on the entire Central American coast, with the exception of the port of Belize—is the sole access point on the Atlantic coast for all goods bound for the interior of other Central American states. Before its recent destruction, the city of Greytown had more than two thousand residents and already at the time of my visit it was starting to reemerge from the ruins. Neglected by the Nicaraguan government, which has refused to establish any civil or political authority there, and barely defended by England, which sees this town as nothing but trouble, Greytown has become a sort of Hanse town, governed by a town council and a mayor, who is currently a Frenchman named Mesnier, a former soldier in Napoleon's Imperial Guard. Given the current state of affairs in Central America, I believe the city will become increasingly important.

It is a quick trip from the port to reach the San Juan River, where several steamers go back and forth, up the river and as far as the city of Granada on Lake Nicaragua. This wide, rather deep river flows between two low banks, teeming with an astounding variety of plant life. For the most part, the surrounding land is swampy and insalubrious, due to the frequent rains. Unlike the rest of the tropics, around Greytown the rainy season is not reliably limited to a few months in the year. The mouth of the Serapiquí River is approximately ten leagues away and flows into the San Juan River from the south. It is beautiful and wide with its source in the mountains around Cartago that are part of the great Cordillera range in the state of Costa Rica. Many of my fellow travelers disembarked at this point, since the Serapiquí is the most commonly used route for people and goods moving between Costa Rica and the Atlantic coast. We watched from the steamer as they got into a *bongo*, which is a large boat that has been carved out of a tree trunk. From there they spent two days and two nights exposed to sun, rain, and nighttime mosquitoes before reaching their destination. Soon however, conditions may improve; there are plans to build a new road from

San José, Costa Rica's capital, to the banks of the San Juan River.

We traveled another fifteen leagues farther upriver, where we encountered the Machuca Rapids, followed by the Los Valos Rapids, but the steamer passed through these with no difficulty. Finally at one in the morning, under a beautifully moonlit sky, we stopped at the Castillo Viejo Rapids. This is a picturesque bend in the river from which several hills rise and form an amphitheater along its banks. Atop one of these hills, on the right bank, stand the ruined remains of a Spanish fort, destroyed long ago by buccaneers. Once the sun had risen, I was eager to climb up to see them. Although it was November, the weather was hot and sultry, and I broke out in a heavy sweat climbing to the top. But the magnificent view was well worth the effort. The large, solidly built fort was typical of the work of those who conquered Spanish America. It wouldn't take much to restore it, but the successive governments since the end of Spanish rule only know how to destroy. Could they even conceive of rebuilding anything?

For more than a year, the main Nicaraguan factions had been at each other's throats. Don Fruto Chamorro[6] was elected according to the country's constitution. Unfortunately his election thwarted the ambitions of others who also aspired to power. They exploited his political blunders to rise up against him in the name of liberty and the rights that, according to them, had been violated. Chamorro was driven out of the capital, León, by a handful of men who dubbed themselves *democrats*, and he took refuge in Granada, León's eternal rival. The Democratic Party established a provisional government in León, headed by Francisco Castellón,[7] who in the past had been plenipotentiary minister in Europe. They enjoyed a string of victories for over a year, and by the time I arrived in Nicaragua, Castellón's armies controlled most of the country and had surrounded Granada, besieging Chamorro and his supporters. Democratic troops were garrisoned in Castillo Viejo, the first military post we encountered while making our way upstream along the San Juan River. In the ruins of the fort I saw four or five half-naked men, in rags, sleeping on the ground under a thatch roof held up by four stakes. They were armed with machetes and guns that had seen better days. The only insignias they wore were soiled red ribbons or pieces of serge tied to their straw hats. They were perfect specimens of Nicaragua's democratic faction as it was then and still is to this day. These were the conditions for the troops stationed at Castillo Viejo on the San Juan River. Actually Chamorro's supporters are no better. Even the most loathsome bandits of Romagna or Calabria stand heads and tails above this sorry lot. Casting one final look in the direction of these pathetic soldiers, I made my way down from the fort, sick at heart at the thought of the atrocities committed daily by both sides.

At the foot of Castillo Viejo half a dozen wood houses stood along the river, bearing the grandiose title of hotels. Here passengers in transit are granted the privilege of paying an arm and a leg for a meager dinner and rotgut. Just like establishments in Greytown and San Juan del Sur, on the Pacific coast, they were run by German, Italian, American, or French proprietors. Along with these hotels, the hamlet of Castillo Viejo was comprised of approximately twenty huts built of mud and branches with palm-leaf roofs, scattered on the hillside—all of which appeared when the Americans started coming through. Passengers transfer here onto steamers that take on less water and can more easily clear first the Castillo and then the Toro[8] Rapids. They say that these rapids were engineered by the Spaniards, who hoped their man-made rapids might impede boat travel on the river and prevent buccaneers from reaching Lake Nicaragua. In any case, it is an undeniable fact that not long after the conquest, Spanish galleons easily made their way upstream to the lake and the city of Granada. Once the Toro Rapids were cleared we transferred once more onto larger steamships. Then we sailed at full tilt along the river that flowed into the lake about ten leagues from the transfer point. As we entered onto the lake, we passed the ruined fort of San Carlos, towering above both lake and riverhead on a promontory to our right. Castellón's forces had recently captured it from Chamorro's supporters after having burned down the customs office depot located there.

Lake Nicaragua is one of the world's most beautiful sites. It is about thirty-eight leagues long and more than fifteen leagues wide at twenty-eight feet above the level of the Pacific Ocean.[9] Magnificent mountains, rich land, and an abundance of minerals surround it. Several fertile and rather large islands emerge from its deep waters. Their names, derived from Nahuatl, are reminders of ancient cities with significant populations. Today those cities are deserted. All that remains are ancient structures and imposing sculptures of men or animals in a style that implies a much less advanced civilization than those of Yucatán and Guatemala. The largest island, called Ometepec[10] (Two Mountains) still has a significant population. It is almost at the center of the lake, although closer to the western bank. My guess is that it is eight leagues long. It has a distinctive shape, like a pair of eyeglasses, with two volcanic cones—one called Ometepec, which is 5,100 feet tall and the other called Madeira,[11] which stands at 4,190 feet—that are like two separate islands linked by a low, narrow strip of land. The island offers an abundant source of wood as well as a variety of fruit, game, and poultry; it supplies the neighboring lakeside residents and the city of Granada. This city, with its fifteen thousand residents, located on a bay on the northwest side of the lake, once had the reputation for being the richest and most pleasant city in the state of Nicaragua. It was also known as the most commercial and industrious city. When I arrived in the country last November, Chamorro had been besieged there for eight months. As a result of the Democrats' blockade, Granada had been largely destroyed, and I was told that there were no more than five or six streets left intact in the area where the beleaguered forces had taken refuge. We learned that the blockade had been lifted last February and that the enemy had retreated. Nonetheless, the city was left in a miserable state.

Across from the island of Ometepec, on the western bank of the lake, I saw the American transit station. It is four leagues south of the city of Rivas (formerly known as Nicaragua). Before the Americans arrived, there were only forests and solitude to be found here. However, once the transit station was established, the woods were razed and a village called La Virgen emerged. It was named for a small statue of the Virgin Mary, found when they dug the foundation of a house. Almost everyone, however, refers to it by it English name—Virgin Bay. Landing in Virgin Bay is not easy, since the pier is too short and the frequent north winds give rise to turbulent waves that are as menacing as any on the roughest seas. This was the case, when I arrived. Consequently, we had a great deal of trouble reaching dry land.

The village of Virgin Bay has a single street running through it, with wood houses that are all hotels just like in Castillo Viejo. Fifty or sixty foreigners from France, Germany, and America, form the town's core population. A hundred or so natives have clustered around the town, living in mud huts along the lakeside. The street starts at the lake and leads to a road built by the Accessory Transit Company. That road goes from Virgin Bay to the small port of San Juan del Sur on the Pacific Ocean, where passengers board steamers that take them to California. Virgin Bay is by far the most colorful and vibrant stop on this route after Greytown. All at once, four to five hundred travelers of all ages and nationalities, male and female, are thrown into this little village. The houses and hotels are all festooned with flags from the United States as well as those from various European countries. Hundreds of mules stand ready to carry passengers and their luggage to the coast at five leagues[12] from the lake through the low mountains. The perfectly passable macadam-covered road cost the company more than a hundred thousand piasters to build but is without doubt the most beautiful in all of Central America.[13]

The women and children were unceremoniously piled into rickety wagons that brought them to San Juan del Sur. These uncovered wagons exposed passengers to the tropical heat and downpours and made for a rather uncomfortable trip. This is an extremely profitable business, and the company has an operating monopoly on both the port of Greytown and the San Juan River. Yet despite signed agreements, it hasn't paid the Nicaraguan government a penny of what it owes for exercising this monopoly. I have been told that since my trip to the area they have built more comfortable carriages that resemble omnibuses like those in New York. But in my experience this company showed very little concern for the well being of its customers, once they had pocketed their money.

The Virgin Bay garrison was dependent on the one in Castillo

Viejo. When someone pointed out the commanding officer to me, the only things that distinguished him from his soldiers were that he actually wore shoes on his feet and that his hat sported a ribbon around the base of the crown instead of a simple red strip of fabric. Sometimes you saw soldiers wearing the bartered castoffs of some English soldier or sailor, with or without buttons, in red or green or blue—apparently color matters very little. These are the big wigs, proud as peacocks, and when they walk down the street, heaven help anyone who dares to look at them the wrong way. Only Europeans and North Americans can bring them down a peg.

San Juan del Sur also has a garrison. This port town, exposed to southwest winds, is funnel shaped and rather cramped. Before the Americans arrived, it was completely uninhabited, just like Virgin Bay. Today it has become a small town of wooden houses, brought from the United States, built on the beach, up against the cliff that flanks the southern end of the port. They are building a pier along this cliff for passengers bound to or from California. A mountain, which was once covered with forests magnificently cascading down towards the sea, abruptly rises up beyond the city. As in Virgin Bay, the population of San Juan del Sur is mostly foreign and numbers in the five to six hundreds, including the indigenous inhabitants. For the time being it is not very big, but the future and the Americans are beckoning. There is an American Consul in the town, named Priest, who also runs the main hotel there. I learned that he recently suffered a great affront from Chamorro's government, which could have serious consequences for the State of Nicaragua.

Here is the account that I heard. In 1855, Castellón's string of victories seemed to come to an end. His southern strongholds fell back into his rival's hands and by the end of January, Chamorro's troops were stationed in Castillo Viejo, San Carlos, Virgin Bay, and San Juan del Sur. Castellón's followers were hunted down and many took refuge on the Isla del Tigre in the Gulf of Fonseca. It seems that a Castellón supporter hid in Mr. Priest's house. The American Consul was sick in bed when one of Chamorro's officers burst into his home and ordered him to hand over the Democrat who had taken refuge in his home. To add insult to injury, the officer wanted to compel

Priest to leave his sick bed and force him to go into town to collect the five thousand piasters that Chamorro wanted all resident aliens to pay. Once again, Priest refused to comply. Their response was to rouse him from his bed by force, and the officer and his soldiers took him prisoner. It didn't take long for Chamorro's men to realize that such insulting and arrogant behavior towards an official agent of the United States had been a great misstep. Consequently Priest was released after two hours. But the United States is not so easily appeased. It will be extremely difficult for the Nicaraguan government to make amends for such an outrage, and since it is penniless, compensation will no doubt have to come in some other form. Never before had there been such an opportunity for the United States to gain a foothold in this beautiful country. And most certainly, Mr. Wheeler,[14] the minister to Nicaragua from the United States, who was in Virgin Bay at the time, wasted no time sending off a communication to Washington to inform his government of all these events. All this occurred in the middle of February, and Mr. Wheeler, who until then had hesitated to take sides in the conflict, soon recognized Chamorro. And although Chamorro died in the meantime, the American minister intended to go to Granada to present his credentials to his successor Mr. Estrada. Meanwhile, this turn of events was of concern in Guatemala, where seeing North Americans getting a foothold in Central America was the greatest fear.

I hope to discuss the rest of my trip in a second letter.

Yours faithfully,
Brasseur de Bourbourg

GUATEMALA APRIL 28, 1855

In Virgin Bay I bid farewell to my travel companions, who were going to California, while I stayed in the village to explore the area around Lake Nicaragua and its islands. Rivas, which is also known as Nicaragua, is located four leagues to the north of Virgin Bay and is the first city of any importance. I traveled there by mule, because mules and horses are the only viable mode of transportation here. And even then the trails are often impassable. And yet, these paths whose trace is so easily lost as you make your way through the woods are known by the rather pompous and not very democratic name of Camino Real.[15] The city of Nicaragua, which gave its name to the entire province, was the provincial capital when the area was under Spanish rule. The earliest accounts describe a city with a large population. Its current name comes from a former president of the modern republic who was a native son.[16] This city boasts eight to ten thousand residents, including those living in what we might call the suburbs. Devastated by the civil war, the city's pitiful state of ruin stands in stark contrast with the cheerful countryside that surrounds it.

Rivas has three churches, none of which are remarkable in any way. The biggest one was destroyed a few years ago by an earthquake and is currently being rebuilt. The surroundings are extremely fertile and the area's sugar and cocoa plantations are considered to be the most productive in Central America. And yet, all over this unfortunate country there is a labor shortage. The most magnificent haciendas or plantations have been abandoned and superb farms with large tracts of land cleared for cultivation can be bought for next to nothing. As soon as calm is restored, Europeans will find that there are fortunes to be made here.

Since independence, the unending civil war throughout the republics of Central America has led to a drastic reduction in the labor force. Both sides have torn workers away from farming using equally brutal means. There is no lottery for drafting soldiers, rather when troops are required in Nicaragua, a platoon of *veterans* comb the cities and countryside. Then, using threats and violence they put pressure on all the *shoeless men* that they encounter. Shoes are the distinctive and unmistakable sign of social class. Those with shoes are ipso facto given the rank of officer. Don't look for education. All you need are shoes. As for drills, they take place during battles, or more accurately, when the *shoeless* are fighting and the officers, who with very few exceptions stay at the rear, push them forward with swords drawn and threats. Their military science can be reduced, more or less, to this: one group gives orders and the other obeys. Nothing is spared in the quest for soldiers. They don't even respect the sanctity of the home. In Chinandega, I witnessed a widowed mother's only two sons taken from her while they were saying their evening prayer at 9 PM. One son was seventeen, the other thirteen! Yes, even children of thirteen are forced to join the militias. Just imagine what kind of soldiers they must be! Consequently, it is no surprise that the siege of Granada—a city with no walls, not fortified in any way—lasted almost a year. Despite this, a great deal of blood was spilled, and in the end Castellón was compelled to lift his blockade.

This explains the scarcity of labor throughout this poor state of Nicaragua. By the end of 1854, the situation was so bad that when it was time to harvest corn—a staple of this country's diet—no one could be found to work the fields. Those who could, headed for the forests to escape forced conscription. Consequently, you practically never saw men in the streets. An American planter, who before the war employed a hundred and fifty laborers on his sugar plantation, was allowed to keep only twenty-five by the government. In need of more men, he planned on hiring a few hundred Chinese workers and bringing them in from Hong Kong or Canton.

The road from Rivas to León, the capital of the state of Nicaragua, cuts through generally flat countryside, for about forty leagues. The topography makes it a promising area for agriculture and for building good roads—no doubt it would be extremely easy to build a passable carriage road. There is a distance of twelve leagues between Rivas and Nandaime, which I was leaving one morning with Joaquim Mathé, an agent for Carmichael's of Liverpool, on our way to Masaya, when a group of fifty soldiers stopped us in a forest by pointing their pistols at our throats. At first we thought they were bandits, but we were soon disabused. They took us prisoner and led us to the Agua Agria Hacienda, which was owned by Chamorro and located at the base of the Momobacho Volcano,[17] southwest of the city of Granada. I showed them my passport, signed in Washington by José de Marcoleta, the minister for Nicaragua, and I strongly protested this violation of international law. They turned a deaf ear. Later, by way of an apology, the officer who had arrested us, read us a letter written by President Chamorro, in which he ordered that all foreigners traveling on the Camino Real be arrested. Prisoners were to be sent to Granada or—if they put up any resistance—shot on the spot. It was quite kind of him to share this with me, but it gives you an idea of the situation. In any case, the next day, after thirty hours of captivity and more objections on my part, they freed us.

We were at the foot of the Momobacho Volcano, which, at 4,440 feet, forms a sort of promontory on the northwest side of Lake Nicaragua. For the time being the volcano is dormant and its crater, opened to the west, is a magnificent verdant amphitheater at the top of the mountain. We were traveling north, and as we lost sight of Momobacho, its brother volcano, Masaya, appeared in the northwest. The sight of this active volcano is quite unsettling. Before the conquest, Indians sacrificed young girls there each year by throwing them into the crater. The Spaniards called it Boca del Infierno. It makes its presence known from a distance. Even before you can see it, you hear its subterranean emissions that sound like continuous artillery fire during a raging battle. In daylight, a tall plume of yellowish white smoke can be seen high in the sky, whereas at night it turns into fire. It reminded me of the pillar of clouds and fire that accompanied the Israelites as they made their way through the desert in their exodus from Egypt.

The city of Masaya, six leagues to the north of this volcano, is a big and beautiful town, but one that has lost half its population. The only thing that separates it from the volcano is a small crater lake of considerable depth. Ephraim George Squier gives an excellent description of it in his highly interesting book *Voyage to Nicaragua*.[18] I arrived at the lake from Nindirí, a village two leagues to the north of Masaya—the cleanest and loveliest of the pueblos in this province. It is funnel shaped with perpendicular walls carved out by fire and large verdant forests towering above it to the southwest. I was led to a hill overlooking the countryside. Before me rose the volcano, whose fiery summit was reflected in the lake in flashes of red. To my right was an enormous lava field that extended over several leagues to the north. At our feet was a path carved deep into the stone, with five or six wooden ladders placed one above the other, which were used by the Indian women of Nindirí to go down to fetch water at a depth of more than five hundred feet. There is nothing more picturesque than these young girls with their copper-colored skin, carrying their clay jugs on their heads with incomparable dexterity, just like the biblical scenes painted by Horace Vernet.[19] On the cliff strange drawings were carved into the walls and painted red, just as Squier described them.[20] These, along with the strange legends that I was told about this lake and volcano, offer evidence that extraordinary religious rites existed in this area at the time of indigenous rule.

The Masaya Volcano stands out against a mountain range that extends along the Nicaraguan coast and forms two vast valleys with the flatlands that I spoke of earlier. At first it appears that the valley where Lake Nicaragua is located ends at this point. But, in fact, the plain extends to the east towards the Panaloya River, which is navigable only by native canoes. The Panaloya flows into Lake Managua, which is incorrectly called Lake León in most of our geography books. Lake Managua, which is the biggest Central American lake, is at a higher elevation than Lake Nicaragua by twenty-eight feet. In my opinion its shores are more varied and charming. The city of Managua is located on the southern shore, seven leagues from Masaya. And like Masaya, it is a partially destroyed city. The government had attempted, before the start of the current civil war, to establish its seat there in order to avoid the petty rivalries between the cities of Granada and León.

As we continued towards the capital city, León, six leagues away from Managua, the fabled view of the volcanoes that line up along the plain became visible. The first cone, jutting out into Lake Managua, is the volcano on the island of Momotombo, the tallest in the state of Nicaragua, at more than seven thousand feet. Then as I scanned the horizon from the southeast to northwest along a stretch of fifteen leagues, I saw a range of cones of various heights, seven of which are volcanoes. They are Momotombo, Axuzco,[21] Las Pilas, Orota,[22] Telica,[23] Santa Clara, and El Viejo,[24] which rises to six thousand feet in elevation.

There is nothing more majestic than this series of peaks as seen from the top of the León cathedral towers one hour before sunset. I could not get enough of this scenery, and each time I went up to look at it, I felt the same thrill as I had the time before. I admired the plain of León, located between these volcanoes and hills along the Pacific coast; it is one of the richest and most beautiful in the world. At sunrise Momotombo forms a bay in Lake Managua, that is still remembered, according to Indian legend, for an ancient city consumed by sinful pleasures that suffered the same fate as Sodom. The memory of the city lives on in indigenous songs and music that I collected. Terror-stricken, the native people point out the ruins of the accursed city, which are still visible beneath the lake's surface. Not far from away, the Spaniards built the first city of León, which in the language of the area was called Nagarando.[25] After a catastrophic flood, fearing that the city would again be destroyed by high waters, they moved it seven leagues towards the interior, in the middle of the plain at its current location. Looking west from the top of the cathedral, you can make out the unimpressive structures of El Realejo and beyond them, the blue waters of the Pacific Ocean.

León, which was once the rival of Guatemala City, is today reduced to a population of approximately twenty thousand residents. Ravaged by war and factional conflict for the last thirty years, this city is a heartbreaking sight. The neighborhood behind the cathedral was once the richest and most beautiful of the city. Now reduced to ruins after being torched at the beginning of the war of independence, the area is overgrown with tropical vegetation. The rest of the city is a shadow of what it once was. With the exception of the home of the vice-consul of England, Thomas Manning, I didn't see a single building that didn't bear some sign of destruction. The cathedral, dedicated to Saint Peter, is the only intact freestone building to be found in the state of Nicaragua. The church, which I believe is the largest in all of Central American, has five solid vaulted naves. This squat, weighty edifice is nevertheless quite majestic, especially once inside. It has survived because of its solid construction, despite the fact that on more than one occasion it has been used as a fort, leaving its damaged towers pockmarked from cannonballs and bullets.

The government house where I saw the director and his ministers in session, occupies one side of the square next to the cathedral. It is the sort of raised one-story building so typical in Nicaragua but in the most appalling state—neglected and filthy. The same can be said for the Episcopal palace across from the cathedral, which has been transformed into military barracks. The galleries, reception halls, classrooms, and auditoriums of both León's seminary and university, with its long history and glorious reputation as a place of high learning, have been given over to the Democratic army's horses.

I won't discuss the depths to which society in general and even the clergy have fallen in this unfortunate region. However, it is not difficult to imagine after twenty-five years of the most savage and barbaric civil war. As for commerce, there is none. A great many families fled or were sent into exile by one party or the other. Capital has dried up, as has the labor force, and the few foreign merchants that had been established here, left, discouraged by the sorry state of affairs. Several Frenchmen lost everything in the siege of Granada. Italians and Germans who had business in that city saw their homes and merchandise go up in flames, with no hope of ever receiving restitution for their losses. In Chinandega an honorable merchant and compatriot, Jules Lefebvre, the proprietor of several haciendas, complained that he would leave the country if only he could find someone willing to buy his land, which he is ready to sell at a loss. No one dares travel the roads or trails since they are swarming with bandits. The city of El Realejo, so renowned during Spanish rule, is no more than a decaying hamlet ever since its port was rendered impractical by an increasingly constricted tide. Is it any wonder after all this that conservatives or, for that matter, rational citizens have turned to the Americans for help? Would Texas or California ever be allowed to deteriorate into such a deplorable state? Would they ever be the theater of the types of abuses committed in broad daylight in Nicaragua? Neither the honest citizens of this country nor the foreigners have a great affinity for those from up north. And yet, despite their natural antipathy, they would welcome a López-style invasion as a positive development.[26] This is something that European governments should take into account.

When leaving León to go towards Chinandega, I entered the city's vast outskirts. Like the rest of the country, this area, inhabited by aborigines, is in a terrible state. This district is called Subtiaba and in ancient times it was inhabited by the Mangue Indians, mentioned in Torquemada's *Monarquía Indiana*.[27] There are two churches and the main one is big and beautiful. The population before independence was substantial. The Indians of Subtiaba preserved their language, which is spoken in several areas within the state of Nicaragua. I could find no relation between this language and those of San Salvador or Guatemala, but perhaps there are commonalities with Trique and Chiapanec.[28] However, I can only base this statement on my recollections.

In the linguistic research I have been able to conduct, I was struck by the past influence and prevalence of Nahuatl over such a large area. Others before me had observed that this language is spoken well beyond the boundaries of the ancient Mexican Empire, situated in the north. Contemporary authors have agreed with early historians in recognizing the presence of Nahuatl among a wide variety of peoples and as far as Veraguas and Panama City. Some have tried to explain this by theorizing that the Tlaxcalan and Mexican soldiers accompanying Cortés and Alvarado in their travels and conquests later settled throughout Central America. This may well be a reason, but it is not a sufficient explanation. A few thousand soldiers dispersed in hundreds of locations over such a vast area could not change the language of ancient peoples that were already living there in so little time, especially when the Spaniards brought their own language with its varying influences. The introduction of Nahuatl must therefore predate the discovery and conquest of America.

However, there is something more compelling that no one has observed until now; something that I noticed thanks to my knowledge of Nahuatl and linguistics that I began to study during my stay in Mexico. I have seen evidence that the names of native animals—mammals, birds, fish, reptiles, and insects—of trees, plants, minerals, remedies, and potions, all derive from the Mexican language. I have found this to be true throughout the areas of Central America where I have traveled both in the native dialects and among Spanish speakers, even when they are of European descent. These words are often admirably imitative and expressive of properties intrinsic to the objects that they designate. Sometimes alternative terms do exist in an area's native language, but the lexicon is incomplete and often the word does not exist at all. I believe that Nahuatl always fills this void, just like Greek and Latin do in our European languages. During my trip I have discussed this with naturalists, chemists, and medical doctors. I have even pointed out to them that commonly used words relating to natural history were not at all Spanish as they had thought, but rather had been altered to sound like Spanish when in fact their origin was unmistakably Mexican. They all marveled at the clarity of these words and their etymologies. They recognized, as I did, that Nahuatl must provide a complete and perfectly exact classification of all aspects of natural history, including the properties of plants and animals. Moreover, this language must have occupied a place among the civilized nations of Mexico and Central America that was analogous in stature to that of Greek and Latin in Europe. *Plantas y Animales de la Nueva España* by Phillip II's physician, Francisco Hernández,[29] abridged by Nardo Antonio Recchi and later the Jesuit priest Juan Eusebio Nieremberg, supported this claim. In my opinion, it is quite impossible for Mexican soldiers following Cortés or Alvarado to have performed such miraculous work. Nahuatl is without a doubt one of the ancient languages of Central America predating Montezuma's Empire, because the Aztec armies never went farther than Chiapas or Soconusco.

Since arriving in Guatemala City, given the supportive and enthusiastic welcome that I have received, I have done my best to gather all the documents that I could find on the ancient history and languages of the native peoples of this area. But I am not merely surveying them. I have been studying them diligently, making copies of several manuscript vocabularies and documents in the original dialects. I have in my possession several in Kaqchikel, K'iche', and Tz'utujil and am attempting to translate them. Soon, I will move to an Indian village in Vera Paz where they don't speak Spanish and where I intend to stay until I have been able to learn their language and customs. This will allow me to put into practice what until now have only been theories and abstractions.

Although I have not made much progress yet in these studies, there are a few facts that I can put forth with certainty relating to Guatemalan ethnography. The first is that although initially the languages in this area seem extremely varied, in reality there are only a small number of them. They are dialects that vary only because they have a mix of foreign words, as well as differences in their pronunciation, final syllables, or vowels. It seems obvious to me that before the arrival of the tribes who controlled this territory at the time of the conquest, the language of the Guatemalan kingdoms must have been either Yucatec Maya or Tzetal,[30] which are very similar. Nahuatl or Mexican may have also been spoken in the region at that time, as it is to this day in a more or less corrupted form. The monuments that I have seen in this area prove to me that a great ancient civilization already reigned here—a civilization on a par with those of the Yucatán Peninsula and Palenque.

During the eleventh century the Guatemalan tribes known as the K'iche', Kaqchikel, Tz'utujil, and Tzotzil invaded the region. They most likely came from the lands closest to Mexico, if not from Mexico itself. This was the time of the collapse of the Toltec Empire, due to internecine strife and a wave of invasions from northern barbarians. When they arrived in Guatemala, these tribes destroyed any obstacle in their path as they conquered these provinces. When the Spaniards arrived, the indigenous invaders were subjugated in turn or in some cases driven into the mountains of Lacandon and Vera Paz. The latter was the fate of the Mam or Poqomam peoples, who today speak a language that is almost identical to the one spoken by the people of Yucatán. There is evidence that the eleventh-century conquerors were few and that they intermixed with the people they vanquished. As told in their earliest accounts, they abandoned their own language and adopted the tongues of the vanquished. The conquering tribes introduced a great many words from their native languages, and the intermingling created the dialects of the K'iche', Kaqchikel, Tzutujil, and Tzotzil, to name just a few, exactly in the same way that the ancient French language was formed from Latin and the barbaric words that the Franks brought to it.

These are my thoughts on the languages of Guatemala as I pass my days copying and studying their grammars, vocabularies, and documents. But as far as I am concerned the strangest thing that I have come across thus far, and the thing that will upset a great many theories, is that the words that don't come from Maya in K'iche', Kaqchikel, and Tz'utujil seem to me to be of Germanic, Saxon, Danish, Flemish, and even English origin. There are things that astonish me, that make me jump out of my chair as I discover them. Is it possible that these gentle people, as well of course as those who once sacrificed human blood, are in fact our brothers? Could they be the ancient followers of Odin and Thor?[31] Is it possible that pirates from the north made their way across the seas to the American continent?

A Tz'utujil manuscript, the *Padilla Codex*, named for the friend who gave it to me,[32] seems to confirm all these ideas. Like other sources, it says that this people's forefathers came to this region from the east, but it designates neither Africa nor the coast of the Mediterranean as their place of origin, rather the far north of Scandinavia. It states that they came from Tullan in the east and distinguishes it clearly from Tula near Mexico City.[33] They came from seven cities and represented thirteen tribes or families, traveling by sea in boats before arriving at their destination. They left a cold and cloudy land that rarely saw the sun. They brought with them their arts, science, magic, song, and music, all of which are contained in books that they call *Vuh* (which is pronounced like *Buch* in German). They engaged in battles at sea and later on land. Another manuscript adds that they arrived from the cold and snow, having suffered terrible hardships on an icy sea, in almost perpetual darkness, and that they went for a very long time without seeing the light of the sun.

Is it possible, that the Antiquarian Society of Copenhagen is right? The Toltecs, Mexicans, K'iche', Kaqchikel, and Tz'utujil may all be their brothers? Could they be Scandinavians? I am not yet ready to fully accept this idea. Before coming to any conclusions, I first must finish translating all these documents, several of which have passages that are still quite obscure. I certainly regret not being familiar enough with the histories and languages of the north. My

English, with little bits of Flemish and German and a few words of Norwegian and Danish are not up to the task. And yet, for the time being I see no other explanation for what I am finding in my documents, except to think that most of the invasions in this area came from the northeast. We would therefore have to accept that in America just like in Europe, barbarian invasions went from the northeast towards the southwest. As for civilization, that is a whole other matter. These barbarians, whether they were Scandinavian or Asian, found an established and fully formed civilization in America. Even the Toltec influence was minimal, although they did put their own particular stamp on the prevailing culture.[34]

These unexpected discoveries are fascinating and continue to engross me. I will continue my research and share my results with you, in a future letter, where I will give you details about my trip to the states of San Salvador and Guatemala.

Yours faithfully,
Brasseur de Bourbourg

FROM GUATEMALA CITY TO RABINAL

An Episode during My Stay in Central America during the Years 1855 and 1856[1]

After leaving Santa Ana la Grande or Sonsonate, Coaxiniquilapa[B1] is the last stop when traveling to Guatemala City from the state of San Salvador. I had spent the first night of February 1855 in the modest hut of Don Miguel Sanchez de Léon, the *colector de rentas*.[2] He had been gracious enough to offer me his hospitality when I arrived at his door in search of shelter for myself as well as for my *mozo de camino*[3] and my mules. I was up before dawn and by five o'clock, and after having taken leave of my host, I got back in the saddle to head towards the capital of the Guatemalan provinces. From Coaxiniquilapa the road continues to climb towards the northeast through the Cordilleras that surround the plateau upon which Guatemala City is built. From these mountains the panorama is varied, with nothing to obstruct the view but scattered clusters of pine trees. You see the blue waters of the Pacific Ocean as well as the lofty volcanic peaks of the Guatemalan plain. My mule was going at a walk or a trot, sometimes preceding, sometimes following the mozo, who was walking the mule bearing my luggage. He was a young *Ladino*[D2] of twenty and my only travel companion. Along the way, he told me the names of

---

B1. Coaxiniquilapa is a village located in the mountains above the Río de Los Esclavos, eleven or twelve leagues to the east of Guatemala City. [The most widely used spelling on maps from Brasseur's period is "Cuajiniquilapa," with alternate spellings of "Cuangunicuilapa" or "Quajiniquilapa." It is currently called "Cuilapa."]

B2. *Ladino* is the name given to the mixed raced people born of whites and Indians or blacks, which implies a superior education or intellect in comparison to both Indians and blacks. [A Ladino is a Spanish-speaking or acculturated Indian, according to Ophelia Marquez and Lillian Ramos Navarro Wold, eds., *The Compilation of Colonial Spanish Terms and Document Related Phrases* (Midway City, CA: Shhar Press, 1998), s.v. "Ladino."]

places as we passed through but this was practically the only subject that would break our long silences. With the grand vistas unfurling in front of me I had quite enough to keep my mind occupied. For those, like me, who have succumbed to its charms, the natural scenery in the tropical regions of the Americas is completely captivating, whether in the *cold lands* of the high Cordillera or in the *hot lands* along the barely marked paths of its forests. I never grow tired of these isolated places in which I spend my life as a traveler. They seem fully inhabited and I have never for one moment felt alone.

We passed the hacienda of Arasola and at around 5 PM I arrived at the point at which the road begins its descent towards the plain. The trail is steep but the landscape magnificent. Every few feet there was a new vista and soon the valley of Guatemala in all its glory was at my feet. Some time later the city appeared, set on the plain like the queen of Central American cities. From a distance it made the most delightful impression, with its soaring churches, towers, and domes looking like a large dull white chessboard laid out on a green carpet. It was hardly an hour before sunset. The sun lit up both the city and the surrounding countryside, illuminating the nearby volcanic peaks in a most unusual way. In the distance, the fading rays of light haloed the mountains of Vera Paz, which were lost in a misty ocean of shadow and light.

The road was excellent, not wild and overgrown like so many roads outside Central American cities. Along the way I saw well-tended plantations. The people, coming and going on foot, on horseback, or in carriages, were from all walks of life. It was obvious that I was about to enter a densely populated area. As we approached, we completely lost the city from sight. We came to the villa de Guadalupe, a charming leafy village with tidy white houses, whose name brought back memories of the outskirts of Mexico City. Night approached and the sun completely disappeared behind the volcanoes. Before we could bid it farewell, the fiery plumes that follow in its wake had gone from the most brilliant purple to the darkest violet. We hadn't yet crossed the plain that separated us from the outskirts of Guatemala when darkness engulfed the entire countryside. The sky was studded with dazzling constellations that provided the light we needed to guide us along our way. A gully—in this area called a *barranco*—with high walls protected the entrance to the city. In

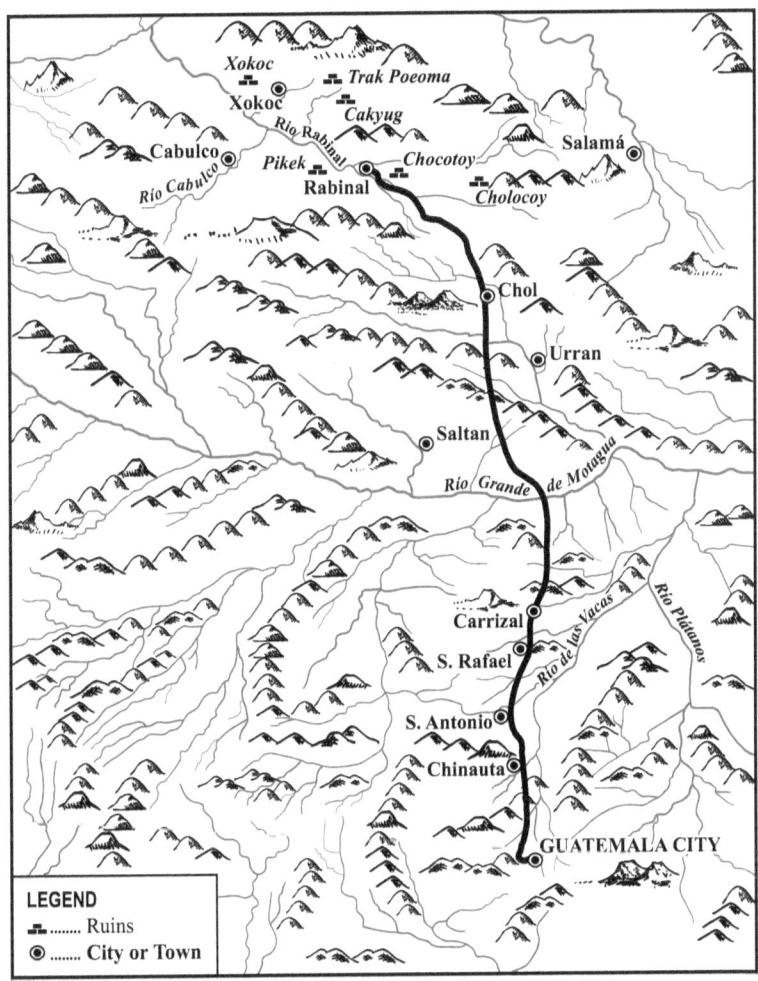

BRASSEUR'S ROUTE FROM GUATEMALA CITY TO RABINAL
Based on an 1859 map of Guatemala, which marks several of the historic ruins around Rabinal mentioned in Brasseur's text. Maximilian Von Sonnenstern and August Van De Gehuchte. *Mapa general de la Republica de la Guatemala.* (New York: Publicado por Maximilian v. Sonnenstern por orden del gobierno, 1859). Accessed at Geography and Map Division of the Library of Congress. Map by Paporn Thebpanya. Copyright © 2017, University of Oklahoma Press.

the dark of night it could easily have been mistaken for a man-made fortification, like one of Vauban's. We descended into it, and then we crossed a bridge at the bottom of the ravine that had been built by the Spanish over an insignificant stream of water. When we reemerged we were at the *garita*, or gate, known as Del Barranquillo.

We were finally in Guatemala City. The customs officials stopped us momentarily. But soon we were riding down poorly lit, deserted streets, with wretched-looking houses. Our path hugged the wall of the Monastery of San Francisco. Despite the darkness, I could still make out this imposing structure, like so many other Franciscan buildings in Spanish America. We crossed the Calle Real, the most beautiful and usually most animated street of the city. But what a difference between what I was seeing now and what I had seen from a distance just two hours earlier! It was only seven in the evening and already the whole place was quiet and deserted. From time to time, we saw passersby wrapped in their Spanish mantas. The lines of one-story houses with few windows gave the impression that the city was nothing but an enormous monastery. I must admit that at first what struck me when I saw these long streets and right angles was the city's monastic austerity, although later when I was able to walk the streets in daylight, I had to reevaluate my first impression.

In Guatemala I enjoyed the hospitality of the general consul of the Netherlands. How I came to have such good lodgings needs a bit of explanation. I have always had good fortune during my travels in distant lands and can thank God for the wonderful people whom I have met, the friendships with compatriots and foreigners throughout Spanish America, and the excellent relationships I developed with the natives of those countries. During a trip between New Orleans and Vera Cruz[4] I had the honor of meeting André Le Vasseur, who in 1848 was named the French minister plenipotentiary to Mexico. He graciously invited me to join him in his carriage for the trip up to Mexico City and after that he often welcomed me into his family's home as his guest.[B3] At

---

B3. Mr. Le Vasseur was instrumental in supporting my research on Mexican antiquities. He gave me the title of chaplain of the French legation and as a result he introduced me to the heads of government and of the diplomatic corps. [This position also gave Brasseur access to the libraries of the area and through his connection to Le Vasseur he undertook a trip through Mexico to San Francisco, California.]

the end of 1854 during my stay in the port city of La Union in the state of San Salvador, I had the pleasure of dining at the home of Bernard Courtade, the French consular agent, where I met Florent t'Kint de Rodenbeek, the general consul of the Netherlands, who was passing through the city at the time. He told me I should consider staying in his home in Guatemala City instead of a hotel when I visited. From the moment that we met, I was fortunate to enjoy both his friendship and generosity. Arriving in this capital for the first time, it was a great relief to find a roof over my head immediately, especially one that would reflect so favorably in the eyes of others. I have nothing but the fondest memories for and gratitude to all those who welcomed me along my way and whenever possible I try to speak of their kindness.

The next day, I visited the French general consul, Interim Consul Alexandre Mellinet, the brother of General Mellinet, who was wounded in the battle of Sevastopol.[5] Once again, I considered myself lucky to find such a friendly and caring welcome. Mr. Mellinet took the time to introduce me personally to the city's ecclesiastical authorities. The archbishop was away on his round of visits, therefore we went first to Don José María Barrutia, headmaster and vicar-general of the diocese. Among the many Hispanic-American clergymen that I had the pleasure of meeting, he stands out as a man of the finest character. Mr. Mellinet then took me to meet General José Rafael Carrera,[6] the Supreme and Perpetual Leader of the Republic, Don Pedro de Aycinena, the minister of foreign affairs, as well as Mr. Charles Lennox Wyke, Her Majesty the Queen of England's chargé d'affaircs, for whom I had a letter of introduction from the late Dr. Drivon, that excellent man, who built the port of Acajutla.[B4] A few

---

B4. Dr. Drivon, the son of a Frenchman born in the West Indies, lived in Sonsonate, where he exercised a great deal of influence by dint of his frank and generous character. His home was opened to all and was one of the most pleasant in that city. His hospitality was what would be expected of a man of such a temperament. Dr. Drivon built the port in Acajutla, four leagues from Sonsonate, by moving the wharf, which he rebuilt at great expense, as well as the government and customs depots. He died in 1856 and is much regretted. [John Lloyd Stephens (1805–52) also meets Dr. Drivon during his travels through the port of Acajutla and Sonsonate; see *Incidents of Travel in Central America, Chiapas and Yucatan* (New York: Harper & Bro., 1852), 1:chap. 15.]

days later, Mr. Wyke was kind enough to honor me with an invitation to dine with government ministers and members of the diplomatic corps, and I was soon admitted into the highest circles of Guatemalan society. Thanks to Mr. Florent t'Kint and José Mariano Padilla's continued friendship I was not just invited to official functions but was welcomed to share in the more intimate family life of some of country's most important families. I will never be able to fully express all my gratitude for their kindness, since it was through them that I met the Larraves, Aycinenas, Piñols, Arrivillagas, Mateos, Pavons, Echeverrias, Rodriguezes, Garcias Granados, etc. I attribute my achievements in this region to my good fortune at having met all these fine people. Finally, I must add, that I owe a great debt of gratitude to the archbishop for the trust he bestowed on me, when he gave me the responsibility of directing several important parishes, including Rabinal's, which was formerly under the control of the Dominican Order.

It was not long before I was informed of the archbishop's return to the city, and Mr. Mellinet graciously accompanied me to the archiepiscopal palace to introduce me. Monseigneur Francisco de Paula García Peláez was a small old man, weak and spindly, at the age of more than eighty. Yet despite his age and fragile constitution, he was astonishingly vibrant and active, traveling by horse up and down the challenging mountains paths of his vast diocese, in order to visit a part of his flock every year. Monseigneur Garca Peláez is the author of a book filled with curious information about the history of Guatemala that ranks among the most important of those rare works on contemporary Central America.[B5] For an hour, he spoke to us about history, literature, and geography and proved to be completely up to date with the most eminent European thinkers. In particular he was a great admirer of Mr. von Humboldt[7] and the Geographical Society of Paris. A few days later, the archbishop honored me with a personal visit at the consulate of the Netherlands.

B5. Francisco de Paula García Peláez, *Memorias para la historia del antiguo reyno de Guatemala* (Guatemala City: Tipografico de L. Luna, 1851).

From Guatemala City to Rabinal

In the meantime, I had started to tour the city and visit its most interesting sites. I relied mostly on Dr. Padilla as my guide. The modern history of Guatemala City is a remarkable one. The current city is the third by this name to have been built by the Spaniards. This has led to many errors on the part of European geographers. When the Conquistador Pedro de Alvarado arrived in Central America in 1523 this region was divided into states of various sizes, the largest of which were the kingdoms of Utatlán,[8] Quauhtemalan, and Atitlán, each named for their capital cities. Together they formed what is today the state of Guatemala. The majority of K'iche' and of Mam speakers lived in Utatlán, which had suzerain control over the two other regions until it was conquered early in 1524. Alvarado ordered King Oxib Queh[9] and his presumptive heir, Beleheb Tzy burned alive and their capital was set aflame. Tecpan Quauhtemalan, from which the Spaniards derived the name Guatemala, was where the royal house of the Kaqchikels[B6] resided and Atitlán was the home of the Tz'utujil royal house. The languages of these two people are dialects of the more elegant and refined K'iche' language, and all three languages are still spoken today in these regions. Alvarado decided to establish his seat of power in their city, thus it became the first Spanish settlement. At first, the Kaqchikels, met Alvarado peaceably and sent a delegation to meet Cortés. However, Alvarado's barbaric rule and the cruelty of his troops drove the area's natives to take up arms against him. He had to abandon Tecpan Guatemala and in November 1527, after many bloody battles, his brother Jorge de Alvarado, whom Pedro had named Governor in his absence, laid down the foundations for the first Spanish city, named Guatemala. It was built at the foot of Mount Hunahpú, which is called the Agua Volcano and was given

---

B6. Tecpan-Quauhtemalan is the Nahuatl or Mexican name for this city, which was called Iximché, meaning "Bamboo Trees" in Kaqchikel. This city is in ruins today. The descendants of these ancient people live in a large pueblo of the same name, that is approximately one league away and which is located sixteen leagues to the northwest of Guatemala City. Utatlán and Atitlán are also names derived from Mexican. The K'iche' called their capital Gumarcaah and the Tz'utujil called theirs Tziquinihay.

the name Ciudad de Santiago de los Caballeros de Guatemala. In 1541 Alvarado was killed by Indians in northern Mexico. That same year a devastating earthquake caused a breach in Agua Volcano's water-filled crater thereby unleashing a torrent of water and mud that wiped out a great deal of the city and its population. Among the dead was Doña Beatriz de la Cueva, Pedro de Alvarado's widow, the newly installed governor of the kingdom.

Many saw these catastrophes as divine retribution, a sign from God as punishment for the excessive cruelty of the conquistadors. The venerable Francisco Marroquín, Guatemala's first bishop, was named as the city's provisional governor. He attempted to improve the lot of the oppressed natives by enacting some of the more liberal measures favoring the indigenous population that the Spanish court had put forth. Moreover, under his auspices, the city was moved to the Panchoy valley, a league away from its original location. Despite continued threats from frequent earthquakes, the city prospered. Gradually it became one of the most beautiful cities in the New World, with an expanding population, increasing wealth, stunning architecture, and its excellent climate. And then, in 1773, a violent tremor completely destroyed it. Those who escaped with their lives took refuge in the surrounding area. In 1776 the Spanish court mandated that the capital be moved to the Ermita valley, six leagues away to the northeast. Thus began the construction of the current capital. Without counting the former capital of the Kaqchikels, three Spanish cities situated in close proximity to one another have born the name Guatemala. The first, at the foot of the Agua Volcano, is now a beautiful village called Cuidad Vieja. Rebuilt by some of its residents after 1773, the second city, which has seen a resurgence in the last ten years, is known as Antigua Guatemala. It has a population of approximately eighteen thousand and is hoping cochineal cultivation will allow it to reclaim some of its past prosperity. The third and current capital is called Nueva Guatemala or simply Guatemala. I hope that these details will help clarify things for the authors of geography books, who have a tendency to copy one another, without consulting sources that provide new information. I have noticed that when it comes to Mexico and

Central America these authors sometimes make the most extraordinary claims.[B7]

From the vantage point of the city, now that the luminous veil of mist that had enveloped it on the night of my arrival had lifted, the Guatemala plateau no longer seemed quite as picturesque. It is a starkly monotonous expanse, clearly inferior in every way to the valley in which Antigua Guatemala is located. Because of the elevation of more than four thousand feet above sea level, the base of the surrounding mountains are not visible, there are nothing but midsections and peaks to be seen. One curious fact is that the water, which supplies the city's fountains and washhouses, flows from the nearby hills of the town of Mixco by way of a three-league-long aqueduct and then divides into two rivers—one that goes towards the Atlantic and the other that flows in the opposite direction into the Pacific Ocean. Another curious feature is that deep fissures have

---

B7. I have traveled throughout most of North and Central America and I must say that, if the geography books on other regions are anything like the ones I know relating to the Americas, then it reflects very badly on the state of geography and leads me to believe that most of our geography books and maps are based on something other than common sense. I will say that several of Victor Adolphe Malte-Brun's are certainly exceptions to this rule. However, the following is a perfect example of the type of mistakes found in those poorly researched books. On p. 145 of a book entitled: *Nouveau discours sur les revolutions du globe*, by J. B. François-Étienne Ajasson de Gransagne and Valentin Parisot (2 vol. in-18, Paris, 1842), one reads the following for the entry on Guatemala City:

> Founded in 1773 in Mexico. A city of Guatemala, which is different from today's city by that name, was built in 1742. Nine years later it was destroyed by an earthquake but rebuilt soon afterwards. In 1773, during the eruption of the volcano upon which the city was built, large cracks formed in the ground, which five days later became a gaping abyss. The city and its 8000 residents were soon engulfed. There is no longer a single trace of this city in the area and the location where Guatemala once stood is now completely deserted.

This is how history is written in France and yet the authors of this scholarly work arrogantly state on p. 13: "Until now geographers have only presented *fiction* (rather than historical facts) relating to the revolutions of the globe." [Brasseur's emphasis. A book by the authors J. B. François-Étienne Ajasson de Gransagne and Valentin Parisot entitled *Nouveau discours sur les révolutions du globe* (Paris: tous les libraires, 1839–40) can be found in the Bibliothèque nationale de France's catalog.]

formed in the ground, like a ring of natural trenches surrounding the city. These gullies, called *quebradas*, formed as a result of volcanic and aquatic convulsions, can be seen all along the plains. In fact, one such gully opened up not far from the monastery of Santo Domingo and it is like an immense garden at a depth of six hundred feet with strangely twisted terrain and deep crevices.

The so-called Gulf Mountains, which are the starting point of the road that leads to the Atlantic coast, are the eastern boundary of the Guatemala plateau. To the south and west three peaks tower above the landscape. The first is Hunahpú or the Agua Volcano, with its remarkably pure line and majestic pyramid-shaped cone, seven or eight leagues away. Further to the east the squat Pacaya appears. In the southwest, only the distant peak of the Fuego Volcano is visible above the Kaqchikel Mountains. To the north, the plateau ends abruptly with a deep valley above which the noble mountains of Vera Paz are visible.

Like most cities built by the Spaniards in the New World, Guatemala is built on a rather inelegant design of gridded streets. The Plaza Mayor, or "Main Square," is a rectangle of 195 meters long and 165 meters wide at the center of the city, where most of the government buildings are located, such as the government palace, formerly the residence of the captains general. With its long arcade, this unimposing building, completely devoid of majesty makes it perfectly obvious that the jittery representatives of the Spanish court, fearful of earthquakes, unconditionally adopted the local custom of building low, one-story structures. The mint and the courthouse are located on the same side of the square. On the north side is the municipal hall, with porticos like the ones that adorn the government palace. Across the way is the shopping arcade and house of the Marquis of Aycinena. Finally, across from the government palace is the cathedral, with its choir school known as the Colegio de Infantes on one side and the archiepiscopal palace on the other. Built at the end of the eighteenth century, the church, while by no means grandiose, is nevertheless a beautiful Italianate structure. The immaculately maintained archiepiscopal residence has an interior reminiscent of a villa in Rome or Albano. Other buildings of note in the city are

La Merced Church and monastery, currently a professed house for Jesuits from Santo Domingo, San Francisco, and Santa Teresa. The so-called Recolección Church, with its two grand square towers, is a picturesque sight to behold, and its nave reminded me a bit of the Church of Santa-Maria degli Angeli near Assisi. I can also add to this list the tastefully elegant University of San Carlos as well as the theater, a building that was still under construction but that was already getting a lot of praise.

Guatemala is now a city with a population of around fifty thousand. For the last ten years, former residents of the Belgian colony of Santo Tomás[10] have settled here, bringing new economic activity and contributing greatly to this growing city. My three months in the capital were spent not only visiting its monuments but also its libraries. These precious depositaries, where clergymen from different orders collected treasures related to the history and philology of the indigenous people of this region, unfortunately no longer contain within their walls more than mere scraps of their past glory. The dire effects of the revolution are everywhere. In 1836 the so-called Liberal Party triumphed, led by Francisco Morazán.[11] At that time—with the exception of the Mercedarian monks, who had found favor with the new leader—the country's clergy was expelled from their monasteries and went into exile along with the archbishop of Guatemala, Francisco de Casaus, who was deported to Havana. The country's archives and books suffered an even worse fate. They were piled into manure carts and brought to the university in complete disarray only to be tossed on the floor in a dark, humid room. There they stayed for ten years until their legitimate owners returned to the country. Meanwhile, anyone was free to pillage and plunder. In fact, an Englishman whom I met in Guatemala City admitted that for a mere three hundred piasters he was allowed to pick and choose whatever he wanted from the collection. The archbishop of London purchased his acquisitions and now one of the most enviable Guatemalan monastic collections can be found in England. The fate of government archives was no better. When the city of San Salvador was declared the capital of the Central American Federation, all documents belonging to the former captains general were relocated.

Today they can be found under the rubble of that Salvadoran city, which was destroyed in an earthquake in 1854. Dr. Padilla, who deplored such a regrettable loss, tried in vain during his short time as minister to repatriate this valuable collection, which had been unjustifiably removed from his country. Along with a group of like-minded guardians of knowledge, he offered to rescue these documents from their fated neglect and destruction. But the petty jealousies that divide the large cities of Central America proved to be an insurmountable obstacle to this noble undertaking. Unless the government of San Salvador decides to perform a magnanimous act—and without a doubt, there is no shortage of pure souls capable of setting aside these small-minded feuds—these archives will suffer the fate of those of the Colegio Seminario Tridentino de San Ramón and the university in León, Nicaragua. I saw what remained of their archives after they were damaged, sullied, and even trampled by horses in the library that Francisco Castellón's[12] army was using as stables.

When the current president Rafael Carrera came to power his first concern was to recall the clergy, who were still a force for discipline and civilization despite their waning influence. Their monasteries, libraries, and documents were all returned to them—but in what condition! Most of the works from the libraries were returned with pages missing or riddled with wormholes. Sullied manuscripts were falling to pieces covered in a pungent dust. These are the gains that had been made by knowledge thanks to the revolution and liberalism in Guatemala. The Morazán administration, which was extolled by the English and the Yankees, was not content to ransack monasteries and to expel their residents, it looted churches, it disposed of the majority of government buildings and took all the profits for itself. They even went so far as to strip the government palace of the beautiful clock that once adorned its façade.

For three months I was engaged in searching through what remained of these monastic riches. In the university library I found among the manuscripts of Father Francisco Ximénez[13] a history in K'iche', with an incomplete translation by Ximénez. I had copied both versions, and was attempting to acquire a working knowledge of indigenous languages, when His Grace the archbishop offered me the possibility of administrating the parish of Rabinal. Archbishop García Peláez, an enthusiast of literature and history, applauded my efforts. He told me that the only way to become well versed in indigenous languages and to understand their customs and traditions was to go live among them while in a position of authority that would be respected by them. I knew that this was all too true and therefore could not refuse the prelate's generous offer. I thanked him profusely but requested a few days to think about it, since, along with the obvious personal advantages of such a position, I would be responsible for people's spiritual welfare. Not long after our conversation, I accepted his offer. Rabinal is a large town in Vera Paz. It was the first town founded by the Dominicans in that area, after the Spanish conquest of the Guatemalan kingdoms. It has a population of six to seven thousand people, and with the exception of three or four hundred Ladinos or people of mixed blood, it is composed of an indigenous population that speaks K'iche'. Like the other parishes of Vera Paz, Rabinal comes under the authority of the Monastery of Santo Domingo in Guatemala City, which provided for all their spiritual needs by sending them pastors who were conversant in their language. But when the revolution disbanded the clergy, it also destroyed the established order in their reductions,[14] which fell under the domain of ordinaries, who were also deprived of resources. Soon, the Church had little choice but to fill their positions with the first person to come along. Unfortunately, when the country regained its sanity only a few poor souls, worn down by exile, returned to the monasteries. And since then both secular and regular clergy have been difficult to recruit. Priests that are well versed in indigenous languages are increasingly rare and their ability to administer sacraments is affected more and more each day. Large villages and towns must often do without a pastor, and the faithful who are lucky enough to have one are not always able to communicate with him easily.

This was the situation in Rabinal. After clashing with an officer in the militia of the nearby town of Salamá, Rabinal's previous priest—a Franciscan—was disgusted with the situation. He abandoned his post and asked the archbishop to kindly send him elsewhere. I was provided with a few more details from another source, which helped me understand the situation that was awaiting me in Rabinal. I was convinced that that my stay among these good and ordinarily obedient people, with only their occasional petty jealousies and minor squabbles, could be quite successful if from the beginning I availed myself of whatever could inspire their respect and confidence in me. With this goal in mind His Grace was kind enough to write Rabinal's indigenous governor and *alcaldes*[15] to announce that he had chosen a new pastor for them. He spoke of me in glowing terms to great effect. Given the rights that my nomination conferred upon me, I wrote them my own letter with specific instructions, but my orders were couched in polite and respectful terms that are rarely used with Indians. I asked them to provide me with porters to carry my belongings and to send me two young men who were equally versed in Spanish and the language of Rabinal, which I wanted to learn. The fact that I was a foreigner and a Frenchman—a nationality unknown to them—along with the words of praise in the archbishop's letter had excited a great deal of curiosity on the part of the residents of Rabinal. Moreover, my request for two interpreters as well as my expressed desire to learn their language had definitively predisposed them in my favor. Not only did they send me men, horses, and everything else that I needed to comfortably make the move to Rabinal, but the church's council of majordomos, composed of the main leaders of the region and descendants of the former K'iche' nobility, decided to provide an escort worthy of the exalted opinion that they had formed of me. Consequently four of them, accompanied by the first officers of each of the town's brotherhoods, were charged with the task of meeting with me in the capital in order to decide on the date of my arrival in Rabinal.

One Sunday at noon as I was finishing my lunch, the entire group arrived, in full dress. They wore baggy white calico pants that went halfway down their legs and were embroidered in different colors. Their pants were held in place by a silk scarf that was wrapped around their waist several times like a thick belt. On top of this they wore an Oriental-style jacket, with tight sleeves, made of a very unusual multicolored cloth, most likely woven by their wives. A madras scarf was tightly wound around their heads in a way that reminded me of the Egyptian headdress, the *calantica*,[16] but in this case, it was covered with a wide-brimmed, black straw hat. With their retinue, the mozos de camino, and their horses, they filled the consul's large courtyard. I stood before them under the gallery and received their first words of congratulations. The chiefs spoke Spanish rather well. A short, straightforward, and good-looking man named Mateo Coloche, who seemed to me to carry the greatest authority, was the first to introduce himself as one of the *fiscales*[17] of the Church of Rabinal. After having greeted me with a great show of respect, he made a speech overflowing with deference, in which he spoke of the great joy that the residents of his region had felt upon hearing the news of my nomination. He then introduced me to the three others: Miguel Pérez, a noble-looking and distinguished elderly man; Nacho (Ignacio) Coloche; and Vicente Toh. The latter was a short, stocky man. His wide, flat face bore a strong similarity to the descriptions that historians have made of Attila and his Huns. He had a striking air about him. And since then I have learned that Vicente Toh was the direct descendant of the former royal family of the tribe of Rabinal, the kings of Vera Paz.

I wasn't yet familiar enough with the customs of the country to be able to fully understand that by coming to meet me in person they were doing me a great honor. The youngest of the four, Nacho Coloche, seemed to realize this and quickly took it upon himself to enlighten me. He was a tall young man with the darkest of complexions who stared at me the entire time with his sparkling intelligent eyes.

"Señor padre," he said, "I feel I should inform Your Lordship that these men are all majordomos of the church of Rabinal, as am I. On top of that, Mateo Coloche also holds the position of fiscal. This means that we are among the most important leaders of the region's families. Our decision to come meet Your Lordship, ourselves, was completely voluntary, and we have never done this for any other *padre cura* before."

The implication of their act was perfectly clear to me now. I thanked them for their thoughtfulness and told them that henceforth

I knew I could always count on their respect and devotion. They, too, I said, could count on me for anything, as long as it didn't violate the law or conflict with my religious duties. I showed them the galleries and the rooms in the consul's house, where they could make themselves at home until my departure, which would be two days later in the morning.

They seemed perfectly pleased with this arrangement. The fiscal introduced me to two young men, somewhere between the ages of fifteen to eighteen, who had been specially chosen for my service. Their names were Akim (Joaquim) and Colash (Nicolás) López. Although they had a Spanish surname, they were nonetheless of indigenous origin. I knew that, as was the case for many others, their ancestors had received their Spanish names from their first godparents at the time of the conquest. Akim and Colash were brothers and great grandsons of Zuyen, the last royal governor of Rabinal, a descendant of the royal family of the area, just like Vicente Toh. They were both physically and intellectually agile, especially Colash, the youngest brother, whose eyes sparkled with intelligence. Naturally he was proud of his origins, and it took him quite some time until he could completely accept the duties required of him in his new role without bristling. In the end, he became more compliant and remained in my service until the very moment when I embarked in Izabal to return to Europe. Since he spoke both Spanish and K'iche' perfectly, he and his friend of the same age, named Colash Tecu, were my best interpreters. He helped more than anyone to learn the language. Moreover, he read and wrote Castilian superbly. At church his talent for singing and playing the violin was nothing less than astonishing for an Indian from deep in the Guatemalan mountains.

In the short time that I had before my departure, I quickly set about getting ready and called on a few people to say goodbye. The rest would have to wait for a later date and I wrote José Milla, who was the *oficial mayor* of the secretariat of state, to ask him to insert a thank you in the *Gaceta de Guatemala* from me to the families who welcomed me during my stay in the capital, begging their forgiveness for my hasty departure. I planned to leave on May 15. Early that day, I performed the Holy Sacrifice of the Mass at the church right next to Santa Catalina. Rufina Alfaro, a *mestiza*[18] of forty-five or fifty whom my friends hired to be my housekeeper, arrived at the consul's house with Dr. Padilla and his two eldest sons. I said my goodbyes to Mr. t'Kint de Rodenbeek and we mounted our horses. The clock in the neighboring convent rang seven as we set out. Our caravan was quite the sight, and people stopped in the streets to watch us pass by. The mozos de camino were up front, having left a few moments before the rest of us. These men, veritable *tlamemes*,[19] were fulfilling the same function as they had during the time of Montezuma. Despite the fact that the Spanish passed laws prohibiting the practice, the custom of using men as if they were beasts of burden continues even today in many provinces and especially throughout Central America. Mules are even harder to come by here than in Mexico and it is widely accepted that Indians are more reliable and less expensive. Native people are the means by which goods—carried on their backs—are transported from one coast to the other and across mountains. They start this difficult trade as children and some continue to practice it for most of their life. On a typical day, they go six or seven leagues, usually carrying forty or fifty kilos. They tie their load with a leather strap, called a *mecapal*[B8] worn over the very top of their foreheads, so that the weight is born by their head, just like the porters in the French city of Lyon. They are dressed in nothing more than coarse calico undergarments that they pull up above their knees or sometimes, they wear only a piece of fabric tied by a string that just barely covers their naked bodies. Each man ties his *matate*[B9] to one side of his load. This is a sort of net made of agave fibers containing his food. On the other side, he hangs his *soyacal*[B10] which is an umbrella made of rolled palm leaves under which he can momentarily take shelter in case

---

B8. *Mecapal* is a Mexican word, but like many others it has become part of the lexicon of colonial language in cases where there was no Spanish equivalent. [In English, *mecapal* is a "tumpline."]

B9. *Matate*, from the Mexican word *matlatl*, which means "net."

B10. *Soyacal*, from the Mexican word *zoyatl*, which is a type of palm tree, and the word *calli*, which means "house" or "shelter."

of a storm. Above his load he places his linen or wool jacket with a blanket that he uses to keep warm and to wrap himself in at night. Beneath his revealing clothing, it is easy to admire the strength of these bronzed bodies, stocky and square shouldered, with their mighty legs and arms, which in comparison, usually look spindly.

Joaquim, along with the others who were on foot, preceded my tlamemes. They were all armed with clubs. Behind them, the chiefs from Rabinal were mounted on small horses that are common in this area. Sitting atop an excellent little mule that had been brought to me from Rabinal, I was bringing up the rear with Dr. Padilla and his two sons. Rounding out our contingent were the representative of the consulate-general of Belgium, Alexandre Biermez, and, of course, Rufina.

As we left Guatemala on the road to Vera Paz, we crossed through the area in the outskirts called La Candelaria to the northeast of the city. This was the first settlement for the residents of Antigua after the earthquake that destroyed their city, when the Spanish court forced them to relocate. We saw many houses and a vast but unfinished church overgrown with vegetation, which resembled a ruin from ancient times. There were a few unprepossessing structures along the road, but they soon vanished and gave way to cob huts surrounded by quickset hedges. I felt that we had left the city far behind. The morning was lovely and warm. The approach of the rainy season, although not yet begun, had declared itself with a few storms, and the sun was hiding behind a drifting curtain of haze that would soon lift. To our right the stubby, uncultivated, and monotonous plain stretched out unchanged to the base of the mountains where the winding Gulf trail began. But the clear-cut shadows that appeared across the plain warned of those large fissures I spoke of earlier. To our left gaping crevices opened up before us—frighteningly deep gullies with magnificent vegetation growing up from their steep walls—giving the landscape an eminently delightful character. After having traveled a league and a half, we entered a narrow gorge with a rapid descent. This deep-set trail, carved out by water flowing through the tuff and sand, was so narrow that you could hardly walk two horses abreast. The place was named Los Órganos for the strange cracks that cut through the gully's walls and look like organ stops. On one side, this twisting path full of switchbacks had a view of the beautiful valleys along the road to Vera Paz, on the other it looked down on the wide quebradas, slashing through the Guatemalan plain. We crossed over one of these ravines on a rustic wooden bridge. Then came a descent so alarming that Dr. Padilla and his sons dismounted, preferring to gingerly lead their horses until they reached the bottom of that diabolical hill. Imagine a furrow cut into the sand along a sheer drop from the highest point of the foothills that buttress the Guatemalan plateau. Then imagine that the path plunges to the bottom of the precipice a thousand feet below. This might give you an idea of how the road to Rabinal begins.

My approach was to put more faith in my sure-footed mule than in my own dexterity, and therefore I made my way down leaning way back in the saddle. On a nearby hillside in the valleys below I could see a charming white church surrounded by a group of equally white houses. It was Chinauta, a small village two leagues away from Guatemala City where we would soon arrive. The Chinauta River, which is also called Río de las Vacas, flowed tumultuously through the valley, where it then separated into several large but much less deep branches. All around us were sandy, pine-covered hills. This was just my first taste of the mountains through which I would be traveling. We all stopped in Chinauta, and while my people from Rabinal had cooling drinks and ate of few corn pancakes, called *tortillas*, in the fragrant shade of the tall trees that line the banks of the river, Dr. Padilla, his two sons, and Mr. Biermez all bade me farewell. I must admit that this separation was quite emotional for me. When I got back on my mule it occurred to me that I was now completely alone with my Indians, all strangers to me, and my newly acquired housekeeper, who was just as unfamiliar. One small consolation was that Rufina spoke a little French, which meant that I could exchange a word or two in my native tongue with someone. Providence, which has so often protected me throughout my travels, continued to do so. That old, dark-skinned woman with her deep wrinkles and those bronzed and olive-skinned natives all showed me the most respectful warmth and affection. They would become such devoted servants that I can't resist taking this opportunity to express my gratitude towards them. How often I think of them, and with such nostalgia![B11] But at that moment, they were strangers to me, and as I followed behind at a distance alone with my thoughts, henceforth separated from the world in which I had previously lived and about to bury myself away with them in complete isolation, I felt an indescribable pang in my heart.

In the end, the sheer variety of the landscape tore me from my melancholy daydreams. We had already forded several branches of the river, and shaded by pine trees, we were gradually climbing into the hills that surround the valley. To our right, we passed the small Indian pueblo called San Antonio, whose church I could make out through the trees. We crossed the river of the same name; a calm stream that was not very deep at that time but that becomes swollen during the rainy season and sometimes has swept away intrepid souls who attempted to brave its fury. Soon we arrived at another valley, which, like the previous one, is surrounded by sandy foothills with conifer forests. And this felt more confining and wild. As we climbed the hills following a twisting path carved into the sand, we soon passed from this valley to the next. My Indians then prepared to take their first break, but only after crossing the Río Quesada, also known as Los Plátanos River.[20] This is a raging stream whose waters wear away at the foothills of shifting sands from which we had just descended. As I surveyed the scene from across the river where everyone was busily lighting their fires, the hills looked to me like the ramparts of a medieval fortified castle eroded by time. The indigenous people of the area, who are much more to the point, call both this place and the river that flows through it Cotoquic Ciwan, which translates as "Twisted Ravine." As soon as they had dismounted, two of the chiefs laid out a big mat covered with a large *pellón*.[B12] This

---

B11. My housekeeper, Rufina Alfaro, once traveled to France and Spain with the family of Monseigneur Viteri, who at the time of his death was bishop of Nicaragua. This girl, who was so kind and devoted to me while in my service, died of cholera last year, in 1857, only a few months after my return to France. I would like to pay tribute to her memory in gratitude for her service.

B12. A *pellón* is quite simply a very thick sheepskin usually dressed and dyed blue. It is used to cover a saddle so that the rider is more comfortably seated.

produced a sort of couch on the shore in the shade of a tall tree whose roots pushed up out of the ground and provided natural supports that I could lean back on.

While their servants were preparing their tortillas and grilled dried beef, Rufina—helped by the royal governor's two grandsons—prepared my lunch. Five or six fires were set along the riverbank at the same time. The chiefs sat directly on mats and others on the sand just as people do in the Orient. Everyone had a task. The scene reminded me of things I had read in the past. I have never traveled farther east than Malta, and yet I have a very clear idea of the Orient. Seeing all these bronzed faces, the way they were dressed, and how they carried themselves, made me feel that I was part of one of those Arab encampments about which I had so often read. The Europeans whom I met in America had often spoken of the gloomy and taciturn Indian character. However, they had only encountered the mostly primitive northern Indians or peons who have been reduced to all but slaves and therefore tremble in fear before those who rule over them with such arrogance. Here, on the contrary, I was taken aback to find a people who were unaffectedly gay and out-going. Although I couldn't yet understand their language, it was obvious that their conversations were full of jokes and quips. The young Colash López, who parried with both exuberance and subtlety, made the solemn Mateo Coloche and the heavyset Vicente Toh laugh until tears came streaming down their cheeks. These scenes were amusing, but they also opened up a whole new world to me. When they saw that I was interested, Colash explained what they were talking about to Rufina in Spanish so as to include me in their conversation.

At one o'clock, Mateo Coloche signaled that it was time to leave. We got back on our horses. Those who were on foot left us to take a different path, which was not as steep but even more water ravaged than the one near Chinauta. We now began climbing the slopes of the Cordillera for more than an hour, squeezed between hedgerows of all manner of withering plants whose yellow leaves showed signs of greening. We were starting to reach the first tall peaks. The forest was thick with holm oak, pine, and fir trees. Delicate moss, both strange and dark, fell from their century-old branches like capricious garlands. Soon the woods thinned and magnificent prairies stretched out before us, rich with feeding herds. We were in the vicinity of the San Rafael Hacienda, at a fairly high elevation. Whenever the woods gave way to a clearing, we had magnificent views of a distant landscape spilling over with vegetation and light. I noticed large boulders all around, scattered through the meadows or on the edge of streams. Sometimes they had been stacked one on top of the other for no apparent reason. At that time I didn't give it a second thought, but later when I passed that way again, I noticed that these stones could be found over a large area. There were no nearby volcanoes, and yet these huge stones seemed to have been gathered together on the highest hills and peaks. I examined some on a hill that looked out over the ranchos del Carrizal. There I discovered a number of blocks that, at least from a distance, might have been the ruins of a crude structure. When I got closer, my theory was confirmed. These large stones that were placed one on top of the other in no uniform way, formed something that resembled a tall tower. Their arrangement immediately reminded me of the Cyclopean structures on the Island of Gozo near Malta. Was I imagining things? I cannot say for sure. What is certain is that ancient tradition in this area speaks of a race of giants whose existence went back several centuries before the Christian era. This proud and powerful race, whose successors were the first Toltecs, was also remembered for its savage hedonism, which, in the end, was its undoing. Could these rocks, these heaps of stone be what remains of their ancient dwellings?

After bypassing these Cyclopean structures, we started to descend towards the valleys below. The view was extraordinary as we left behind the cool shade of the Vuelta Grande, the Río Grande de Motagua's vast river basin. Every wonder of nature seemed to have been gathered in one place; it was a feast for the eyes. In the distance surrounded by luxuriant vegetation I could make out a silvery vein, which reflected the light of the setting sun. It looked like a lake nestled between the high, sunlit cliffs that jutted out like enormous staggered terraces. That was the Río Grande. Nacho Coloche also pointed out the Hacienda del Saltan, owned by Canon

Ocaña, which was the agricultural center in the rich Urran valleys. The majestic Mount Tumabah or the "Trumpet of Stone," towered over everything. The Indians say that this is where thunderstorms originate. This is where the Heart of the Mountain (*ri Qux huyu*)[21] gives the signals for earthquakes by playing his resounding trumpet. Even farther away, one can make out the nine cones of Beleh Qeché, the main mountain range of Vera Paz, which sits like a crown in the background of this amphitheater, with its admirable outline standing out against the dark blue sky. Below us there was a series of valleys and we quickly descended towards them along alarmingly precipitous trails. When we had gone three hundred meters I could already see a few houses with red-tiled roofs that pierced through the foliage, but they soon disappeared from view as we rounded a bend in the road. Suddenly the loud, creaking sound of a sugar mill could be heard. It was the *trapiche* on the Sarzal Hacienda, where we were going to spend the night. The sugarcane fields went for as far as the eye could see. Interspersed were rows of banana trees heavy with long bunches of fruit hanging in the shade of their broad leaves. At the time of my visit the property was in shambles and José María Azmitia—who was the brother of the esteemed magistrate, José Antonio, president of the supreme court—was living there.

I was up before dawn the next day. At six o'clock the caravan was back on the road. I left not long afterwards, accompanied by Rufina and my two young servants. Leaving Sarzal we went up hill and down dale, towards the Río Grande. These woods cut through Guatemala's hot lands. We were traveling at the end of the dry season otherwise it would have been extremely difficult to pass through this area on horseback. Along the trail, large trees that had collapsed from old age lay across the path. The vegetation is in a state of indescribable chaos. There are yellow and green leaves side by side on the same branch as well as splintered tree limbs and coils of creepers like the most tangled skeins of yarn. The Indians rely heavily on their machetes. Using these large knives they slashed open new pathways, which led us to continually change course as we followed them through the brush.

Two immense foothills remained to be climbed before arriving at the banks of the river. When we emerged from the brush, we started on a bumpy path that I could hardly make out but that my party perceived to be carved into the cliff. We cut across a mountain ridge with sheer drops on either side. From these gaping abysses, whose depths were partially obscured by vegetation, rose the roar of nearby waters rushing to join the Motagua River. If it weren't for the surefooted Hispanic-American mounts, no one in their right mind would dare expose themselves to such obvious peril. We descended into a chasm and crossed a stream whose rumblings just moments ago had seemed so formidable. This gorge was breathtakingly beautiful, and on its terraced hills, lustrous foliage and tree ferns stretched towards the blue sky. Everything, including the gleaming streams of water piercing through this leafy scenery, derived brilliance from the sun and its warmth. I hardly had time to take it all in. The river was already to my left, flowing magnificently between two soaringly tall green-and-yellow rock walls. The sound was no longer the murmur of streams propelled into waterfalls. It was muffled, harmonious, and indistinct like the waves from a distant sea. A few steps farther brought us to the river's banks of fine white sand. We picked the safest spot to cross and fortunately, it was easy to ford. An enormous boulder had fallen from the mountain into the sandy riverbed and stuck its head up from the water, giving us a sense of its depth. When I passed through this same location the following July, it had rained a great deal in the mountains around the towns of Sololá and Joyaba, which feed the Motagua River. This stone that had acted as our gauge was completely submerged under the yellow waters, and I had no choice but to cross by way of a *garrucha.* This word translates as "pulley." In fact, there is a long cable tied to two large trees on opposite sides of the river and a pulley with a sort of basket. One by one everyone crouches in the basket like a monkey and using a rope that slides through other pulleys attached to trees on the riverbank, you are pulled left and right, suspended between water and sky. Belongings and merchandise also cross in this way, although animals are forced to swim from shore to shore.

I was sincerely grateful that this time I didn't have to put my fate in the hands of such an uncomfortable contraption, which certainly has its dangers. While the Indians, squatted in the shade on the left bank of the river, preparing their frugal meal of tortillas, frijoles, chilé, and dried meat, as they had the previous day, I dismounted across from them under the canopy of a bamboo shack, where the man who worked the garrucha lived. Rufina, with the help of my two young interpreters, was already busy making my meal. At nine thirty, we got back on the road. I crossed the Motagua, the boundary between the states of Guatemala and Vera Paz, and as soon as I got to the other side, I started the climb up the cliffs that are the entryway to the mountains of Vera Paz. This section of the journey was truly precarious. I am convinced that the men in my party, who were on foot and wanted to take the shortest possible route, decided to lead me onto the worst trail in the entire country. For a quarter league, I had to climb the slope of one of those gigantic foothills that abruptly ended at a precipice overlooking the river. In fact, the path was so steep that I had trouble keeping my balance on my mule. The trail, partially carved into the cliff, looked like a deteriorating staircase zigzagging through the woods, where roots and uprooted trees had become one with enormous rocks that seemed to have rolled down from the summit just to raise the level of difficulty on this horrendous path. After a half hour we arrived at the top of the first hill. We then continued along the crest on arid, stony ground sparsely covered in scrawny patches of grass withering in the blistering sun. My view was obscured by the forest and mountains that seemed to be stacked one on top of the other. From time to time I turned around to gaze one last time on the river, hemmed in by the fiery fawn-colored cliffs, and the Guatemalan mountains that we had crossed over the last two days.

As we continued to climb, I admired the plunging views of the valleys, where the roar of the Motagua could still be heard. From this higher plateau we could also start to make out the peaks of the volcanoes of San Salvador to the east and to the south the majestic cones of the Agua and Fuego Volcanoes on the Guatemalan plain. You could say that the same things always dominated these magnificent vistas. But what diversity, what majesty, what grandeur! This scenery is ever the same and ever changing! The soil became increasingly arid and stony. We continued to ascend along a steep, slick slope, on a path of blue-green shale. After climbing for two hours and cutting through a pine forest, we arrived at a charming clearing with a few old shacks as well as some newer houses. This is the aptly named hamlet of El Rodeo, which means "the long detour." My people stopped for a half an hour. Rufina offered me some *chicha* as a refreshment. I was curious to try this drink that was often mentioned in indigenous tales, and so I accepted. I understand that it is sometimes made of fermented maize or fruit with water and sugar or honey. Rufina's had pineapple chunks and was slightly sour and effervescent. It was quite pleasant to drink and packed a bit of a punch. In fact, given the hard climb that we had just completed, it was positively delicious! At twelve thirty, we started off once more on a path that marched us up and down two or three mountains, all with pine forests, through which terrifying precipices to our right or to our left could be seen and where the sound of roaring water was ever present. We moved between temperate and hot zones. From the heights of the sierra, which reminded me of melancholic Alpine landscapes, you could gaze down to the bottom of the abyss to find abundant tropical vegetation.

    Finally we reached the pueblo of Chol. This village is located on a plateau with steep cliffs all around and a screen of high mountains beyond. As we came around the road, its white church appeared suddenly. It had a beautiful Spanish gate with a bell, which acted as a bell tower and was surrounded by a few equally white houses. We were fifteen minutes away. I set off at a full trot with my mule followed by the Indian leaders, and soon we were galloping through the streets of Chol towards the *convento*. I dismounted in the courtyard and under the canopy I was greeted by the owner of the Saltan Hacienda, Canon Ocaña, who fulfilled clerical duties in the area when necessary. Chol, like other towns and villages, had no permanent priest. The canon embraced me and did me the honor of opening his home to me as a fellow cleric. My servants congregated under his gallery while my housekeeper prepared dinner. Chol's presbytery was modest in size for this country. Beyond the stables an enclosure for a now-neglected garden stretched out in terraces down to a sudden drop at the edge of a stream, whose water was flecked with golden sand carried down from the mountains. The church was rather beautiful with a ramshackle interior that resembled that of most Central American churches, since clergy had become so difficult to recruit. The Dominicans, to whom Spain had given the reduction of Vera Paz, founded the village of Chol. It was named for a barbarian tribe from the region near the Mopán River and Lake Petén Itzá that had been converted by the Dominicans. In order to prevent contact with their brothers, who had remained idolaters and persecuted the new converts, the tribe was moved by the clergymen inland towards previously subdued provinces, where the Chol people comingled with other populations. I spent the night in Chol. The next day, May 17, was the day of the Ascension. Early in the morning I celebrated a mass that my Indians attended showing great religious devotion. At six o'clock, I was back in the saddle after a cup of coffee. My men and I were off again scaling the final mountain that separated us from Rabinal. As soon as we left Chol, an unrelenting climb began. The orange and banana trees that had brought shade to the outskirts of the pueblo were soon replaced with cold-climate conifers. The ground consisted of slippery bluish shale, which made our task extremely trying. Shimmering silver-flecked talc rose from below as my mule made its way, stumbling against enormous blocks of stone that had been scattered about—who knows how at such an altitude—in every direction. Gradually we arrived at a habitually foggy zone. The morning wind sporadically carried up the billowing clouds, which then came back down as a light mist. Through the veil I could make out pine-covered peaks and terrifying precipices above which, to the west, the majestic Tumabah Huyu towered above the surrounding valleys. It quickly vanished as the fog rose up around me. Suddenly in this spot the forest was splendid. Water flowed abundantly through little ravines from which a variety of plants sprouted, some of which I recalled having seen in European hot houses in the past. These woodlands, streams, and vistas were the most beautiful that I had seen in the cold lands of Guatemala. We were still hugging these mighty peaks of the Cordillera while admiring sweeping views of the mountains in the provinces we had just left behind to the east and south.

Just before arriving at the top of Beleh Qeché I wanted to look back once more. The expansive horizon unfurled before me. At my feet were the bottomless voids, with their screen of vigorous plant life in infinite colors shimmering in the light. Further, there were the jagged mountain ranges that offered up their tawny and red indentations to the brilliant sun. It was a sea of mountains, summits, peaks, and volcanoes, and as I contemplated this scene, I compared it to my memory of the glacier that I marveled at one summer morning from the summit of Rigi. The difference between the two scenes was the difference between life and death, numbing snow and the warm life-giving colors of the tropics. Fog hovered above some of the valleys, obstructing the view. Colash López, who had been studying my likes and dislikes with a keen eye for the last two days called out to me: *Aquí señor, aquí esta la capital.*[22] And once the fog had finally dissipated I could in fact see Guatemala City in the distance, sitting in the middle of its plateau like the queen of these regions. As the crow flies, I was at least twenty leagues away. But I could still make out that square city, looking very much like an ivory chessboard. Its brilliant white towers and domes stood out against the gold and clay surroundings with the same clear-cut outline of mountains under an equatorial sky. This panoramic view is the most extraordinary one that I had contemplated in Central America. I did not tire of it. And each time that I passed this spot, I stopped to admire it once more. It will never fade from my memory. Since then, whenever the thought of death has entered my mind, I have thought that it would not be a bitter thing and that my tomb would not be a burdensome weight if I could rest facing the wonders that the Creator placed there in such abundance.

We continued through a magnificent forest and finally reached the top of Beleh Qeché. Our group stopped here for a few moments. In that brief interlude, I saw a group of Indians arriving toward us from several directions dressed in ceremonial garb. Men and women filed past, kneeling before me to receive my blessing with a mix of respect and curiosity on their faces. They were my children and my vassals. *Oh r'al, oh qahol La, Lal ahau!* they said to me with jubilation.[B13] Someone brought me a large horse and placed my saddle on it. It belonged to the Indian governor, Jacinto Osorio. I understood that they were bestowing a great honor on me by insisting that I ride this horse when I made my entrance into Rabinal. I acquiesced and once again we started off. We were on a hillside across from Rabinal. I was getting my first peak at the plateau of Vera Paz. The views were very different here—less all encompassing as the panorama I had just left behind. The scenery was just as imposing. Below me was a precipice with the undulating terrain of the last of Beleh Qeché's hills, which meet the Chuch u Pam Hugu, or Santa Cruz Mountains, to its northeast. I also could see the wide valley bathed in sunlight with isolated hills, which had broken free from the surrounding mountain ranges, casting dark shadows in every direction. At a distance in the center of the plain was the pueblo, with its banana and sugar-cane plantations and tall orange trees that fragrantly shaded the base of the tall tumuli containing the remains of town's former chiefs. The church, with its Moresque dome and its large presbytery, was bigger than most cathedrals and towered over the red roofs that surrounded it.

"There is Rabinal!" called out Nacho Coloche, with an excitement in his voice that betrayed his admiration for his region. "Señor padre," he continued, "this is your new homeland, we hope that you will like it and that you will live here forever!" Certainly he could see the gratitude in my eyes and he seemed pleased. However, I didn't respond since my thoughts were of France, despite myself.

B13. "We are Your Grace's children and vassals, my Lord." *R'al qahol* is an expression that is often repeated in K'iche' histories and has the connotation of sons of a same tribe, who are the subjects of a lord, who is also the father and chief of this tribe—a sort of Scottish clan leader. [Allen J. Christenson (e-mail communication, November 16, 2015) offered the following reading of the K'iche' text in this passage: "This would be very interesting if [Brasseur] got this information from living K'iche' consultants, but I suspect it is [his] own interpretation based on archaic texts like the *Rabinal Achi*." Christenson translates this phrase as "we are your children (daughter or son of a woman) and your sons (sons of a man), lord." "Meaning that they are acknowledging him as their priest father. He overstates things by including 'your grace' and that they are declaring themselves to be his vassals, or adopting him as their 'clan leader.'"]

I continued to admire the scenery in silence. Colash and his brother pointed out all the notable sites around Rabinal. I asked him if there were any ancient ruins in the area. Above the town, he pointed out Cakyug, where the former lords of the valley dwelt before the Dominicans forced those who lived there to relocate to the current city. This barren hill, standing like a sentry over the irregular mountains of Tikiram,[23] separates the valley of Rabinal in the north from the higher plateaus of Vera Paz. My young interpreter pointed out some indistinct masses, which later I determined to be the ruins of a great palace, flanked by two *teocalli*.[24] As we continued west we saw other enormous hills, looming over the plain. The Poqomam people had built their mighty city of Nimpokom,[25] whose walls, twenty palaces, and many teocalli were located in those august mountain tops. From Nimpokom and Xeokok[26] to the deep gullies where the Usumacinta's waters flow, from the trail I was traveling with its sites that stir up the imagination to the high hills that bear the ruins of the nine castles of Zamanib[27] and the ancient city of Joyaba, I was surrounded by the ruins of cities, castles, abandoned temples, which stood watch silently over these plains and the surrounding valleys. In the distant landscape, I could see the dark blue outline of Mount Meawan[28] against the bright sky in the west and beyond that the banks of a river. There are impressive ruins to be found there as well. The region's histories are filled with wondrous stories that invoke the name of Meawan, which is tied to the fabulous legends of the earliest times of Guatemalan civilization.

I continued to descend towards Rabinal's valley. The forest was splendid and dark with its clusters of tall trees in tiers that were almost perpendicular to the foothills that audaciously emerged from the plain. As we got further down, the landscape was no longer as sublime, but at each turn it still provided the most stunning scenery. The sky was pure and clear, and a gentle warmth brought the natural world around us to life. Within an hour we had reached the valley. I could see a few houses grouped together on the hillside above the trail. This hamlet, called Chirrum,[29] depends on Rabinal, which is just one league away. We stopped for a few moments by a large stream with crystal clear waters in the shade of some trees.

But soon we pushed forward again and as we made our way along the path, we were accompanied by that flowing water as it rushed towards the two rivers that encircle Rabinal.

Rabinal was founded by the illustrious Bartolomé de Las Casas, also known as the "Protector of the Indians." This zealous Dominican, along with fellow evangelists from that distinguished ministry, used kindness and persuasion to subjugate the rich province of Vera Paz. They therefore succeeded in bringing this land, which had previously been the birthright of the kings of Zamanib and Chamel, under the dominion of the Catholic kings of Spain. Whereas neighboring kingdoms had already been brought completely under Spanish control, for ten years the warriors of Tetzulutlan[B14] opposed Alvarado's lieutenants in a display of unparalleled bravery. However, in 1537—in the hopes of saving them from their assured destruction—Las Casas undertook their spiritual conquest and the history of this campaign of conversion constitutes one of the most captivating chapters in the history of this period. The princes from the Rabinal tribe, who were the sovereigns of Zamanib and Cakyug, were the first to heed the voices of these Christian missionaries and the rest of the region's population quickly followed suite. As a testament to the glorious achievements of the order of Saint Dominic, this area that until then had been dubbed Tierra de Guerra,[30] by the Spanish, would be officially renamed Vera Paz by royal patent. Fearing that these new converts could easily return to their idolatrous beliefs if they continued having contact with their infidel kinsmen, the Dominicans

---

B14. "Tetzulutlan" was the Nahuatl or Mexican name given to the whole region that is known today as Vera Paz. Among the princes who ruled over this area the most well known were those from the city of Chamel (later replaced by the Christian town of Chamelco, at approximately fifty leagues to the north of Guatemala) and those from Zamanib, an important city whose ruins can still be seen today on the high plateaus of the mountain of Xoyabah, to the west of Rabinal and at about thirty leagues northwest of Guatemala. The natives call these ruins Beleheb-Tzak Belehb-Cuxtum (the Nine Fortresses and the Nine Castles).

persuaded them to move from the mountains down to the plains and into a small town. The first town that they built was Rabinal, which was named after the area's royal family. With the establishment of other towns soon to follow, the former indigenous cities, which had already lost a great deal of their population due to this forced migration and to epidemics that had devastated Mexico and Central American in the sixteenth and seventeenth centuries, were completely deserted. Approximately fifty years after having come under Dominican control, the Indians of Vera Paz were pushed to extremes by contemptuous and greedy Spanish colonists, who had settled among them in their towns without regard for royal statutes and despite all the best efforts of the clergy. The Indians therefore took up arms and revolted en masse. The population was inflamed. Rabinal, as well as other towns of Christian origin, were sacked and missionaries feared for their lives. Only the chiefs stayed faithful to their allegiances. Eventually heeding their leaders, the people once more accepted their obligations. In fact I have in my possession a letter written by Phillip II to Don Gaspar Toh, the descendant of the kings of Zamanib and Cakyug, in which the king of Spain pompously honors him for services rendered to the crown. Rabinal was rebuilt one league to the east of its former location with much less of its past splendor since the native aristocracy, which had already lost much of its political power, now saw its sources of wealth disappear, as well. For example, the natives refused to rebuild the aqueducts that had been destroyed during the revolts in their former city. They feared that restoring an abundant water supply would lure Spaniards back to their town. Only the monastery and the church were rebuilt in grand style and Rabinal's church is one of the largest and most beautiful in Central America.

    The order of Saint Dominic, to which the missions of Vera Paz had been entrusted, preserved nearly absolute power for close to three centuries. The fact that the indigenous people had been greatly weakened and that their numbers were decreasing day by day, insured that the clergy could maintain peace and keep control of the area. Thus, after the first generation of chiefs who had embraced the Catholic faith died off, their authority gradually passed into the hands of the fathers who exercised power in the name of the king and the Church. But to be fair, they never used that power to the detriment of the population in their charge. Thanks to their vigilance, Spanish greed was constantly frustrated in its efforts to subjugate the native population, and it was only after years and years that a small number of new colonists finally succeeded in penetrating this rich region. As far as religion was concerned, the Dominicans proved to be tolerant towards the Indians. If they are criticized in Europe for their severity and austerity regarding faith, one could almost argue the contrary is true in Central America. They had the wisdom to understand that the natives, who, in a sense, had been torn violently from their idolatry,[B15] could not immediately turn into perfect Christians. Acting benevolently—and one can hardly find fault with their intentions—they did their best to assimilate those indigenous rites that they found unobjectionable into Catholic forms of worship and they attempted to translate the veneration for ancient idols into Christian imagery. They sometimes tolerated customs, which might seem odd from the perspective of French-Catholic tradition. And they closed their eyes to superstitions that the Church most certainly did not condone but that only time and preaching would successfully persuade the natives to disavow. In this way, they avoided antagonizing those who had not been convinced to recant the practices of their ancestors. They treated them like children who would rebel against too much rigidity. How many local superstitions remain from the pagan times of our ancient Celts, Gauls, or Romans in France and Europe where Christianity has been freely preached and practiced for more than fifteen centuries?

The Dominicans remained the uncontested masters of Vera Paz and the Indians, who recognized them as their protectors and their leaders as well as their spiritual fathers, transferred the feudal

---

B15. The Indians were not exactly forced to renounce idolatry. A great number embraced the Catholic faith of their own accord, not to escape persecution by Spanish clergy, who had always been like fathers to them, but in order to obtain the Church's protection from the violence of the conquistadors. The monasteries were a refuge, in Spanish America just like they had been in the Middle Ages in Europe, for those seeking refuge from the evils perpetrated by feudal lords or those seeking power.

services that they had been forced to perform for their indigenous lords to their monasteries. These ties deteriorated when the religious orders were expulsed from Central America in the wake of Morazán's rise to power. At that time Ladinos and mestizos, who until then had been restricted to very a limited percentage of the population in the indigenous towns, started moving to those areas in growing numbers. The *doctrinas*, as they were called, were granted to secular clergy as parishes or they were just completely abandoned, as I mentioned earlier. The return of the Dominicans after ten years in exile did not do much to remedy the situation. In the intervening years, many of the former clergy had died and as a result of the suspension of ties with Spain the order had stopped recruiting. Consequently many reductions, which had been under the control of the Dominicans in Vera Paz or of the Franciscans in Quiché and Kaqchikel, are currently in a fairly deplorable state. Rabinal, which has a pastor one day but not the next, is not what it was a century ago. But a self-respecting priest who could gain the respect of the people, who attempted to learn the language of the country and make himself understood by the indigenous people, and who wanted to put himself above the factions created by the antagonism between the often warring Indians and Ladinos races could still make an enviable place for himself in this region. Both materially and spiritually speaking, he could bring about the greatest good for all levels of society.

Before leaving for Rabinal, I was already aware of all of this. As I descended towards the valley, I was deep in thought, reflecting on the situation and my discussions with the archbishop. With all this in mind, as I rode along the twisting and shaded paths of the Chirrum River, I mapped out a line of conduct for myself in my new post. We had been riding along for fifteen minutes or so, getting farther from the mountain's base, when a considerable number of Indians and Ladinos came to meet me. Among them were members of the municipal council. One by one, they all greeted me with the utmost respect. The alcaldes and governor were not far behind with the rest of the civil and military authorities, all gathered together in a nearby prairie. In their right hands, the alcalde and governor each held an emblem of their authority, a long walking stick with a silver knob. The governor was preceded by three Indian *alguacils*,[31] each armed with a white six-foot-long rod, the last vestige of the sovereign power, which the indigenous governors continued to embody long after the Spaniards had stripped them of their thrones. The Ladino schoolmaster, Don Salvador Blanco, had been designated to speak on behalf of the rest. After a solemn oration, delivered with great ease and which lasted several minutes, he introduced me by name to all the dignitaries surrounding him. I thanked them in a few words, without dismounting, and we set off again towards the center of the parish.

Most of my greeting party was on horseback and, along with the rest of my escort, I had a cortège that would have been the envy of many a European bishop. At the front, the church banners waved, adorned with feathers and flowers followed by a dozen indigenous musicians playing all sorts of barbaric traditional instruments, such as the *tun*, chirimías, flutes, and the *teponaztli*,[B16] hollow wooden drums with leather. They produced a chorus of sounds that were at times muffled and rhythmic in a melancholic way and at others wild and shrill, to the point of making my ears ring. The crowd, which

---

B16. The *tun* is a sort of trumpet, which often lends its name to the bayle known as the *Rabinal Achi*. The *teponaztli* is a Mexican name for a sort of hollow wood drum, which the Maya called *tunkul* and that has a muffled sound from a distance. The K'iché call it a *gocin* or *gocinabul*. [In Brasseur's 1862 publication, the title *Rabinal Achi* is followed by the subtitle *The Dance Drama of the Tun*. Tedlock (*Rabinal Achi*, 1) explains that "when the characters are not engaged in dialogue they dance to the music of trumpets, which gives the play its other title: *Xajoj Tun* 'Dance of the Trumpet.'" Breton "decided not to translate" the term *tun* in this context. "Although today that word designates the large drum with vibrating blades that accompanies two large 'trumpets' in certain evolutions of the dance, all the ancient dictionaries I consulted list this terms under wind instruments: 'trumpet,' 'clarion,' flute' or 'horn.'" *Rabinal Achi*, 3n3. In Brasseur's 1862 publication of *Rabinal Achi* he describes the instruments in question by saying:

> the K'iche' Tun, called *Tunkul* in Yucatán and *Teponaztli* in Nahuatl is still today the preferred instrument of the indigenous natives . . . . It is a sort of drum made of large hollow tree trunks, with only two long opening running lengthwise, which the musician plays with two drum sticks that have rubber balls at the ends. Along with the tun came the Gohom, which is called *Tlapanhuehuetl* in Nahuatl. It resembles our drums. Brasseur, *Rabinal Achi*, 9–10.]

was already quite large, grew as we slowly made our way along the road. After a half hour through the parched countryside, as we were about to enter the small town, the path was so congested that we had trouble advancing. Men, women, young, and old—all dressed in their finest clothing—swarmed the roadside and filled the air with their cheers. I was starting to think that I was truly an important figure!

Bamboo arches, adorned with foliage, had been erected at the end of the main streets, which were wide and cut at right angles like those in Guatemala City. From the top of the church steeple the signal of my approach was sounded. The bells rang out, joining the blasts of fireworks and cannon fire that went off from the terrace of the town hall. The noise and confusion were enough to make a gunner from the battle of Sevastopol go deaf. We finally came to the town square. It was quite large and spacious. The church's tall majestic portal occupied an entire side of the square. Along another side sat a discrete cemetery and across from there was the great courtyard leading to the monastery—its high galleries decorated with flowers and foliage—which is the size of an immense public square. I dismounted amidst an attentive and curious crowd, whom I urged to enter the church. Without losing any time, I donned the rochet and cope with a glorious stole, and I asked my interpreters to lead me into the building. The vast naves were filled to capacity. After spending a few moments in prayer at the foot of the altar, I climbed to the cathedra and did the unexpected: I gave a short address in Spanish. This calculated move produced exactly the effect that I had intended. Given the character of such a community, it was important to impose myself. It was essential to put on a beguiling show with the greatest impact in order to have my authority respected. I knew that the majority of the people of Rabinal did not understand Spanish, but I merely needed to display myself with a flare and let them see me speak. In a few words I reminded them of their duties towards God and the Church. I led them to understand that as the envoy and proxy for the archbishop, I came here to work for their spiritual and temporal happiness. In return, I demanded not only their respect and affection, but more importantly, their absolute obedience.

They listened to me in rapt silence. And then the crowd accompanied me with enthralled respect to the door of my house. The chiefs took their leave of me one by one. When I entered into the presbytery's large room, I found their wives and the wives of the most important Ladinos, all dressed in their finery, to welcome me. One of them, a descendant of one of the most important families of the area, added as she kissed my hand that she hoped that I would "reign" for a long time on Rabinal: "Y nosotros todos los hijos deste [sic] pueblo de Rabinal esperamos que Su Merced largo tiempo reinará sobre nosotros!"[32] As incredible as it may seem, the choice of words was accurate in every sense of the term and anyone who wants to exert authority upon the Indians will find it to be true. The fact is that for the short amount of time that I was with them, I governed this population on both the temporal and spiritual level. In fact Mr. Lennox Wyke, the British chargé d'affaires, who was visiting me one day while I was at the home of the general consul of the Netherlands in Guatemala City, made an astute remark when he saw several Indians come into the room: "Your subjects are looking for you." He was joking, of course, but the comment had some truth to it. I was able to send away the host of people who continued to mill about my house, but a few señoras remained insisting that they wanted to share the honor with Rufina of serving me the dinner that they had prepared in anticipation of my arrival.

This was the start of my administration in Rabinal, where I am certain that the memory of the *padre francés*[33] persists and is as deeply engraved in the hearts of the Indian and Ladino residents as it is in mine. I will never forget this period in my life, which despite a few clouds here and there, was fascinating and has remained one of my fondest and most satisfying memories. Almost always, I found the men of the parish to be dutiful and ready to obey my every wish. And I only have praise even for those I had been warned to watch out for. The commander of the militia, a Ladino who was feared by all, was as gentle as a lamb in my presence.[B17] On more than one

---

B17. Less than a year after my departure from Rabinal, this Ladino, whose name was Francisco Martínez, was killed along with several others in an Indian rebellion. He was universally despised.

occasion when the people of the area felt that they were in danger of seeing some of their children taken away from them either for corvée labor or to be drafted into military service, I simply wrote a few lines to the provincial *corregidor*,[34] General Paredes, who lived in Salamá, and I was always able to obtain a satisfactory response in favor of my subordinates.[B18]

Even though the feudal obligations that compelled Indians to work for Dominican monasteries had nominally been abolished since the revolution, in most of the towns of Vera Paz and the other provinces of the republic there was clear evidence that these bonds still existed. According to the concordat between the Holy See and General Carrera, a tithe continued to be levied on whites and mestizos that went to the archbishopric and the metropolitan chapter. Moreover, the first fruits of the earth and the first animals born of the herd were to be paid to the chiefs of the different parishes.[B19] The Indians had other duties. Their chiefs provided corvée labor for public-works projects for both religious and administrative concerns. They also collected contributions for the upkeep of the church and for the priest's allocation, according to a fee set by the higher ecclesiastical authority, which provided for servants for the presbytery and the altar. The size of most of these old monasteries usually required a large staff and each one had its own allocation of funds calculated based on the circumstances and the town. The sacristan was always a native chief chosen by the spiritual administrator of the parish. He carried out his duties until the end of his life, unless the administrator had serious cause to request his dismissal. He was responsible for the silver and vestments. For example, during the time that I was

---

B18. General Mariano Paredes was an officer of merit. He had been the president of the Republic of Guatemala between Carrera's two terms in office. He died of cholera in a camp in Nicaragua near the Granada border during the first expedition against William Walker in 1856.

B19. The reader should not be too shocked by this state of things. If tithes and other compulsory payments in kind were still being paid, it is important to keep in mind that in Guatemala these replaced the salary allocated elsewhere for the clergy. It should be noted as well that in that republic there are no feudal, land, personal, or window taxes of any type. The government has no revenue sources except for customs tariffs and their monopoly on distilled alcohol, gunpowder, and tobacco.

in Rabinal, the church still possessed chalices and patens valued at closed to fifty thousand francs. Other undersacristans worked with him and discharged several other duties.

As for the domestic staff, the situation was the same, and in several parishes, such as San Juan Sacatepéquez, there was a head of the household staff with the title of *Tata Alabon*, or the "father of the young." In Rabinal, my old housekeeper performed these duties, which were regarded as elevated in status and comparable to the role played by intendants for lords in ancient times. The most well regarded among the Indian señoras and Ladinas treated my housekeeper Rufina as their equal, and the Indians always greeted her by calling her señora or *nuestra madre*.[35] Along with my attendants, Joaquim and Colash, there were two other young men who also spoke K'iche' and Spanish who were employed by me as regular servants. Two men were in charge of the stables and two others carried the firewood and *ocote*.[B20] Another two were in charge of providing the house with water. The kitchen had a titular cook, a Ladina, along with a young housekeeper and two *molenderas*, or grinders, to grind the corn on a stone expressly used for this purpose in order to make tortillas or to grind cocoa for my chocolate. All these people ate at the presbytery and the master of the house paid the bills. Moreover, there were the laborers that the municipality, known as the *cabildo*, sent me each week to clean parts of the monastery.

I hope that the reader will forgive me for going into so much detail. But this provides an accurate picture of the feudal system that is still preserved in a great many Guatemalan parishes, especially in those where the indigenous people have remained the majority population. Following the conquest, when the Church superseded the authority of lords and idolatrous priests, any status that it conferred on the native population was naturally considered to be a great honor—even if it was only temporal in nature. To support the Church, twelve confraternities were established, each one dedicated to parish saints. Their leaders were elected annually and given the

---

B20. Ocote comes from the Mexican word *ocotl*, and designates the long slivers of wood and pine that are lit at one end, which are used by the poor for light and are used in all homes in the less formal parts of the house like in the kitchen, etc.

Indian title *cahauixel*,[B21] which is poorly translated into Spanish by the term *mayordomo*, or "majordomo." They are generally chosen among the most influential families and are responsible for managing the holdings of these brotherhoods, which include farms[B22] or money. They use the revenues to maintain their patronal chapels and vestments as well as fund festivals and pay the officiating priest for his services. They also select the sacristan and three other officers from among past and present majordomos, who have the title of fiscal and are equal in status and dignity with the sacristan. They are responsible for the choir and teach singing and music to young parishioners who are selected based on their abilities and voices. They are also responsible for collecting the names of children to be baptized—as well as those of their parents—and proclaiming Indian banns of marriage. And finally, every Sunday when the priest has concluded the mass, they sing recessional hymns or recitatives in their native language or Spanish which thereby instruct their assembled brothers in Christian doctrine.

The celebration of the festival of the patron saint Joseph had been planned for the Sunday following my arrival in Rabinal. In fact it had been delayed because there had been no priest until then to say mass. This was among the festivals paid for by the Ladinos, since each racial group had its own festivals. In the sixty or eighty years since they had settled in this town, the Ladinos had obtained the right to establish several brotherhoods, whose patron saints were different from those celebrated by the indigenous brotherhoods. On the occasion of this solemn ceremony, they had decorated the church extravagantly with draped fabric, flowers, and an ample supply of tinsel. On Saturday night a delegation came to notify me

---

B21. *Cahauixel* means "father." The root of this word is *cahau* but here it is given an active form and implies a form of generation that is both active and actual. Thus in this language, when speaking of God the Father they always say *cahauixel*; when speaking of God the Son they say *qaholaxel*, instead of saying *qahol*, which simply means "the son"; and for the Holy Spirit they say *uxlabixel*, which expresses in an admirable way the ongoing workings in a spiritual sense of paternity, filiation, and divine spiration.

B22. The ruins of the great ancient city of Nimpokom are part of a hacienda belonging to one of these brotherhoods.

that they were waiting for me in order to fetch the saint from the home of the majordomo, where the patron saint is usually kept the week before the festival, in a home chapel erected expressly for this purpose. A procession formed at the foot of the high altar. The crucifix and candlesticks were at the front with the thurifers. Behind them were the fiscales and choirboys. There was a host of violins and cellos, flutes and drums, as well as other instruments, which accompanied a Latin chant of which I did not understand a single word, on a tune that was not lacking in melody but was more gay than solemn. I followed behind, wearing my cope, bringing up the rear of the cortege, which exited the church as the bells began to peal. A servant stood alongside of me holding a large umbrella, in lieu of a parasol, above my head.

The effigy of Saint Joseph sat in a place of honor in the majordomo's home. Its altar was covered in flowers and was brightly lit. When I arrived four of the Ladinos leaders placed the statue on a richly decorated stand that they carried on their shoulders, while four other men held a golden silk canopy above it. We made our way back to the church, which I entered carrying an altar candle. Back in the sanctuary I incensed the effigy, and after the appropriate prayer, I returned to the presbytery. A few moments later, an officer of the brotherhood came with an offering from the majordomo. It was a dish of choice meats and a large basket of cakes covered by an impeccably clean napkin. Early the next day the bells started chiming. A festive atmosphere reigned throughout the entire town. Half an hour before mass, the majordomos from all the Indian brotherhoods arrived at the door to my room in their ceremonial dress. Each held a six-foot-tall silver scepter, with a likeness of his patron saint, radiant and wreathed with flowers. They knelt in a sign of greeting and then led me to the sacristy walking somberly in rows of two. After the Eucharist they walked me back in the same manner and took their leave after having received my blessing. These long-standing rituals were repeated each Sunday and for each brotherhood's feast day. In the afternoon I heard a great ruckus of drums and trumpets. The mystery was soon resolved. Led by their majordomo, a delegation from the brotherhood had come to invite me to join their festivities.

The great courtyard of the monastery was packed with people. A dozen Ladinos masked and in fantastical disguises, greeted me with a dance. These were the characters of the baile,[36] or "ballet," an essential feature of any religious festival—which in fact are the only type of festivals still celebrated in this region. Under a gallery, they had prepared a platform for me, where there was an armchair and a mat at my feet. The dance performed was not particularly interesting in this case. At the end there was *besamanos*[37] and the sound of fireworks bursting in the air. As was customary, I gave the performers a few coins and then they went dancing off through the crowd to repeat their piece elsewhere.

As I mentioned, this dance was performed by one of the Ladino confraternities. The bailes done by indigenous brotherhoods during their festivals are of a completely different nature. Before the conquest of America, we know that dance played an integral role in the religious rites of all the nations on the continent, no matter their degree of civilization. Most processions included ballets, which were performed either in the courtyards of temples or royal palaces. Those danced at the temples were purely religious in nature and related directly to the deity being celebrated. The others were more historical or warlike in nature. Often they were merely gestural. At other times, they wove in songs that were more like monotonous recitatives, accompanied intermittently by musical instruments. When the missionaries, charged by Spain with their conversion, got to know the indigenous people of these lands, they were horrified to learn the idolatrous nature of these theatrical performances. They were so deeply rooted in the customs and mores of the culture that it would have been impractical to suddenly forbid them. Any attempt to do so would have been not only futile but would have jeopardized the fragile peace. In their anxious attempts to resolve this situation, they proposed alternatives with Christian themes that would be performed in accordance with the festivals of the Christian calendar. As a result, there are indigenous towns and villages that perform something called *Baile de la Sierpe*, the "Ballet of the Serpent," drawn from the legend of Saint George and the dragon or others with dances that tell of the

Moors' defeat in Grenada or Cortés's conquest of Mexico.

However, these efforts to wipe their historical and religious ballets from the memories of the natives were completely unsuccessful. They needed to look no further than the names of their people and places for constant reminders of that past. In those areas where the missionaries refused to tolerate them, the ballets were performed during secret meetings. It created a sort of freemasonry, in which members were admitted only after passing a series of tests. In several parishes the clergy relented and eased their restrictions, which meant that, once again, these works could be performed as they had been in the past. This was the case for *Hunahpú Coy* (the Hunahpu Monkey)[38] in the Altos and for the *Xtzul*,[39] whose subject is related to the marvelous legend of the dance of the thirteen precious stones found within the Gagxanul Volcano. Although some condoned such tolerance, others objected vehemently, especially since it became customary for these performances to take place not only in the presbytery but sometimes within the church itself—an act that the dissenters considered to be a sacrilege against the divine faith. Most often the actors, wearing masks and costumes, came to mass along with the rest of the faithful, but when entering or leaving the church they performed a few steps of the ballet in honor of the patron of the festival. I personally saw this as perfectly harmless despite the fact that it is contrary to European custom.

The more lenient clergy claimed that this was the only way of preventing secret cabals that were a far greater danger to faith and public safety. Moreover they tried to calm any fears on this subject by maintaining that performing these ballets within the confines of the church forced the devil to pay tribute to God by converting these idolatrous spectacles into acts that honor and benefit the Church and its saints. In any case, these performances continued to take place with more or less pageantry in Indian areas far removed from the central authority. At times they ceased if a hard-line pastor intervened. But they later reemerged and were staged with even more zeal if his successor proved to be the least bit accommodating. This was certainly the case with *Rabinal Achi* when I first heard about it. My curiosity had already been piqued by details relating to these types of ballets that I had read in Juarros[40] and Ordoñez[41] as well as in works about the history of the conquest of Mexico. After arriving in Rabinal, one day I went for a ride in the surrounding hills. Colash and his brother told me of a fascinating legend—*Rabinal Achi*. I immediately started peppering them with questions to find out more about it. They were already quite aware of my interest in the ancient customs of their country so they were not in the least bit wary of my questions and did not hesitate to give me details about this play. In fact Colash, who was rather bold, assured me that his elderly uncle, Bartolo Sis,[42] had in the past been one of the leading actors in the play.

I was intrigued by this revelation. I was determined to learn more. A few days later, when the chiefs of one of the more important brotherhoods came to see me for one of their festivals, I suddenly interrupted their greetings to ask them if they planned on that day to perform *Rabinal Achi*. They were rendered temporarily speechless by my point-blank question. They looked around at each other, at a loss for words. Finally, still disconcerted, they told me that this was something that had been long relegated to the past, a memory that was now all but forgotten. They added that in the past there had been reasons to stop performing this baile. Not wanting to insist too much at this time, I merely told them that I was particularly interested in it. Moreover I explained that as far as I was concerned, seeing *Rabinal Achi*, which was based on actual events from their national history, was much more compelling than watching a performance based on the story of Cortés and Montezuma, which was a degrading reminder of the humiliation to which their race had been subjected. They left in a state of befuddlement. Later, however, I learned that most of the indigenous population greatly appreciated what I had said. That was a turning point. After that my influence grew beyond my expectations.

One night I was lost in thought watching a purifying *aguacero*, or "rain shower," when an Indian woman came to my door. She was a respectable-looking elderly woman in an ordinary striped skirt wrapped around her in the same way as the goddess Isis is depicted on Egyptian monuments. She was wearing an embroidered *huipil*, resembling a short chasuble, which covered her shoulders and chest. Her braided hair, tied with two big green and red ribbons, looked like a diadem crowning her head. Colash López had brought her to me explaining that she was his uncle Bartolo Sis's wife. She didn't speak a word of Spanish, so Colash did the talking. He told me that her husband was sick, described his ailment, and asked me for a remedy. There was no doctor or apothecary in Rabinal. Consequently I carried with me a small travel pharmacy, which had already given me the reputation for being a veritable Hippocrates. Luckily for Sis and for me I was able to recommend a relatively simple treatment, and in a few days he was feeling better. He paid me a visit as soon as he had recuperated. He was an Indian in his fifties. Although he was relatively poor in comparison to other residents of the town, I was surprised by his eloquence and poise. After having thanked me, he told me that his nephew had said that I was curious to learn about *Rabinal Achi*. He was more than happy to provide me with all the details I wanted on the play. I assured him that this would make me very happy. He added that he had learned it in the traditional way under the direction of his father and his grandfather. He had even performed one of the leading roles in a performance that had taken place thirty years earlier before a Dominican priest. Since that time, he explained, it had been abandoned for a variety of reasons. However, he was concerned to see that his people's ancient culture was being forgotten and that it was threatened with extinction. Therefore he had decided to assemble this work in order to pass it on to his children as their patrimony. He concluded by suggesting that he could dictate it to me.[43]

I was thrilled by this proposal. We made plans for him to return in a few days, once he was fully recovered from his illness. He kept his promise. Having learned from Colash López that his uncle was particularly fond of anise cakes and coffee with milk, I asked my housekeeper to prepare these things as a treat for him at our morning meetings. At the time, I had not mastered the K'iche' language and this project was by no means an easy one. Nevertheless, I was able to complete it using the spelling adopted for K'iche' by my predecessors. For twelve days Bartolo Sis, Nicolas López, Tecu, and I locked ourselves away for the entire morning. Intellectually the two young men proved to be up to the task with which I was entrusting them. They were completely unfamiliar with grammatical terminology and yet they were able to explain the structure and composition of each sentence in this indigenous play with incredible clarity. At the end of every page, I translated it word for word, and they gave me as much information as possible.

This work was extremely useful to me. Very quickly it taught me more about the language as a whole than I could have ever learned in books. Once I had mastered my subject, I started to recopy the play making a clean version of it and translating it as I went along into French.[B23] However, I was not completely satisfied with the results. What I really wanted was to see the play performed as it had been in ancient times. Over and over, I brought this up with the chiefs, but since they didn't know about my work with Bartolo Sis they gave me the same old story and avoided giving me a straight answer. One day, after one of these discussions in which they were less than forthcoming, I reacted impatiently: "Well if you don't know the play, I do. I can even dictate it to you." I proceeded to recite a few lines that I had learned by heart and added bombastically: "I know more about your history and traditions than you do. This is why I have come here, for I am the person who knows all: *In in, in ux Etamayom*.[B24] They were flabbergasted by my speech and especially by the quotations, such as my last line, which according to one history was pronounced by one

---

B23. I am currently completing a Spanish translation of this play, which I hope to publish with a French translation and the original K'iche' text, along with the music that accompanies it. [Brasseur's bilingual translation was published in 1862 along with a K'iche' grammar under the title *Gramatica de la lengua quiche: Grammaire de la langue quichée, espagnole-française mise en parallèle avec ses deux dialectes, cakchiquel et tzutuhil, tirée des manuscrits des meilleurs auteurs guatémaliens. Ouvrage accompagné de notes philologiques avec un vocabulaire . . . et suivi d'un essai sur la poésie, la musique, la danse et l'art servant d'introduction au Rabinal-Achi, drame indigène avec sa musique originale, texte quiché et traduction français en regard*. (Paris: A. Bertrand, 1862).]

B24. "It is I, I who is the one who knows all." *Etamayom* is the present participle of the verb *etamah*, "to know," and is frequently used in ancient histories as a synonym of the word "seer" in the sense of a prophet, etc.

of their ancient legislators. At the same time, I seized the notebook in which I had begun to recopy the play, and I effortlessly declaimed one or two pages.

I was thus able to convince them that I had a thorough knowledge of their culture, and they admitted in their guileless and unpretentious way that I knew their own histories infinitely better than they did. After several moments of stunned silence, they humbly told me that they were ready and willing to do whatever I asked of them and that they would perform *Rabinal Achi* whenever I wanted. Their one complaint was that, unlike today, in the past they had a great deal more money to spend on expensive items like feathers and fabric that were necessary to make their costumes. I replied that I would gladly cover their costs. Since we were in September or October I wanted to give them plenty of the time to prepare their show, therefore I suggested setting the performance date for next January during the festival of Rabinal's patron saint, the Feast Day of the Conversion of Saint Paul.[44] They appreciated my offer and, in fact, seemed overwhelmed with joy at the prospect. The news spread quickly through the pueblo and surrounding area. Everyone seemed amazed that a padre, a foreigner, who was of neither Indian nor Spanish origin, was so interested in indigenous culture. I was surprised to see the enormous prestige that all this brought me. I ordered wool damask and trim in Guatemala City, and the tailors quickly got down to work. Meanwhile the actors learned their parts, and each evening, in one of the participant's homes, they rehearsed.

In the midst of all this I learned that French and English forces had taken the city of Sevastopol.[45] I was living in the middle of nowhere, but that didn't prevent me from wanting to keep up with what was happening in the outside world. Each month I received a package of English, French, or Spanish newspapers that the French chargé d'affaires, Mr. Mellinet; Mr. t'Kint de Rodenbeek; or Mr. Wyke were kind enough to send when they had finished reading them. The entire American continent breathlessly waited for news from the Crimea and even isolated Vera Paz was stirred by the rumors of these momentous events occurring in a far-off land. Before my arrival in Rabinal, the residents had no idea what a Frenchman was and had never even heard of France. But all that changed. Sometimes when the chiefs of the brotherhoods were meeting with me, I tried to give them an idea of the powerful nation from which I came. In terms they could understand, I described the city of Paris, explaining that this city alone had a population greater than that of their entire state, and I told them the houses surpassed the heights of even the tallest domes of the churches of Guatemala City. I had shown them articles in newspapers such as *L'Illustration* and *Illustrated London News* that described the wonders of the Universal Exposition or the meeting between the queen of England and our emperor, Napoleon III. Those who were literate were struck with admiration when they read the name Napoleon, and Colash López, recalling conversations he had had with me, told them that Napoleon's uncle had won great battles in the past. Showing them images of the current war, I had repeated the name of the French emperor. I told them that, at that very moment, he was beating down the gates of a great enemy city whose ramparts were stronger than the mountains of Tikiram or Beleh Qeché. They listened in rapt silence when I discussed the topic, engrossed in my stories, and when they took their leave, saying that they had never heard anything so extraordinary, their farewells were laced with ever-growing respect. I also recounted for them the ancient histories of their own ancestors, reminding them of the legends concerning the great King Gucumatz,[46] who rebuilt the temples and palaces of Utatlán so gloriously and who conquered distant lands such as Xibalba (Palenque).[47] Sometimes, I regaled them with the heroic deeds and misfortunes of King Qikab the Enchanter,[48] whose magic drum was located deep within the surrounding mountains. Sometimes, instead I told them about great European monarchs. They never questioned a single word; the padre francés always told the truth.

In September Mr. Mellinet had sent news assuring me that Sevastopol would soon fall. He had received letters announcing that his brother, the general, had been critically wounded but that luckily his life was not in danger. When the mail from Europe was due to arrive, I sent Joaquim López to Guatemala City asking Mr. Mellinet to send him back to me as soon as there was news of Sevastopol's fall. As it happens, by the time Joaquim got to the capital everyone was talking about the great military victory and General Pélissier's[49] promotion to the rank of marshal of France. Mr. Mellinet wrote to say that he planned a big celebration to mark the occasion and that he regretted that I could not join them. I received his letter at around two in the afternoon on Sunday, October 28, as I was sitting down to eat. As soon as I broke the seal and read the first lines, announcing the victory, I called one of the available sacristans. I instructed him to call his companions immediately and ring the bells. Since I could not be at the French legation in Guatemala City, I decided to celebrate the triumph of our forces in the Indian way in Vera Paz. At the same time, I told the alguacils to position the cannons on the cabildo's terrace and pack them as they would for their most important celebrations. At that hour, the town's residents had finished eating and were quietly napping under their porch roofs or dozing in their hammocks.

It came as quite a surprise to hear the bells and cannon fire echoing off the surrounding mountains. It wasn't long before everyone was up and the town was all abuzz. The alcaldes came running to find out what the commotion was all about. A whole host of others, including the governor with several brotherhood chiefs, were not far behind. They asked my permission to interrupt my meal. They entered the dining room. One of them respectfully broached the subject that had brought them there, while others interrogated Joaquim about what was happening in Guatemala City. I answered with the utmost gravity using the words of a book in the K'iche' language: "Are rumal ri qhakat chirech ri Rahawal frances Napoleon u bi, chila chi Sebastapol ru bi ciwan-tinamit" (It is because of the victory of the Emperor of France, whom we call Napoleon, over the fortified city of Sevastopol). Without waiting for more details, some of them ran off to explain what was happening to those who were gathered outside. I suppose that they did not really grasp what I was saying, but the resounding names of Napoleon and Sevastopol were enough to give them an idea of the importance of the news I had just received. Those who remained listened as I provided more details and as they left, I heard them discussing the great power of this heretofore-unknown nation, of which I was the sole representative in their country.

This momentous occasion temporarily interrupted my otherwise uneventful existence among the natives of Rabinal. Meanwhile, the preparations for the feast day when *Rabinal Achi* would make its return were well under way. On Saturday, January 19, 1856, everything was ready for the first public performance. In the afternoon, I was told the participants were waiting to receive my blessing in the church. I made my way through a large crowd, dressed in my rochet and stole. The entire cast was present and dressed in their new costumes. Each wore a feathered headdress of fan-like plumes. These were nothing like the ones seen in the opera *Fernand Cortez*,[50] and more like the ones worn by Comanche or Apache chiefs portrayed in George Catlin's Indian Gallery in London.[51] Even more extraordinary were the wooden masks covering their faces, each one skillfully carved and painted to convey the character being portrayed, with slits for the eyes and mouth. They reminded me in every way of the masks of Greek and Roman theater.

In ancient times, when the Indians were the uncontested masters of this land, any ceremony was first and foremost prepared in a religious context. The same continues to be true for their descendants. In the past, dances and staged productions were done in order to honor the gods. Today they still honor divinity. Since the festivals of the Catholic calendar are at once civil and religious in nature, the church is there to consecrate it all, just like in the past. When they saw me arrive before the sanctuary, the war cry, at the beginning of the play, rang out through the nave. The tun and the teponaztli played a few melancholic notes, while the actors solemnly performed one of the dances from the ballet. Then it was my turn to speak. I reminded them that when their fathers ruled over this land, religion was always an integral part of their festivals. The play that they were about to perform abounded with memories of that period when, according to one indigenous author, their ancestors still worshiped wood and stone. "Today," I added, "despite the secular nature of this performance, God does not proscribe you from making it part of your festivities. But never forget that you are Christians now and that all the honor goes to Him, as you have so clearly demonstrated by asking for my blessing in His name."

As I spoke, I sprinkled them with holy water and made the sign of the cross. They each passed before me, one by one, and greeted me in the traditional way of their ancestors. They then formed a quadrille and left the church dancing to the sound of their instruments.

The novena for the Conversion of Saint Paul had begun. The next day, Sunday, the parish celebrated Saint Sebastian, one of its patron saints. After the customary mass, a platform was erected under the gallery of the great courtyard, which was promptly invaded by a sizable crowd. This would be the first time that the actors of *Rabinal Achi* performed the entire baile for me. This play has four characters with speaking roles: Goptoh, the chief of the house of Rabinal and the King of Zamanib; his son, the Galel Achi,[B25] who is usually referred to as Rabinal Achi and whose name translates as the "warrior" or "hero of Rabinal"; Qeché Achi, the prince of the house of Cawek, which reigns over the K'iche' people; and a slave girl, Ixok Mun. There were substantially more nonspeaking roles in the past, but they now include only the Queen Mother, wife of the King Goptoh; Rabinal Achi's young wife and Princess of Carchag, Precious Emerald; twelve high-ranking warriors called the Eagles; twelve more high-ranking warriors called the Tigers, and several male and female slaves. What sets this play apart is that the stage director—who is both the head of the orchestra and the teponaztli master[B26]—along with two other musicians, are an integral part of the performance. The play has only two acts with four separate scenes. The first scene is supposed to take place outside the walls of the palace of Cakyug, the home of Rabinal Achi. The second scene takes place within the walls of that palace in the presence of the

---

B25. The word *galel* or *ca'el* is a title that literally means "he who wears a bracelet." The word *achi* is basically like the word *vir* in Latin and means "hero" or "warrior." When the two words are united they form a royal title.

B26. Even today, in many towns the teponaztli master is an important figure. He is usually the living depositary of ancient traditions and leads gatherings having to do with ancient customs. Usually, he has one of the best seats in the church and everyone has a great deal of respect for him.

king. The third scene transports the action once again outside and the fourth returns the actors within the palace.

The performance starts with the melancholic and muffled sound of the teponaztli while Rabinal Achi, Ixoc Mun, his favorite slave, and several Eagle and Tiger warriors dance in a ring, slowly circling each other, despite the lively music. Suddenly Qeché Achi jumps into the center of the group making threatening gestures pushing them to quicken their pace. He suddenly stops and although he is already a prisoner, he attempts to lasso Rabinal Achi and hurls insults at him. The entire first act consists of verbal attacks and counter attacks between Qeché Achi and his captor Rabinal Achi. In fact, the K'iche' prince was guilty of having insidiously lured ten of King Goptoh's sons into a trap. Then in a treacherous act, he abducted Goptoh himself, in order to take possession of his rich territory. We never learn the fate of the ten sons, but we know that by virtue of Rabinal Achi's powerful arms, his father was liberated from the fortress where he had been imprisoned by Qeché Achi. The enraged Qeché Achi is broken and becomes his rival's prisoner. Their dialogue might strike a European audience as terribly monotonous. Rabinal Achi calls the sky and earth as his witnesses when formulating his accusations and Qeché Achi, using the same expressions begins by repeating almost word for word most of his adversary's speech, before answering. Then Rabinal Achi reiterates Qeché Achi's words before launching a new series of accusations. The whole scene unfolds like this, periodically punctuated by the sound of warrior instruments that accompany the performers, who dance austerely in a circle. In the end, just as he is about to be brought before the king to hear his sentence, Qeché Achi, asks for a reprieve in order to say his good-byes to his family. He offers all his riches in return.

"In truth," he says "I have sinned like this because of my sad heart. I accept my punishment between the sky and the earth! My mouth and my face have no more to say. But the squirrel and the bird standing before me, my lord, will inspire you (will sing),[52] to perhaps grant me this favor and allow me to carry the news of my sentence to my lord, the chief of my race, in his great fortress and in his great castle. Then allow me to send a messenger from there into your mountains and valleys![B27] 'For that is where we will sever your root and your trunk,'[B28] were your words between the sky and the earth. Let's make a final pact, oh my brother, oh my elder: I will dress you in my plunder. I will give you my gold and my silver, as well as the son of my arrow and the son of my shield, my Aztec club and my Yaqui ax, with my clothing and sandals. They will serve your children well, here, between the sky and the earth[B29] and they will be the guarantee that I pledge so that you may happily grant me permission to return to my mountains. These are the words that you have spoken to the face of the sky and the earth. Sky and earth be with you, oh valiant warrior, oh Rabinal Achi!"[53]

But Rabinal Achi must consult his father, King Goptoh. This is the start of the second scene. Goptoh congratulates his son on his victory. He calls him by his name, but he addresses him by these words that he bestows on him like titles: "My Anger and my Valor!" and he orders that the captor be brought before him. In the second act, this is what I am calling the third scene, Rabinal Achi brings Qeché Achi to Goptoh, who rebukes him once more for his misdeeds. The K'iche' prince repeats the king's speech, which is full of humiliating admonitions, and then haughtily adds: "And I too, I am a brave warrior, a hero! In truth, if I bow my shoulders down, if my face knows humiliation, here is the sign of my humility: It is my arrow and shield. Ah! If I could only destroy your grandeur and your power at this moment! If only I could beat your mouth from above and below! I will attempt this now, oh great lord."

Having said this, he moves menacingly towards the king. But a slave blocks his punch, by grabbing his arm. Goptoh reminds him again of a series of misdeeds and finally sentences him to death. Qeché Achi repeats his speech. He responds by providing an inventory of the riches and grandeur to be found in Goptoh, king

---

B27. "Mountains and valleys" is an expression that usually connotes prairies.

B28. "Sever your root and your trunk," in other words, extinguish the race.

B29. The phrase "between the sky and the earth" that is frequently repeated alludes to the castles built by princes on the most inaccessible peaks of the Cordillera Mountains.

of Zamanib's palace, all of which the king has just mentioned in his speech. He lists twelve refreshing beverages, twelve succulent dishes, lustrous fabrics embroidered by the Queen Mother and the young queen from Carchag,[B30] a pearl, whose beauty is unrivaled.[54] "Since I must die," he adds, "allow me to enjoy these things just one more time. Let me drink from the cup, sit at the king's table, don those tunics embroidered with gold, dance with the young queen and joust with the twenty-four heroes, known as the Tiger and Eagles at Zamanib's court."[55] Goptoh accords him his wishes one by one. Qeché Achi then gives the signal to the musicians himself, and orders them to play his people's national anthem, composed of a few melancholic notes that reminded me of the French cavalry regiments' reveille.

Each time that Queché Achi has taken advantage of one of the reprieves accorded him by the king, he returns to thank him. But then he issues yet another challenge to the king. Finally, he returns with the king's Eagles and Tigers after jousting with them with no more demands and he mournfully exclaims: "And now, if only you could give me still a few more days and a few more nights to go bid farewell to my mountains and valleys!" The final scene ends with this speech. He nears his place of execution and then disappears for a few moments. He returns and calls to the Eagles and Tigers who are to be his executioners. "Eagles and Tigers!" he cries, "you must have thought 'He is gone.' But no, I just wanted to say a final farewell to the image of my mountains and my valleys, where in the past I wandered while hunting for food. My anger and my valor have done me no good! May the sky and the earth hear me! This is where I must die and end my life between the sky and the earth. My gold and my silver will therefore go to you. My Aztec club and my Yaqui ax will go to you! My ceremonial robes along with my sandals will go to you! But you will go into my mountains and my valleys. You will bring the news of my fate to the face of my lord and my father. For in that place, my lord, my father will say: 'My Anger, my Valor is busy

---

B30. Carchag is today called San Pedro Carchá, a rich town twenty-eight leagues north of Rabinal, on the farthest edge of Vera Paz, along the Petén Itzá border.

looking for my sustenance, busy hunting for my food.' This is how my lord speaks. But he will say nothing more. I await only death. I await the end of my days, here between the sky and the earth. Sky and earth, listen to me! Yes, it is all too true. I must die here and finish my life between the sky and the earth. If only I could change places with the squirrel or the bird who die on the branch of a tree or on the flower's calyx, searching for food between the sky and the earth! . . . Hey! Come here Eagles and Tigers! Since it must be this way, do your duty and fulfill your mission. Show your fangs and your claws. My face will not flinch when you tear me to pieces. I alone am valiant, since I came from my mountains and my valleys. Sky and earth be with you, Eagles and Tigers!"

Then the Eagles and Tigers surround him. They put him to death and the play ends with all the actors dancing in a circle, with the exception of the K'iche' prince. The music that I asked someone to note down during the performance is solemn and melancholic in general, but extremely simple. Mr. Gevaërt,[56] the young and brilliant composer of *Quentin Durward*, with whom I have shared this music, found it to be quite original. I would add, moreover, like the play, the musical portion of the performance is brief and highly repetitive. Despite this repetitiveness, the dialogues between Rabinal Achi and Qeché Achi and the back and forth of their confrontational taunting are truly beautiful, with very lyrical passages. During one of these skirmishes Qeché Achi says: "Sky and earth, listen to me! To whom will I tell the name of my mountains and my valleys? Will it be to you, my friendly singers, my birds with your brilliant yellow feathers? I am the son of anger, the son of valor! My lord, the Yaqui of Cunen, the Yaqui of Chahul, king of Balam Achi Balam Qeché, honored me ten times by coming down the path of clouds and fog to my mountains and my valleys . . ." Later, Rabinal Achi, remembering the tragedy of his brothers and their abandoned homes, calls out in grief: "Today the halls where they feast are empty. Everything has been consumed there. There are only ruins to be seen, only rubble covered in brambles. Only silence dwells in their homes, interrupted only by the cricket's chirp within their castles!" In one of their first dialogues, Qeché Achi turns towards his rival and accuses him of having been the instigator of the conflict between them. He exclaims: 'Why did you arouse your anger and your valor?' This is what your mouth says . . . But the herald, the messenger from between the sky and the earth comes from here, from the dominating walls of Cakyug and Cilic Kagocanic Tepecanic, which are the names we give to these walls and this façade of your castle.[B31] . . . Let's act as good and loving brothers. Let me see the K'iche' king's anger and the valor. Let him take his share of these beautiful mountains and these beautiful valleys. Come, my brother and elder. Inherit these beautiful valleys, here, between the sky and the earth. Split open the ground. Sow the furrows where the heads of our squash press against each other, the heads of our white squash and our white frijoles! This is how your challenge spoke, this was the call of your herald to my lord. . . ." Later in the play, Qeché Achi remembers the war cry that was let out by the head of his family. He majestically invokes the K'iche' god: "Rise up, Tohil! And return to this place.[B32] For I have given shelter to a herald of arms, a messenger from between the sky and the earth. Take your strength and power in hand, the son of your bow, the son of your shield and come to the bend of the mountain and the opening of the plain!" He continues: "Then, I in turn let out my challenge and my war cry four times . . . and I came to Xolchacah. . . . This is where I heard all twelve of them, wild Eagles and Tigers, who sounded the battle trumpet and the drum of blood. The sky was agitated, the earth trembled from the thunderous boom and the daunting stirrings of the twelve, of the wild Eagles and Tigers, congregated with their male and female slaves. . . . That is when I began to sing out to the face of the sky and

---

B31. The names of Cilic-Kagocanic-Tepecanic can be translated as "where the viper climbs and lashes out in anger." [In Brasseur's 1862 publication of *Rabinal Achi* in the *Gramatica de la lengua quiche*, he gives this place name as Cakyug-Zilic-Cakocaonic-Tepecanic, with the following footnote: "Cakyug-Zilic-Cakocaonic-Tepecanic is the name of the main city and translate as 'Fire kept by the viper who slithers and climbs in anger.'" (40)]

B32. This invocation reminds me of the beautiful words of Psalm 67: "Exsurgat Deus et dissipentur inimici ejus; et fugiant qui oderunt eum, a facie ejus" (Let God arise, and let his enemies be scattered; and let those that hate him flee from before his face).

the earth: 'Won't you come, despicable prince, odious prince! What is this? Won't I succeed in severing the root and the trunk of the king of Chacachib and of Zamanib or of the Caok of Rabinal?'"

I could cite many more passages like these. But I hope that these few quotations give readers a sense of this fascinating and singular warrior drama. The text alludes to the customs and practices of the people of Vera Paz as they must have been in the thirteenth century—the period when the events in the play mostly likely occurred. There are several references to fortresses and castles located in the clouds, which, interestingly enough, echo Germanic customs of that same period. It is noteworthy that Qeché Achi speaks of the custom, of casting your vanquished enemy's skull in gold or silver and using it as a chalice. I have found no comparable evidence elsewhere in the annals of these regions of such a practice from more barbaric times.

The baile that I have just described is, if not the only surviving dramatic work by ancient Americans that is known, then without a doubt an extremely rare artifact. It was performed over a period of approximately twelve days, both before and after the Feast Day of the Conversion of Saint Paul, during which the most solemn performance was given. I noticed that there were always two or three actors prepared to play a single role, in case someone needed to be replaced. This was no doubt necessary since both the length of the play and the wooden masks worn in hot temperatures must be very draining for the performers. News of the performance attracted a huge crowd to Rabinal during the festival, and since the fair was also held at this time, there were twice as many customers as in previous years. In particular, indigenous people came from as far as fifty leagues away—from Retalhuleu in Guatemala as well as border regions of Mexico, like Soconusco and Chiapas, San Salvador and other parts of Central America. My support for this production that is of such cultural importance for the Indians, the costumes I provided, my knowledge of their traditions and languages, not to mention my status as a foreigner, were all fodder for conversation. I had become the focus of their curiosity and the name of the padre francés was on everyone's lips. I am convinced that during the rest of my time in Guatemala, because of my support for these performances, my reputation, and more importantly the friendship expressed by Indians towards me, were greatly enhanced and went well beyond the boundaries of my jurisdiction.

    There is very little left for me to say about the ballet-play called *Rabinal Achi*. I will only mention that later, when it was time for me to leave Rabinal, I had to pretend that I was taking a brief trip to Guatemala City. Otherwise, it would have been difficult to tear myself away from my affectionate Indians. I left in the middle of the night. But despite my precautions, the most important chiefs, who had learned of my departure, came rushing to the presbytery. With tears in their eyes, they begged me to return quickly and not to abandon them. I didn't know how to respond, and I was so moved by their pain that I believe I would have yielded to it, if I did not feel the desire to return to France so that I could publish my work on Mexico and Central America.[B33] Bartolo Sis, who had dictated the baile to me and who was confined to his bed due to illness, could not come to say good bye to me at that time. When he learned from his nephew Colash López that I was not going to be returning to Rabinal, he cried out in distress: "Oh! Our father will never return. I can die now, since I will never see him again." I note these moving expressions of devotion that I earned at so little cost and am torn between gratification and regret. As for poor Sis, he languished for a few weeks after my return to Guatemala City and died before the end of 1856.

    B33. *Histoire des nations civilisées du Mexique et de l'Amérique Centrale Durant les siècles antérieurs à Christophe Colomb, écrite sur des documents originaux et entièrement inédits, puisées aux anciennes archives des indigènes,* 4 vols. (Paris: Arthus-Bertrand). [This was written while Brasseur was in Rabinal and published upon his return to France between 1857 and 1859.]

VOYAGE ACROSS THE ISTHMUS OF TEHUANTEPEC
IN THE STATE OF CHIAPAS AND THE REPUBLIC
OF GUATEMALA IN 1859 AND 1860[1]

CHAPTER I

From New Orleans to Coatzacoalcos[B1]

On May 12, 1859, I boarded the American steamship, Coatzacoalcos, chartered by the Louisiana Tehuantepec Company to carry passengers whose lucky, or perhaps unlucky, stars were guiding them

---

B1. Guazacoalcos is the American corruption of Guazacoalco, which is a softer Spanish version of the original Mexican Coatzacualco. Initially it was the name of a town on the river's banks, from which the waterway's name is derived. [In referring to this river, in the southern part of Veracruz, Brasseur uses the spelling "Guazacoalcos" often seen on contemporary maps of his period. Other common spellings at the time include "Guazacoalco" as well as "Coatzacoalcos," which is also the name of the port town at the mouth of the river on the Gulf of Mexico. I have taken the spelling "Coatzacoalcos" when referring to the port town, river, and American steamship on which Brasseur traveled, since it seems to have been the most accepted English spelling. A note in John J. Williams's book *The Isthmus of Tehuantepec: Being the results of a survey for a railroad to connect the Atlantic and Pacific Oceans, Made by the Scientific Commission Under the Direction of Major J. G. Barnard, etc. Arranged and prepared for the Tehuantepec railroad company of New Orleans, by J. J. Williams, principal assistant engineer* (New York: D. Appleton, 1852), which Brasseur relied on a great deal for his topographic descriptions of the Isthmus, says the following:

> Many disputes have arisen with regard to the orthography of this name. In the official dispatches of Hernán Cortés to the Emperor Charles V, he writes it in no less than six different ways, viz., *"Mazamalco," "Quacalco," "Cuacuacalco," "Cuicicacalco," "Guazacualco"* and *"Guazaqualco."* The veteran soldier Bernal Díaz del Castillo, who resided more than thirty years in the province, calls it *"Cuacazualco."* De Solís, on the other hand, writes it *"Guazacoalco,"* and the Abbé Clavigero, who, from his extensive knowledge of the languages of Mexico, is perhaps the best authority, writes it after this manner, viz., *"Coatzacualco."* (19)

towards California via the Isthmus of Tehuantepec. I was not one of those passengers. My intention was to go to Mexico City by way of Tehuantepec and the state of Oaxaca. I was pleased at the prospect of getting to know the isthmus, about which so much has been written. I was also eager to travel this new route, which a company in New Orleans had recently opened to great fanfare. After several days of driving rain that made the poorly paved streets of the Crescent City[B2] practically impassable, the weather took a beautiful turn with a distant clear sky hanging pure and serene over the low-lying banks of the Mississippi River. The ship's rackety engine had been warming up for the last two hours, while passengers came and went from land to ship and back again; a bell rang out announcing immanent departure. At nine o'clock in the morning, they detached the steamer from its moorings on the wharf and tranquilly it moved midstream. The Coatzacoalcos was a big beautiful vessel, with a large saloon that took up almost the entire deck and wide walkways above and on each side. The handsome and practical cabins, on either side, were furnished in the comfortable style typical of American steamships. There was only one drawback—the ship, built for traveling on rivers and coastal lagoons, was not seaworthy. Thus Captain Wilson, the ship's commander, informed us when we came on board that it could be precarious if the weather took a turn for the worse, since this ship could easily sink in a storm. But in the United States they show little concern for this type of accident; Americans always seem to expect good fortune to smile upon them.

At ten or twelve nautical miles from New Orleans we started towing a smaller river steamer called the Alleghany Belle, which was more like a ferryboat and was going to transport passengers back and forth from our final destination, the port of Minatitlán, to the interior of the isthmus on the Coatzacoalcos River. Thus our ship, along with its escort, made its way majestically down the deep Father of Waters, which narrows slightly, as it flows towards its mouth. Nothing is more monotonous than this river's banks,

---

B2. Americans call New Orleans the "Crescent City" because it is situated on a crescent-shaped bend on the Mississippi River.

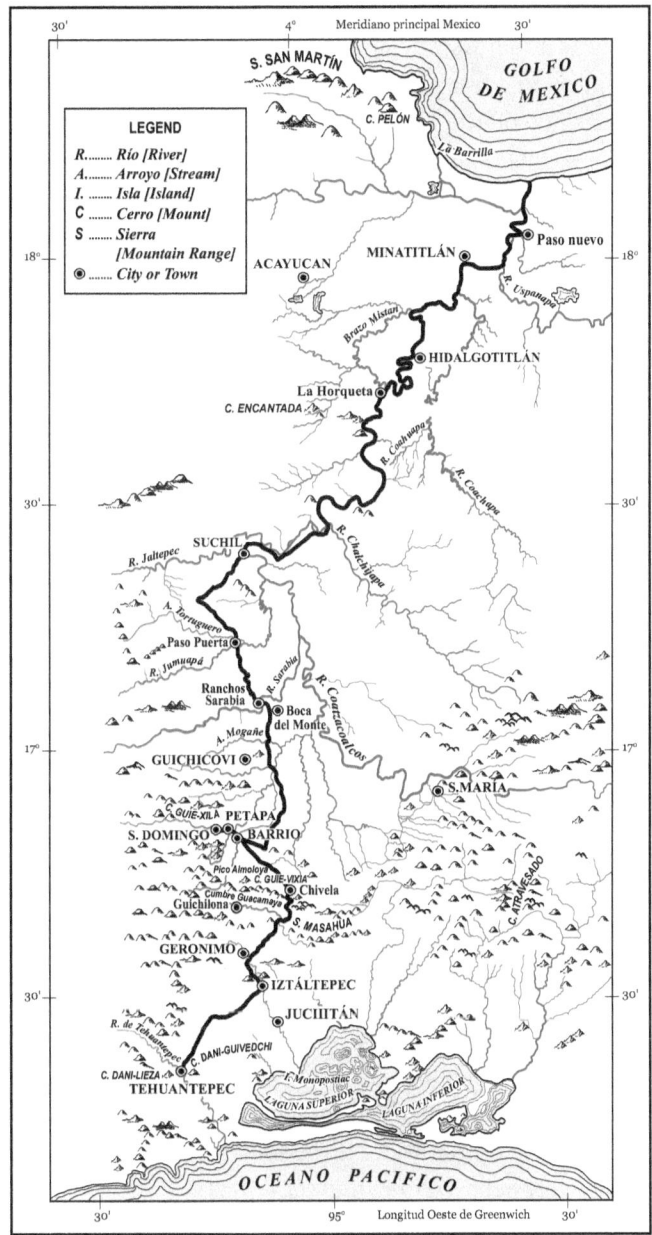

BRASSEUR'S ROUTE ACROSS THE ISTHMUS OF TEHUANTEPEC
Based on the Comisión de Cartografía's *Carta de reconocimiento del istmo de Tehuantepec. Formada para la aperture de un canal interoceanico por la commission Mexicana nombrada al efecto, 1871* (s.l.: s.n., 18710). Uncatalogued map, Geography and Map Division of the Library of Congress. Map by Paporn Thebpanya. Copyright © 2017, University of Oklahoma Press.

especially as it follows its course towards the Gulf of Mexico. With the exception of a few plantations, whose roofs harshly reflect the bright sunshine off their large red tiles, there is nothing distracting to the eye or imagination as you gaze out at this sea of vegetation. It is hard to imagine where Chateaubriand[2] found the remarkable images in his Mississippi scenes. To get a sense of its true grandeur, all you can do is summon up your geographic imagination and recall the many rivers and waterways that feed into it, starting at Lake La Biche[3] and Saint Anthony Falls thousands of miles away. With the exception of periods of flooding when the entire landscape seems to become one with the network of lakes that stretch out between New Orleans and the gulf, the river is hardly more than two miles wide as it reaches the ocean. In the swampland where the river's many estuaries wind through thick forests, the splendid vegetation is already exuberantly tropical. The majestic American cypress lifts its haughty head letting down braided garlands of threadlike Spanish moss,[B3] in anticipation of equinoctial America's approaching temperate climes.

The ship, carried by current and steam, sailed rapidly towards the gulf. The mild temperature and the serene landscape led us to believe that the crossing would be without incident. Sitting at one end of the ship, I enjoyed the peaceful scenery along the river's banks. The monotony of it all was actually stimulating and never wearisome. As the ship approached the ocean, the terrain lay so low that I wondered whether it was solid ground or a thick swamp of aquatic plants. This is the land of perpetual fevers, where reptiles and insects of all kinds dwell. One sees only untamed isolation bound by a sterile and unchanging horizon. A few scattered shacks and roaming livestock are the only signs of a human presence here. Otherwise, it seems that water is the sole mistress of this place that is so completely exposed to raging sea winds.

As evening approaches, these outposts of terrestrial life disappear. The setting sun makes the separation complete and now, only the ocean remains. And yet, for more than an hour after having left

---

B3. Tillandsia usneoides.

behind the estuaries of the Mississippi, I could still clearly see, in the radiant starry light, the muddy yellow waters of the Mississippi that had been carried towards the gulf, unadulterated by seawater. The river's varying shades can be seen from as far away as thirty miles from the its mouth and even when we reached the gulf, the smell of fresh water endured. I spent the hours following supper contemplating all of this. The night was so beautiful and tranquil that no one thought of going to bed. The air was dry and warm so several passengers decided to sleep on deck. Under that deep blue sky, next to which even the most splendid Italian nights pale in comparison, there is a mysterious pleasure in gazing at those countless, exceptionally bright stars, shining in the clear evening air.

It wasn't until the next morning that I started to mingle with and get to know my fellow travelers. There were no more than thirty of us on board, only a dozen of whom were headed to California. The rest were either employed by the Louisiana Tehuantepec Company or were hoping to be hired by them once they arrived on the isthmus. At that time, everything was still in a state of confusion. The company was only a few years old and in that brief time it had already gone through two reorganizations. In fact, this story goes back as far as the Mexican conquest. Hernán Cortés was the first to point out the importance of a passage across the Isthmus of Tehuantepec to the Emperor Charles V. After Cortés's *Letters from Mexico*,[4] the oldest existing document on this subject is a report by the engineer Agustín Cramer, the king of Spain's commander at the Castle of San Juan de Ulúa, who, in 1774, was sent by Antonio Bucareli, the viceroy of Mexico, to study the feasibility of a route from the mouth of Coatzacoalcos to the port of Tehuantepec. When Mexico declared its independence, Tadeo Ortiz and Juan Orbegozo did studies—the former for the federal government and the latter for the State of Veracruz—to determine whether an interoceanic route was viable.

However, recently the project has taken on more urgency. On March 1, 1842, José de Garay, who proposed that the Mexican government establish communication between the two coasts, obtained the exclusive privilege of executing this major undertaking. Garay in turn entrusted the survey to a scientific committee, which included Cayetano Moro;[5] Théodore de la Trouplinière, a French engineer; and General José Robles, who was a colonel at that time. According to Michel Chevalier,[6] between 1842 and 1843 they accomplished a great deal of the work on the site, which the North Americans were able to build upon when they took up the project. José de Garay published an interesting report in Mexico City in 1844, which was also the blueprint for Major John Gross Barnard, the chief engineer for a project exploring a projected Tehuantepec railway in 1850.

In the end, Garay was not able to fulfill his contract on time. It was annulled not only because he could not meet the deadline but also because the Mexican Congress had not ratified it. Consequently, Garay sold his privilege to Hargous Brothers[7] in New York. The Mexican government was troubled to see the grant in American hands, especially since it yielded foreigners practically exclusive rights to thousands of square miles of land, from coast to coast and in some of the richest states of Mexico. The government, therefore, refused to approve the deal based on these irregularities. But the new grant holders were well connected in the capital and it became impossible to rip this prey from their hands. They greased palms and made promises so successfully that they were provisionally allowed to survey the land, and while waiting for the Mexican Congress to make its final decision, the steamship Alabama landed at Minatitlán in December 1850, carrying workers and engineers led by Major Barnard and sent by A. G. Sloo of New Orleans.

As a result of this expedition, a survey was completed of the proposed railway between Minatitlán and the port of La Ventosa, on the Pacific coast. Major Barnard charged a naval officer named W. C. Temple with surveying the Coatzacoalcos River at Minatitlán, while Pierre E. Trastour, a Frenchman, charted the Pacific coast. Their work was more or less completed in 1852. But the constant upheavals in Mexico's government and politics, not to mention many other circumstances, slowed construction of the railway. Meanwhile, a passable route was opened between La Ventosa and Tehuantepec and later from Tehuantepec to Suchil, at the mouth of the Jaltepec River—the point at which the Coatzacoalcos River becomes navigable. The rest of the trip towards the Atlantic coast was to be done by steamship to and from Minatitlán. This route was opened to American shipping in 1858, thereby finally making the trip between New Orleans and San Francisco possible.

The grant was extended beyond what had already been agreed upon by previous governments with a treaty that was sealed with Benito Juárez, the leader of the Liberal Party.[8] The American minister proceeded to recognize Juárez as the president of the state of Veracruz, instead of Miguel Miramón,[9] the president of the opposing Conservative Party in Mexico City. Created in New Orleans, the Louisiana Tehuantepec Railway Company established a steamboat route from New Orleans to Minatitlán and later to Suchil. Eventually it provided a coach that carried trunks and passengers from Suchil to La Ventosa once a month, where a steamship brought them to San Francisco in California. Newspapers in New York and Louisiana sang the praises of the new enterprise. At the time that I booked my passage, I saw a magazine that was filled with illustrations and sketches of the isthmus's landscapes with the sole purpose of luring customers. Like many others, I was very impressed and although I had been considering boarding a schooner for Yucatán, I let myself be enticed by a trip to Mexico and Central America via the Isthmus of Tehuantepec, which I was eager to explore.

The most important passenger on the Coatzacoalcos among those who were employed by the company was John McLeod Murphy, who is now a state senator for New York.[10] The principal investors of the company had sent him on an assignment. He was traveling with Louis Hargous's son because his father wanted the young man to get to know the land and people of Tehuantepec as soon as possible. I had met Mr. Murphy seventeen years earlier, in 1843, when he was a midshipman with the American squadron cruising Mediterranean waters.[11] I often dined with him and other officers at the Hotel Favre, now called the Hotel Fœder, in Genoa. We met in the offices of the Louisiana Tehuantepec Railway Company's president Mr. La Sére,[12] to whom I had been introduced by Louis Hargous and we soon recalled our previous acquaintance. We became the best of friends once again on board the ship from New

Orleans. Murphy is a distinguished and clever fellow, with a keen sense of humor. As far as I am concerned, his only real fault was his propensity to drink grog or cocktails on an empty stomach. Aside from that, he was a charming travel companion and unfailingly obliging. He was beloved by his associates and employees, and the masses—who *elected*[13] him senator—praise him to the hilt. He went from being an officer cadet in the navy to an engineer, and during Major Barnard's expedition he put all his energies and talent into supervising the construction of the road between Suchil and Tehuantepec. Now he was returning apparently with the same goal. As I mentioned, he had been entrusted with a confidential assignment, but more on that later.

I had hoped to catch sight of the Pico de Orizaba when we reached the Gulf of Mexico, since, as I knew from previous journeys, it can usually be seen from a great distance at sea when approaching Veracruz. But we only got our first glimpse of land when we reached the mouth of the Coatzacoalcos River, on May 16. At dawn, we could spy the uneven peaks of the San Martín and Pelón Mountains, which rise up along the coast in front of the Sierra Madre, between the Papaloapan (also called the Alvarado) and Coatzacoalcos Rivers. But their peaks were soon hid behind the clouds that in this season so often veil the high mountains as the sun rises in the morning sky. When we arrived at the bar at the mouth of the Coatzacoalcos with such splendid weather, I was completely lost in admiration for the imposing landscape that unfurled before my eyes displaying all the wonders of the tropics. To our left, for as far as the eye could see there were lush forests and rolling plains stretching towards an interminable horizon. To our right, only the hazy outlines of the Sierra de San Martín, vanishing in the distance, limited the boundless expanse. The mouth of the river, which is five hundred meters wide flows between two low hills. At the top of the tallest one, part of a range of sandy hillocks at the foot of Mount Pelón to the west, are the ruins of the old Spanish fort, called the Battery, and a tower that is used as a lookout post for the Mexican Customs Service.

At the mouth of the river is a bar, where the water is never deeper than six meters. However, the river widens to double its initial size, forming a bay where ships are completely protected from the gusting northern winds, which cause so much trouble in Veracruz's harbor. It is as if nature had specifically created this site to be a great maritime city. Accordingly it attracted the attention of the earliest explorers, who took interest in the advantages and security the area provided. In his correspondence with the Emperor Charles V, Cortés explains that he learned about it from Montezuma:

> I asked this prince to tell me if there was a river or cove along the coast where ships could safely enter and drop anchor. He answered that he did not know but that he would ask someone to draw the entire coast with its coves and rivers, and then I could send Spaniards to explore, adding that he would provide guides for them. This is exactly what he did. The next day they brought me the entire coast painted on cloth. One could see a river that flowed into the sea and according to the drawing it was wider than the others. It seemed to be situated between the mountains that we call the Sanmyn[B4] and the bay was such that the pilots until then had thought that it divided the land of a province called Mazamalco.[B5] Montezuma told me to decide whom I wanted to send. And he personally assured us that they would see and be informed of everything. Therefore, I chose ten men, several of whom were pilots and naval experts. With the recommendations that he gave them, they started out. They sailed along the entire coastline from the port of Chalchihueca[B6] that we called San Juan, where I had landed. They went for more than sixty leagues without finding either a river or a cove where the ships could have entered, although on this same coast there were many very large ones that they sounded from boats until they reached the province of Quaçalco,[B7] where the aforementioned river can be found.

B4. This is an abbreviation for San Martín.
B5. This is apparently an error made by the copyist for "Guazacualco."
B6. This is a reference to Chalchiuheuecan, a Mexican city near the current location of Veracruz but which no longer exists today.
B7. Another spelling of Coatzacualco. These variations are typical in Spanish manuscripts.

The lord of this province, Tuchintecla, received the men very well and gave them boats so that they could reconnoiter the river. They determined that at its mouth it was two and a half fathoms deep. *Several great cities*[B8] were scattered along its banks. The entire province is quite flat. Moreover, it has a rich abundance of all the products of the land *inhabited by an enormous population*.[14]

Along with this passage that is so fascinating when establishing a history of the Isthmus of Tehuantepec, in another letter to the emperor after the conquest of Mexico City, Cortés writes that when he sent Diego de Ordás[15] with Spanish troops to found a colony on the Coatzacoalcos River, the latter found the entire province stirred up and ready to resist the conquerors of Mexico. Not far from the river was the city of Coatzacoalcos that Burgoa[16] called Pechugui,[B9] where a princess reigned who still today is well known in local traditions and who was probably Tuchintecla's widow or daughter. When she learned about the conquerors' cruel deeds, she refused to recognize Ordás's mission and received him with arms in hand, as an enemy. A few days later, the Spanish captain approached the city from the river and under cover of night seized it by storm and abducted the princess, whose tender heart could not resist her captor's charms for very long. Heeding her wishes, the population submitted and the other princes came to pay homage to the Castilian crown. With the entire province reduced to obedience, Ordás was victorious in love and war, and proceeded in founding a colony called Espíritu-Santo, near Pechugui, which today consists of only a few huts.

In general, travelers to the region are amazed that the Spanish did not do more to exploit the invaluable commercial advantages of the Coatzacoalcos River. But there is nothing really surprising about it, because neglect was part and parcel of their colonial policy. It

---

B8. Today as is the case in many areas, these cities have been deserted but ruins can be found in the forests. [Emphasis is Brasseur's.]

B9. Pechugui was the Zapotec name of the city that the Spanish—basing themselves on its Mexican name—called Coatzacualco. In ancient times it was the commercial hub of the isthmus in the north, just like Tehuantepec was in the south.

first began when the daring exploits of English, French, and Dutch pirates became a source of serious concern. The Spanish reacted by abandoning most of the settlements that the first conquerors had founded on American shores. Too weak to defend such extensive positions, they concentrated all their strength in the interior and limited their commercial activities to the port of Veracruz on one coast and Acapulco on the other. As a result, these remained the only two ports opened to the seas that lap up against Mexican shores. Similarly, in Honduras, when buccaneers sacked the port of Trujillo in 1643, they abandoned that port to relocate the capital to Santa María de la Nueva Valladolid also called Comayagua.

Since Mexican independence, the world would have gleefully taken advantage of everything the Coatzacoalcos River had to offer, were it not for the civil war, which continuously saps the vitality of Mexico and is propelling it towards total ruin. Until now, this sorry state of affairs has benefited the Americans whose intrigues have only exacerbated the situation. Since becoming concessionaires of Garay's grant, they have had their eye on Minatitlán, where they established their main depot and center of operations. This village, founded at the beginning of the revolution, was named in honor of General Mina.[B10] It superseded the hamlet of Fabrica, located on the left bank of the Coatzacoalcos twenty miles from its mouth at the point where the river is no longer navigable. Its location was superior in all aspects, not the least of which was the fact that it was much more salubrious than Fabrica's. It has the same ease for navigation towards the interior. Both above and below the city the river has major tributaries which lead to the saltwater lagoons that follow along the shores between the Alvarado and the Champotón Rivers, which is on the Yucatán border.

B10. Mina-ti-tlan may well sound like an authentically Mexican name, but etymologically it is absurd. *Ti* means "elegance" or a "tie," and *tlan* indicates a "position between, in the center or near." It implies a sort of generality or plurality, so Minatitlán is literally "Between or Near the Minas." The Mexicans, who came up with this name and others like Hidalgo-titlán, did not understand a single word of Mexican. [When Brasseur refers to the Mexican language he means Nahuatl. The general that Brasseur is referring to is Martín Xavier Mina y Larrea (1789–1817).]

When the steamship passed the bar and made its way up the river, the passengers' faces lit up. For the Americans, it was as if the whole world was theirs for the taking. Coming from Europe or the United States and after being on board ship for several days, I have to admit, the tropical landscape offers incomparable charms. Nature is more beautiful and smiling. Even for those who have contemplated these regions in the past, the colossal size and fertility of the forests, the brilliance and variety of the foliage, the unaccustomed splendor of the sun, that luxury of light, water, and vegetation, all in one place, whets the appetite for a completely different landscape. Most of the passengers of the Coatzacoalcos arrived here with the hope of settling on the isthmus and finding lucrative employment. Thus they looked upon this wild paradise, in which every turn in the river offered up a new and more delightful perspective, with a hungry fervor. We stared out in wonder as we passed lagoons and rivers with long expanses of calm clear water, glimmering blue under the morning sun that suddenly and furtively darted under shaded arches of trees gently bent over the river. Waterfowl with dazzling plumage lined the banks, hunting their prey among slender bamboo and reeds, whose supple stalks and foliage elegantly reflected off the still, glassy sheet of water. Fiery flamingos and golden fawn herons swayed on their long legs, feasting on little fish, until the steamship's clamor brought terror to their ranks and they took flight, dispersing among the mangrove trees that cover the nearby swamps in luxuriant green. A variety of pheasants could be seen perched in tall trees, while bands of green parrots and swarms of parakeets flew swiftly over the river above our heads, their cries piercing the silence of the woods, defying man's murderous hand.

Nonetheless, under the clusters of swaying forest trees, which stretch out all around into the maddening distance and are seemingly impervious to sunlight, are many dwellings scattered between the milpas[B11] and prairies. The Indians, who have settled here, are not alone. There are North Americans, Europeans, and especially Frenchmen, who drew hard lessons from the disastrous experiences of the

---

B11. *Milpa* is the Mexican term for a "field," usually of corn, that has been cleared or sowed. The term is commonly used in the Spanish that is spoken in this area.

first colonists along the river,[B12] and have now created a comfortable existence here. However, as we made our way down the river, I could hardly make out the huts concealed in the all-encompassing sea of green. The prairie pushes its way, here and there, to the riverbank, slashing through the great forest. Scores of deer, cows, mules, and semiwild horses graze freely in the tall grass. With the roar of the steam engine, they prick up their ears, caracole, and flee at a gallop from the savanna into the forest. The outsider, tempted to follow them, would be stopped in his tracks. The sun hardly filters through this impenetrable thicket and inspires an anxious curiosity. A vast array of often unseen reptiles, insects, and other animals, study this bold adventurer, who dares invade their dwelling place. Hummingbirds flutter about in the canopy as their beating wings make a buzzing sound. Grimacing monkeys play in the towering trees, while squirrel monkeys hang from the branches with eyes fixed on these intruders, but soon frightened by their own temerity, they beat a hasty retreat. Even the boldest hunter finds many obstacles in his dangerous incursion. Beneath the surface of the seemingly clear waters around the mangrove trees, whose branches are intertwined with a multitude of other aquatic plants, are swamps of muddy sludge. Unable to continue walking, the hunter wants to go back. His foot slips and sinks even deeper. Sweat pours from his brow. Mosquitoes hungrily bite his face and hands. He returns exhausted and almost unrecognizable to his cabin. Only the Indians, in bare feet and armed with machetes,[B13] can clear a path. They know the

---

B12. Laisné de La-Ville-l'Évêque, along with other Frenchmen, had obtained a land grant on the shores of the Coatzacoalcos and attempted to found a colony, which through negligence, ignorance, or the dishonesty of the concessionaires had the most unfortunate results for the colonists that were sent over. It started in 1830, and while most of the hapless Frenchmen were expecting a land of milk and honey, they instead found poverty, fevers, and insects when they arrived. Most perished and it was only after incredible suffering that others succeeded in creating a better lot for themselves in this land. [The name of the Frenchman who was granted a concession to create the French colony of Guazacoalco is sometimes spelled Laîné de Villévêque. For a firsthand account written by one of the colonists, describing the catastrophic conditions in the concession, see Pierre Charpenne, *Mon voyage au Mexique, ou Le colon du Guazacoalco* (Paris: Roux, 1836).]

B13. Machete is a sort of cutlass in the form of a saber.

forest's twisted maze. They walk confidently in the swamp, following the trace of wild animals, and armed with only a leafy branch they defy even the cruelest tiger. Neither thorns nor venom deter them, because they know that they are the masters of these wilds.

Five miles downstream from Minatitlán we passed the mouth of the Uspanapa River, the Coatzacoalcos's most important tributary. It descends from the high mountains, which are home to the Zoque[B14] people, and which are located along the isthmus's border with the state of Chiapas. In comparison to the meandering Coatzacoalcos, the Uspanapa is a more important route towards the interior since ships with greater tonnage can make their way further inland on this river. Although its source is unknown, the Indians claim to go upstream by boat for twenty days in a temperate and magnificent landscape, rich in wild cotton and cocoa, as well as gold and silver mines. When writing to Charles V, Cortés described the area as heavily populated and flourishing. However, according to the region's indigenous people, there remain only ruins of ancient cities, whose populations disappeared under Spanish domination. When arriving at the Uspanapa River, one can see the Indian hamlet of Paso Nuevo,[17] with huts made of palm leaves standing on the land where once Ordás had built Espíritu Santo, which like the ancient city of Pechugui, is now shrouded by the forest's impenetrable vegetation.

CHAPTER II

An American Wedding.
American Politics in Minatitlán.

At around seven o'clock in the morning, Minatitlán's first huts appeared. They leaned towards the river, flanked by the green branches of mangrove trees that smothered them in their unhealthy shade. A bit farther along the bank, European and indigenous employees of the Louisiana Tehuantepec Company were busy

---

B14. The Zoque people are an ancient and civilized population that inhabited the western part of the state of Chiapas in Mexico.

hewing and sawing wood on an exposed beach with an American-style landing wharf. The *Suchil*,[18] a small steamship that ferried passengers and mail to California, was docked there. It was warming up its engine and ready to sail upstream as soon as the passengers made their transfer.

"Since you aren't going any farther than Tehuantepec you're not in a hurry," Murphy said to me. "So, why not stay in Minatitlán with us for a few days, and we will leave together. The *Suchil* will be back the day after tomorrow."

I accepted his offer and waited. Farther up the beach, there was a crowd of residents from every level of society eager to hear the latest news from the United States. I noticed a house built of uniform wood boards, supported by pilings that raised it considerably above the ground, and with crudely constructed balconies that looked out over the plain. This was the home of an American merchant, who also ran a hotel where there were lodgings for all comers. As I gazed out at this new city with curiosity, the Coatzacoalcos docked at a wharf across from the wide street leading to the port. The crowd quickly clogged the riverbank exchanging handshakes in the way Americans do. I soon learned that Minatitlán had the honor of receiving a high-ranking diplomatic figure—Robert McLane,[19] Washington's envoy extraordinary and minister plenipotentiary to Mexico. Instead of going to Mexico City and associating himself with other resident foreigners, who had recognized Miguel Miramón, Mr. McLane stayed in Veracruz where he had just recently presented his official letters of appointment to Benito Juárez, the liberal faction's president. Since he was rather bored in Veracruz, which offered very little in the way of entertainment, the new minister had come as far as Minatitlán, in order to see for himself the progress the Louisiana Tehuantepec Company was making in this enterprise that he had so heartily support. He had found lodgings at the home of A. C. Allen, the American consul to Minatitlán. Mr. Allen was on board apprising my friend Murphy of the news. I was soon introduced to this gentleman, who—I was told—was a prominent and influential merchant in this region, where he had lived for years and which he knew exceedingly well. He shook my hand and graciously invited me to stay in his home for as long as I was in Minatitlán. In the meantime, he grabbed Murphy and me by the arm determined to find us a morning cup of coffee.

I gratefully accepted his invitation. We quickly climbed the incline that separated us from the street and while we walked up towards the city, the *Suchil* whistled and started its journey upstream towards its namesake, the town of Suchil. Minatitlán was in a charming location on an exposed hill that overlooked the river between two swampy but richly forested valleys. Strictly speaking, the town consisted of a single street that ran from the port to the foot of a hill where the newly built church stood. Not far from there, the road forked to the right and left of the hill, receding into the countryside. This area and especially the church overlooked a vast, pleasant landscape with large tracts of forests on one side and woodlands full of fluttering hummingbirds on the other. The American consul owned a lovely property, which had not been completely cleared at the edge of town. His home, outwardly very rustic, was what his compatriots call a *log house*.[20] However, it was completely enclosed and the interior provided a certain degree of comfort. The house had a large room that was both a sitting and dining room. To the left, was the master bedroom and to the right a guest room with three beds donned with mosquito netting. McLane already occupied one bed. The second had been offered to both John Hargous and to Murphy, who declined it, and the third was intended for me.

McLane was finishing his coffee when we entered. He rose politely and after Allen introduced me, he welcomed me graciously. He was still a young man, probably not yet in his forties. His perceptiveness was immediately apparent on his face, which, for an American, was rather delicate and distinguished. He was neatly dressed in a clean black suit. His manners and bearing conveyed that he was a man in many ways outwardly superior to many of his compatriots of equally high moral character whom I have known.

When Allen introduced me and added the customary nicety a *French clergyman*,[21] I couldn't help noticing a look of approval from McLane, which I attributed at first to our shared religious faith. While I drank a cup of coffee with milk, I noticed that he was engaged in lively conversation with Allen, and I was especially intrigued because I suspected that I was the subject of their discussion. They waited for me to finish my coffee and promptly shared their scheme with me. Here is what it was all about. A young American resident of Minatitlán, a carpenter in the employ of the company, had fallen in love with and desperately wanted to marry a young lady, the daughter of a European merchant, who had been away for the last three or four months. As a Catholic he had already gone to the priest of Acayucan since Minatitlán was under his jurisdiction. However, when the priest learned that the young woman was a Protestant, he refused to marry them unless she consented to being baptized immediately. The young woman, however, refused his conditions. Meanwhile, the father was expected back shortly and all concerned anticipated that he would absolutely forbid the marriage. He was rich and the young man had nothing. Thus the two desperate lovers, who saw no way out, came to Mr. Allen pleading to him to help and advise them. The perplexed consul, in turn, spoke to Mr. McLane about it. The latter advised them to wait for the steamer, since the captain promised to bring back a Protestant minister of any denomination when he returned to the colony. All this had happened on the eve of our arrival. Unfortunately for the hapless young lovers, instead of a Methodist or Presbyterian *clergyman*,[22] they ended up with a Catholic. Neither McLane nor Allen was in the least bit troubled by this detail. After all, McLane assumed the French were all good natured and not especially punctilious. As soon as the word *clergyman*[23] was uttered, they rubbed their hands with glee, believing they could count on me to resolve all their problems.

I had hardly finished my coffee before they took me aside. They explained the situation and the urgent need to marry the couple who, for one reason or another, could not wait any longer. At last they pleaded with me to help them unite these two lovers as quickly as possible.

"And what about the priest!" I cried.

"The priest refuses to marry them. He is demanding that the young woman, who is Protestant, first be baptized."

"This is not absolutely required," I replied. "We could write to the archbishop of Oaxaca or to the pope to ask for a dispensation."

"A dispensation! But that would take six months and these young people need to be married immediately."

"I am quite sorry. But I am even more helpless than the priest, since I don't have the slightest jurisdiction in this country, where I am a total stranger. A marriage performed by me under these circumstances would be completely null and void."

It was difficult to explain the concept of jurisdiction to Allen, whereas McLane, by virtue of his position as a diplomat, was able to grasp my explanation more easily. But despite my reasons, they both seemed quite exasperated by my reply. As for me, although I was sorry that I was not in a position to help them, I was even more astonished by their irritation and especially by the relentlessness with which two men in their position were pursuing the issue. McLane did not even know the young people in question and his intention was to return to Veracruz within two or three days. The two Americans remained silent for a few moments, glancing at each other. McLane broke the silence first:

"Tell me, sir," he said as he turned towards me, "what would you do in our place, if we asked your advice on such a matter?"

"My goodness, Mr. McLane, when one is as unscrupulous as this young man, who cares little whether he is married by a Catholic, Methodist, or Presbyterian, he might as well find someone who can perform a civil ceremony."

"A civil ceremony?" exclaimed McLane.

"Of course, American law regards those types of marriages as perfectly legal. You and Mr. Allen have as much right to marry this young couple as any of our consuls or government ministers abroad do regarding those who have no need for the church..."

"I had no idea that such a law existed in the United States," cried Allen. "Do you think that such a marriage would be valid?"

"Valid? Yes... in the eyes of your legal system... Of course I am merely pointing out a fact that may be of interest to you at this moment."

"That is perfectly correct," added McLane. "We perform marriages like that every day. I regret not having thought of this sooner.

Allen, you are the United States consul to Minatitlán, you are the one who should unite this poor young couple."

"Me?" exclaimed Allen blushing to his ears. "I wouldn't know how to go about it."

"I don't know any more about it than you do, my dear Allen, but I am positive that you will perform your duties splendidly. This kind gentleman, who has more experience than you in these matters will give you a phrase or two."

"You have everything you need." I replied laughing, "Any Episcopal prayer book has what you are looking for, in detail."

"An Episcopal prayer book! I bet we won't be able to find a single one in all of Minatitlán," said Allen.

"There must be one on board the Coatzacoalcos," I replied. "I saw Captain Wilson holding one."

"Then all is well, my dear Allen," said the envoy, gleefully. "You look respectable and dignified. Tonight you will make an excellent minister. Inform the engaged couple and then go see Captain Wilson to ask whether we can use the saloon on board. That way we can celebrate the wedding on territory that is unquestionably American."

McLane and Allen shook my hand, thanking me for having come up with this expedient solution. I went out to stroll around the town, laughing to myself at the thought of the complacency with which these gentlemen were going to pull off this wedding in the absence of the bride's father. Murphy is Catholic, and I was eager to tell him about this adventure, which I felt that I did not fully grasp. But he had left me at the door of the consul's house and was making the rounds, paying visits to his many friends in Minatitlán.

Quite naturally I walked towards the church. The buildings on the main street were almost all made of wood boards and several were two stories tall. They all had shops stocked with American merchandise, and I counted as many as six *bar rooms*[24] before reaching the end of the street. At all hours of the day these establishments served every manner of fermented liquor, which are dreadfully adulterated and falsely sold as cognac, rum, or Bordeaux wine. Behind these houses were several other small dwellings built of wood, cob, or sun-dried bricks that are called adobe. Some had tiled roofs, while others were conical and used palm leaves. This was a charming scene—this variety of homes in the distance, spread out over the hillside or in the swamp in the fragrant shade of orange, coconut, and mango trees.

They were digging up the hill upon which the church of Minatitlán stands. It was a modest looking wood board building, in the style of the finest houses in the village, but it was brand new. Its construction had been funded by subscriptions collected on site and elsewhere by the colector de la aduana,[25] Don Francisco Soto. Several workers were busily cleaning it, and I learned from one of them that it just so happened that the next day was to be its inauguration. For the ceremony, they were expecting the priest from Acayucan, the vicar of the province, as well as the priests of Chinameca and Cosoleacaque. This explained why people had been streaming into Minatitlán since the morning. Indians, Mexicans, Ladinos, and foreigners were all arriving from neighboring villages to take part in the celebration. Don Francisco Soto was organizing the ceremony and paying all the expenses. It just so happened that, as I was leaving the church, he arrived accompanied by Murphy, who promptly introduced us. He sung the praises of señor colector's religious fervor and selflessness. Soto quickly joined in, elaborating on what Murphy had said, since he was thrilled to have this opportunity to give a French traveler *who was writing everything down*,[26] irrefutable proof—in great detail—of his integrity and his unwavering love of God.

Murphy was surprised not to find Allen with me. I apprised him of our discussion and when he heard the details he burst out laughing: "Poor McLane, poor McLane!" he repeated, "He is nursing his wounds after what happened in Veracruz."

I didn't understand what he meant.

"You are puzzled![27] Tonight at the wedding I will explain everything and you will understand."

We all walked around the area outside the church and then returned to the consul's house together. In the meanwhile, our host had informed the couple about what had been decided with the United States minister. He then went on board the Coatzacoalcos, where the captain, thrilled at the honor, put the ship at McLane's complete disposal. The news that a wedding was going to be celebrated on the steamer caused a great deal of agitation in Minatitlán. The town was already brimming with señoras, niñas, and señoritas[28] who had come from the surrounding region for the celebration on the following day. But un casamiento americano[29] was completely unexpected. It was one more festivity and for these childlike people, who would like nothing more than for life to be a perpetual party, it was one more blissful event. Two for the price of one!

The nuptials had been announced for eight that evening. As soon as the sun set the riverbanks were overrun by crowds of people eager to see what might unfold. My cabin, where I had temporary left my belongings, was at the far end of the saloon, where the mahogany table that would serve as the altar had been set up. It was decorated with vases filled with flowers next to which Captain Wilson's prayer book[30] earnestly lay. I entered with Murphy. The room was adorned with garlands, and the flags of Mexico and the United States hung together, on either side of the room, forming a banner that flapped gently in the evening wind. The ship's lamps, along with every candelabra that could be rounded up for the occasion, shone brilliantly on the Mexican ladies who were already crowding onto the ship. Young and old, mostly dressed in white, they were all adorned in the elegant style and charm with which Spanish American women seem to be born and nevertheless, can come as a surprise to a visitor when encountered in a place like Minatitlán. The caballeros[31] were in their finest clothes—in other words, white jackets or in European frock coats. Only a few wore the traditional ranchero attire that was so common only ten years ago. Clearly the advent of the Americans had brought changes to traditional dress. The ladies were seated and the gentlemen stood, forming two separate groups. They all spoke in hushed tones, with each new arrival attracting great curiosity and, in light of these elaborate preparations, there was a rising sense of naïve expectation at what this casamiento americano might bring.

At exactly 8 PM, McLane and Allen appeared, both in formal black suits. They were followed by Don Francisco Soto and the most prominent indigenous and foreign residents of the village. Only the betrothed couple kept us waiting and in fact they did not arrive until a half hour later. The young girl was on Captain Wilson's arm, since he had volunteered to stand in for her father. Friends of the couple accompanied them. Neither the bride nor the groom seemed the least bit embarrassed at being the object of so much curiosity. McLane stepped forward and led the young lady by the hand to the table, whereas Allen, visibly moved, prepared to fulfill his daunting responsibilities. In the end, he managed it all wonderfully and the happy couple was united according to the Episcopalian rite. McLane then took the floor and gave a speech[32] addressed to the newlyweds, which I was too far away to hear. He then kissed the bride in a fatherly way. The young woman consented willingly to all this, accepting paternal kisses first from Allen and then from Wilson, who were thrilled to have been lucky enough to play a role in such an occasion. The captain then led her to a sumptuously laid out table. The United States minister, the consul, and other guests, both invited and uninvited, followed the newlyweds. The ship's staff in dress uniform served a splendid supper of patés, ham, cold meats, pastries, all types of canned food, fruits, ice cream, and sorbets, as well as chilled champagne and fine Spanish and French wines. There was an abundance of everything and all the guests ate and drank until they had their fill. The captain served as a dignified host. In fact, after such an event, the stature of the Louisiana Tehuantepec Company was greatly enhanced and would no doubt remain so. No wedding was complete without dancing. The music, arranged by Don Francisco Soto, arrived after supper—violins, cellos, and flutes started playing. McLane had the first dance with the bride. It was all too appealing. What Mexican woman could resist being swept up in the excitement? Everyone joined the ball. They danced quadrilles and polkas until two in the morning and as they left, the Mexican, Creoles, and Ladina women from Acayucan all repeated enthusiastically: "Ha qué gusto, qué bonito, qué lindo es un casamiento americano!"[33] (What a delight, how beautiful, how lovely an American wedding is!)

Never before had they been in such a splendid saloon, never before had attended such an orderly reception, and it was highly unlikely that any of them would ever attend such an occasion again. This was one of the last nights that I spent on the Coatzacoalcos and consequently

I was there to take in the whole show. From time to time, I left the suffocating heat to step out on deck. The evening was extraordinarily beautiful. The sky was clear with sparkling stars. The moon, which had risen on the horizon, gave off such a pure glow that objects were illuminated as if by daylight. As I left the saloon, it was aglow in artificial light, brimming with intensity, reverberating with the booming sound of music. The view of the river, with its dark waters vanishing into the distance between the two banks with the motionless thick forest canopy radiating in moonlight brought an indescribable calm to my soul. I will never forget the odd juxtaposition of the two scenes.

I was there alone, contemplating the scene, when Murphy interrupted my musings. McLane had just retired for the evening and the ball was winding down.

"Well," he said laughing, "the show has come to an end, and everyone is going to bed. Come drink a glass of punch and then you can do the same."

"Wait a minute! You had promised me an explanation. From my perspective, the actions of Mr. McLane—the envoy extraordinary and minister plenipotentiary of the United States to the Mexican government—are completely inexplicable. In my opinion, this whole wedding was highly unusual and certainly a person of his stature in Europe would have jeopardized his reputation if he had done such a thing."

"Bah! We see things quite differently in America. From the Yankee perspective, McLane's reputation not comprised in the least, in fact, he will use this to his advantage, to enhance his popularity. You see, he has just made a diplomatic blunder and fears the consequences. Therefore he is looking for ways to make up for his mistakes."

"A blunder? What do you mean?"

"He recognized the Juárez presidency without having been fully authorized to do so by Washington, and . . ."

"Really! That is incredible! Didn't his diplomatic dispatches instruct him to take those initiatives? That is quite serious."

"What makes it worse is that these are nothing more than shady backroom deals. Juárez was only officially recognized as the president of Mexico in order to benefit Mr. La Sére."

"Come on, then, tell me the story. I had heard rumors in New Orleans, but I could hardly believe them."

"Really? Everyone knows about La Sére. Basically, he is an excellent man, but there is no doubt that he is the most enterprising and cunning fellow around. He wants to be elected to the United States Congress, so he is using all the means at his disposal. After having been president of the Louisiana Tehuantepec Railway Company for some time, he saw that his tenure might be coming to an end, and he wanted to be reelected to this position at any cost, since it was a great source of his influence in New Orleans. But how could he pull this off? The stakeholders, especially those from New York, didn't think very highly of him. But then came La Sére's masterstroke, as a result of which he was able to win back all those who had previously tried to push him out. He would end his term with an act that was capable of producing the greatest profit for the company. McLane had just arrived in New Orleans as he made his way to Mexico, in his new role as minister plenipotentiary. La Sére was more or less aware of his mission. The new envoy had been instructed to go to Veracruz, appraise the situation carefully, and try to get to know both parties equally. He was only supposed to present his letters of appointment either to Juárez or to Miramón once he was thoroughly informed on their respective positions, so as to be able to judge which of the two had the right or the most likely chances for success. McLane is very able, but La Sére is in a league of his own. He cajoled and flattered him. He manipulated him to the point that when McLane sailed for Veracruz, La Sére was on board. During the trip, La Sére kept pressing his point. He praised Juárez and his qualities. Moreover, he argued for his legitimate claims to the presidency. He tried to convince him that Juárez was the Union's most zealous friend and that he was ready to make great sacrifices for these American friends, as long as the United States recognized him as the rightful president of Mexico. In other words, La Sére earned McLane's complete trust. He turned the new minister's head with images of the glory that awaited him if he were able to obtain new concessions on the Isthmus of Tehuantepec and insure American control in the area through a new treaty. They arrived in Veracruz. They disembarked. And then La

Sére crowned things off with one last maneuver—a splendid dinner on board their steamer for Juárez, his ministers and friends, and McLane, of course. Champagne flowed. Seated between Juárez and La Sére, McLane was lauded. He was intoxicated by praise and his head was spinning with all the compliments that were lavished upon him in toast after toast. He finally exclaimed unwisely as he raised his glass: 'I am seated between two presidents.'[B15] I would like to drink to the health of the constitutional president of Mexico!' He had made the plunge. There was no going back. A few days later, perhaps with some regret, McLane officially presented his letters of appointment to Mr. Juárez and recognized him as the true and legitimate president of the Mexican Confederation. Immediately afterwards, Juárez signed the extension of the privilege of the Louisiana Tehuantepec Company, which increased the land grant to ten leagues from the one league that had previously been granted. Furthermore, through a clause that has not yet been made public," added Murphy with a smile on his face, "we have been given the port and territory of Huatulco,[B16] which they say are both first-rate."

"And this special mission that you have been charged with," I interrupted "is related to all this, no doubt."

"That's true," he answered "I won't lie to you, but for the time being don't let on that you are aware of anything. I have never been able to get along with Mr. Sidell,[34] the chief engineer for the transit route and railroad across the isthmus, and I was determined to resign. So in order to keep me occupied without putting me under Sidell's command, they commissioned me to explore Huatulco and its surrounding area. My intention is to head there with my associates once I arrive in Tehuantepec."

"And Mr. McLane?"

"Well, McLane is no longer feeling very grateful towards Benito Juárez," laughed Murphy. "Now, he is kicking himself. Washington

---

B15. The president of Mexico and Mr. La Sére, the president of the Louisiana Tehuantepec Company.

B16. This is the most beautiful and secure port in the state of Oaxaca on the Pacific, which has been neglected for quite a long time due to substantial depopulation in that part of the country.

took a dim view of his premature actions, since it is impossible for him to go to Mexico City as a result to ascertain what the rest of the diplomatic corps is up to. It was a great blunder and they are leaving it completely up to him to resolve the situation as best he can."

"But what possible connection does any of this have with this evening's wedding?"

"The wedding? Probably more than you could imagine. Through no one's fault but his own, McLane has just set his career back by several years. He is trying to find a way to regain those years. He is young and no doubt has the time. But he has to curry popularity and get good press. That is the only solution. His secretary was noting down exactly what was happening. He will embellish the story and soon enough we will see it appear in the New York Tribune or some newspaper of that stripe. Our Yankees will be astonished to learn that a lovely couple was rebuffed in Minatitlán by Roman Catholic priests, hostile to their union, and that the two lovers found protection against Catholic intolerance thanks to Mr. McLane, who arranged for Mr. Allen to sanction their marriage in the name of American freedom."

"That is fine, my dear friend," I exclaimed, "but you know that this could make an interesting article for a Parisian magazine and that I am prepared to write it."

"As long as it is not right away, I don't care. It will be more than a year before you return to France. By then the subject will have changed."

"So what terms are Mr. McLane and Mr. La Sére on now?

"They have not seen each other since the treaty was signed. A few days ago, a friend of Mr. La Sére traveled from Veracruz to New Orleans. Mr. La Sére asked him for news about our ambassador. 'He is quite bored in Veracruz' his friend told him 'and regrets not being able to go to Mexico City.' 'Poor McLane!' cried out La Sére with a knowing smile. But he could care less. He was reelected president of the company and now he is scheming in Baton Rouge[B17] in order to insure his election to the legislature."

B17. Baton Rouge is the capital of the state of Louisiana and located on the Mississippi River.

Having said this, Murphy took me in to have a glass of punch and then shook my hand wishing me a good night.

The next morning, the distant sounds of fireworks and bells, of cannon and gunfire, woke me from a deep slumber. I had finally managed to fall asleep after the grueling events of the previous days, despite the mosquitoes that had invaded my cabin. The celebration of the benediction of the church of Minatitlán was being announced with great fanfare. It was 7 AM I dressed quickly and after the usual preliminaries, I set out calmly into town. The weather was wonderful but it was very hot. The streets were lively and gay like the people, and along the way I met many others who, like me, were making their way to the church. On its esplanade, crowds of natives hurried, not wanting to miss the ceremony. Men and women, young and old, mestizos and Creoles all jostled one another. Meanwhile those who had arrived early were stretched out on mats set up outside the church and were relaxing or preparing food. Their dress was not particularly remarkable. The men had wide white cotton jackets and pants that went down to their heels; on their heads were crudely made hats woven from palm leaves. The women, with their long braids falling over their shoulders, wore colorful cloth skirts and on top they were wrapped in a huipil or a loose-fitting tunic of white muslin.

I found the priest from Acayucan in the sacristy. As the provincial vicar he had been asked by the archbishop of Oaxaca to preside over the celebration. We had met through Don Francisco Soto the day before. He was with the priests from Chinameca and Cosoleacaque awaiting the appointed hour to start the ceremony. The latter was going to sing mass, Acayucan's priest was going to give the sermon, and Chinameca's was going to have the role of subdeacon. They had invited a fourth person to fulfill the role of the deacon but he had not arrived and since it was getting late, the priest of Acayucan asked whether I would take the stole in his place. Quickly each of us was dressed in our vestments. Under a glaring sun, the benediction ceremony took place according to the usual rites of the church. I was sweltering and sweating under my dalmatic. As was the custom, no one was allowed to enter the church until the end of the ceremony, which took place outside. The esplanade and the hillside were teeming with crowds of people, who all rushed into the church as soon as the doors opened. What an extraordinary crush of people! It was a free-for-all the likes of which I have rarely seen.

The mass started immediately afterwards, despite the pandemonium. It was accompanied by shouts, incoherent singing, fireworks, and gunshots—all intended to deafen the least Christian of those in attendance. Moreover, the moment the officiant and his ministers appeared at the foot of the altar, the choir began singing the Introit, or the Kyrie eleison, in such a ludicrous and offensive way, to my ear, that I didn't know whether to laugh or to cry. My God, what a choir! Even now, when I think back on that day, my ears ring with the earsplitting sounds. The orchestration was commensurate with the singing. The most awful hullabaloo was no match for this supposed sacred music, which must have affected my hearing for an entire week. It was even more oppressive than the heat, if that can be imagined. In fact it was all equally bad—the precentor, the music, the priests, and even the public! Never in my life will I attend such a mass again. The sermon, preached by Acayucan's priest, was no better. The climax came when he extolled the superiority of American institutions and Yankee civilization with the utmost solemnity, and then called on heaven to bless the liberal faction and their weapons.

It was certainly a great relief when this was all over. Immediately afterwards, Don Francisco Soto came to the sacristy to invite me and the other officiants to his home. An impressive lunch awaited us there, as did a great number of invited guests—Mexicans, Creoles, mestizos, Americans, and other foreigners. Everyone paid tribute to the customs officer's boundless generosity. He was toasted by all. Speeches[35] were made in Spanish and in English. The priest of Acayucan didn't fare much better here than he had in his church sermon, yet the Liberal Party enthusiasts greeted his words with rousing applause. Chinameca's priest—of the three clergymen, he was the one with the lightest skin—whispered his objections to the display in my ear. He confided that, in his opinion, the tone of both the speech and the sermon were a bit too revolutionary. All this certainly astonished me considerably. Until then, from the newspapers I had read, I was under the impression that Juárez had little or no supporters among the Mexican clergy and that the priests were the most vehement enemies of both the Americans and the Liberals. In Minatitlán I began to see things differently. However, it wasn't until my stay in Tehuantepec that I realized the obvious contradictions in the current political situation in Mexico.

I didn't want to impose on McLane, nor frankly, for the sake of my privacy, did I want to share a room with others at his house, so I decided to return to the Coatzacoalcos that evening to sleep on board. Unfortunately, the mosquitoes kept me up all night. I spent part of the evening in battle with these annoying insects and part of it walking the saloon and the deck. As morning approached, worn down and no longer able to resist exhaustion, I threw myself on my bed fully dressed. I nodded off. But I had hardly dozed off when I was awoken by a sharp whistle, like that of a distant steamer. It was the *Suchil* returning with the San Francisco mail and passengers from California en route to New Orleans. I got up, grumbling at my bad luck in getting any sleep. It was not even 5 AM and the sun had not risen. But we were asked to yield our places to the newcomers, who soon appeared on the little steamer. It was quickly hitched to the Coatzacoalcos and they hastened to remove the belongings of the passengers, who had remained on board, and in no time at all, the Californians were invading our cabins. By six o'clock all was set. Captain Wilson waved goodbye. The cannon gave the signal before departure. The Coatzacoalcos, having cast of its moorings, sailed rapidly towards the mouth of the river and quickly disappeared from sight.

As soon as I had insured that my trunks were in safekeeping on the *Suchil*, I went on shore. I walked to Mr. Allen's home, and after a cup of coffee, I threw myself on the bed that he had offered me, in the hopes that an hour's nap might make up for my sleepless night.

The next day, on May 19, it was our turn to leave. We had been in Minatitlán for three days. Murphy, who was always looking for a good time, was not was not very enthusiastic about leaving. But the captain of the *Suchil* informed him that if he wanted to arrive in Suchil without too much trouble, he would have to take advantage of the rising water, brought on by the mountain rains. However, if he waited a day or two more, the water would subside and the only way upstream would be by rowboat. That possibility was too daunting for Murphy not to comply, since it would mean that instead of a trip of one day and one night, it would take three or four days to reach our destination. This was not a pleasant prospect. After some discussion with Allen, he realized that there was no alternative and gave the order to start up the engine. I bid farewell to the good consul, who for his part was preparing to accompany McLane back to Veracruz. By 8:30 everyone was on board the *Suchil*. Only Murphy was missing and he arrived at nine. We immediately cast off and were soon sailing up the Coatzacoalcos.

CHAPTER III

The Isthmus of Tehuantepec.

THE LOUISIANA TEHUANTEPEC COMPANY: ITS PROGRESS AND WORKING CONDITIONS

The Isthmus of Tehuantepec truly begins once you leave Minatitlán. Geographically speaking, this isthmus extends from the southwest in the state of Oaxaca to the northwest in the state of Veracruz and borders both the states of Tabasco and Chiapas to its east. Of all the interoceanic routes in the Americas, this one is the closest to New Orleans and New York. It is also the shortest and most convenient way to get to California, while presenting the most healthful climate. From the mouth of the Coatzacoalcos—located at in the northern latitude at 18°8'20" and at the western longitude at 94°32'50" from the Greenwich Meridian—it is approximately 143 English miles to the port of La Ventosa on the Pacific Ocean, located at a latitude of 16°11'45" and a longitude of 95°15'40" from the same meridian. Both of the isthmus's coasts go east to west. Its topography can be divided into three very distinct regions.

THE NORTHERN REGION

The first, in the north, covers the forty or fifty miles in from the Gulf coast. It has large fertile valleys, showered by the waters that descend from the Cordillera towards the Gulf of Mexico. As we have already seen, these valleys, which rarely rise to more than two to three hundred feet above sea level, are in general densely forested. The most remarkable of these is the Coatzacoalcos Forest, named for the river that flows through it from south-southeast to north-northwest. To the west of the Coatzacoalcos's mouth rise the high volcanic peaks of San Martín and Pelón, which we glimpsed from afar when at sea. These mountains, part of the great Tuxtla range, turn towards the north almost forming a right angle with the coastline to the east and give a singular character to the coast where La Barrilla is located. From the Tuxtla Mountains to the Jaltepec River, which is the main tributary on the left bank of the Coatzacoalcos, the only mountains worth noting are the Encantada Mountain—rising at eight hundred feet above the surrounding plains at thirty miles from the gulf—and Mount Tecuanapa, at twelve to fifteen hundred feet above sea level. Besides these two mountains, this entire northern section is a broad plain, covered in dense forestland.[36]

Nevertheless, there are a certain number of large towns and villages, some of which have a considerable number of inhabitants. Three miles from the right side of the Coatzacoalcos, in a delightful location with a salubrious climate, is San Cristóbal Ishuatlán.[37] This town is not far from Paso Nuevo and together they boast a population of twelve to fourteen hundred people, who are Indians for the most part. Three miles to the east of Ishuatlán is an indigenous town of Santiago Moloacán, with eight hundred inhabitants. What sets this town apart is that it has a considerable spring of petroleum oil, which covers several acres. On the Coatzacoalcos's left bank, at about seven miles west of Minatitlán, there is a village called Cosoleacaque, inhabited by more than two thousand peace-loving and industrious Indians of Aztec origin, who all speak the Mexican language. Two or three miles farther west is Otiapa with a mixed population of Indians who speak Mexican and of mestizos. Further north is the town of Chinameca with a population of fifteen hundred Aztec Indians, who are just as hard working as those of Cosoleacaque.

However, of all these towns the most well known is Jáltipan, which according to some is the birthplace of Marina, whose legend is still alive today among the Indians. Marina, who was first Cortés's slave and later his mistress, played an important role at the start of the conquest. On the same side as Jáltipan is the town of Texistepec with a population of more than two thousand Indians who speak Mexican, and finally, there is Acayucan, the court of the former royal family of the region, which has become the capital of the district of the same name since the Spanish city of Espíritu-Santo was abandoned.

The political leader or prefect responsible for the jurisdiction of Coatzacoalcos resides in this town and its population, which is as high as six thousand inhabitants is mainly composed of mestizos and Creoles, as well as some foreigners. Acayucan enjoys a mild and salubrious climate and is located twenty-seven or twenty-eight miles from Minatitlán through which its goods are connected to the sea, but its main trade is through the San Juan River. Acayucan is the main trading center for the Coatzacoalcos valley and its surrounding region. If it weren't for the wars that have ravaged Mexico, Acayucan could prosper and flourish, instead unfortunately, it has been greatly impaired. Just a few years ago annual exports of cotton and *ixtle* (or Bromelia pita) from the isthmus, through the port of Veracruz alone, came to more than $1,256,000.

With its fertile soil, climate, and geographical location, the Coatzacoalcos valley should be considered one of the most extraordinary places on earth. The land yields one hundred times what the hand of man sows, and for the same amount of work it produces at least six times as much as the United States does, although its land is more prized. It is difficult in such a quick overview to give a precise notion of the variety and wealth of the economic production on the isthmus in general and the Coatzacoalcos valley in particular. This land yields a wide variety of valuable timber as well as India rubber, vanilla, sarsaparilla, indigo, dragon's blood, cacao, coffee, sugar, tobacco, cotton, corn, honey, pita, etc. And with a minimum of effort, these products could enrich the population, which is enterprising and industrious. In the north it takes a year of hard work to raise a single corn harvest, whereas in this area, they can produce as many as three yields, with less toil. In order to prepare their milpas, or fields, the natives merely burn the forest down to midtrunk. It is almost always women and children who sow the seeds using only a pointed stick with which they make a hole in the ground for the grains, which are then covered over using their feet. The most fertile land yields a return of up to three or four hundred fold and the less fertile soil up to sixty or eighty. But the average estimate for the isthmus is one hundred and fifty fold. Apiculture was one of the most important industries to have existed before the conquest. And as a direct result of Mexican piety, the production of raw wax alone could ensure a man's future wealth, given the large quantities consumed in churches and oratories. Unfortunately, today no one collects the wild hives that can be found everywhere in the forests and even in the walls of houses.[B18]

Among the plants that grow wild on the isthmus, one of the most curious and least known in Europe is ixtle, which is similar to agave but different in certain regards from the *Agave americana*, or the maguey plant, found in Mexico or the *Agave sisalana* found in Campeche. There are countless varieties of this prolific plant, which produces pita and a wide array of fiber ranging from the most common hemp to the finest flax. It grows anywhere regardless of the climate or the season. The ease of growing this plant as well as the simplicity of extracting and preparing its fibers, is such that is widely used. Indians use it to make thread, ropes, mats, bags, and clothes as well as the hammocks, where so often they are born, where they rock back and forth and rest during their lifetime, and where, in the end, they die.[38] Their ancestors used these fibers as it is still used to this day: to make paper that it is exquisitely beautiful and extremely resistant. The juices that are extracted from the plants are used to make caustic to heal wounds. In the morning they gather the dew that collects in the hollow of the plant's large leaves in order to wash with this liquid, which preserves them from skin disease, protects their complexion, and prevents premature

---

B18. The walls of the house that I used to live in in Rabinal were a like sponge, riddled with holes, because bees had made their cells there. Of course, the walls were made of adobe or unfired bricks, which had been dried in the sun.

wrinkles. Their thorns are used to make pins and needles. Moreover, in several regions they extract a delicious distilled beverage from the plant's roots, which in Guatemala is known as *comiteco*. The cultivation of ixtle is extremely widespread on the Isthmus of Tehuantepec, mainly around the small Indian towns of Chimalapa[39] and San Juan Guichicovi.

However, the population of the isthmus seems to remain indifferent to the immense wealth of resources around them. The Americans, on the other hand, were beginning to discover the area and all its potential. This explains why they were unrelenting in their attempts to appropriate Garay's grant. They opened a route that many thought would be paved with gold. For a year or so, this route was overrun with travelers either going to California or coming to the isthmus to try their luck. Unfortunately, intrigue, dishonesty, negligence, and foolish pride, were on full display. A coherent plan on the part of the employees of the company, however, was nowhere to be seen. Thus bankruptcy was all but inevitable. As a result, despite the large amounts of capital that had been sunk into it, this much-vaunted route has been completely abandoned. Nonetheless, the advantages of this project are such that the Americans, who made one attempt, will no doubt try it again in the foreseeable future.

THE CENTER REGION

The center of the Isthmus of Tehuantepec, which is its second distinct region, is particularly remarkable because of its great diversity. The great Cordillera chain, which goes by several other names, extends in a single unbroken line for the entire length of the two American continents. Instead of the lofty volcanoes, which are such a striking feature elsewhere along this chain, the mountains spanning this section of the isthmus from east to west, suddenly dip down. The mountains seem to divide the landscape in two as if Providence was explicitly pointing to the shortest route from one ocean to the other. Here the Cordillera approaches the Pacific coast with its southern slope ending abruptly, almost in a straight line from east to west over quite a considerable distance. To the south of the Jaltepec River, we encounter a series of high plains circumscribed by these mountains through which course the Jaltepec and Chalchijapa Rivers, both tributaries of the Coatzacoalcos that descend from the west from the high Sierra Mixe. Further south, are the hills of Xochiapa, where the Malatengo, Almoloya, and Chichihua Rivers flow down to the Coatzacoalcos as if paying tribute to the great river. They have opened up a natural passageway through the range, which otherwise would have presented an insurmountable obstacle to the construction of a canal or railroad. Between this range and the Summit Pass, there are rolling plains known as the plains of Xochiapa, Chivela, and Tarifa. These plains are divided up by a series of low hills that rise gradually and become more uniformly level as they approach the Summit Pass, which leads to the Pacific Ocean. To the south, they are bounded by the Guacamaya and Masahua Mountains, which both end in rugged limestone peaks with an elevation of fifteen hundred to two thousand feet above the Pacific. These are the only connecting links uniting the high chain of the Cordillera in the state of Oaxaca to the mountains that extend to the east towards the state of Chiapas and the Guatemalan Republic.[40]

THE SOUTHERN REGION

By a narrow natural gap in the mountains, one suddenly descends from the elevated plateaus to the low plains of the Pacific coast. This brings us to the third region of the isthmus. The average area of these plains is twenty miles from the base of the mountains to the coast, at an inclination of ten to fifteen feet per mile, until reaching the lagoons of Tehuantepec. Thus they form an immense inclined plane, 250 feet above the sea, gently and uniformly sloping towards the Pacific Ocean. At certain locations, there are hillocks or isolated hills of volcanic origin, which make the landscape extremely picturesque. Eight rivers descend from these mountains, flowing through the lower plains, to empty into the lagoons, which are connected by a narrow outlet called the Boca Barra. The largest of these rivers is the Loteca or the Santa María River,[41] which descends from the mountains of Oaxaca to the northwest of Tehuantepec and then cuts across this city and discharges itself into the sea in the bay of La Ventosa.

We were sailing up the Coatzacoalcos on the river steamer the *Suchil*. It was not a large boat but had cabins, which were rather well laid out and, although far from as luxurious as those on the *Coatzacoalcos*, they were comfortable and well ventilated. The river—swollen from the first May rains, which had begun two days ago in the mountains of Guichicovi—rolled its rapid muddy waves, carrying along plants and trees torn from its banks. Several miles outside of Minatitlán, we passed the mouth of the Coachapa, a tributary of the Coatzacoalcos to its southeast. During the rainy season this river has the curious distinction of flowing into the Coatzacoalcos again thirty miles higher up, where it unites with the Coahuapa River to form a large, hilly, forested island. Further up, the Coatzacoalcos itself divides into two branches, the Mistan and the Apotzongo branches, which circumscribe the twelve-mile-long island of Tacamichapa. This island is claimed by the town of Jáltipan, which asserts its rights based on the tradition that maintains that the Spanish crown gave the island to the celebrated Marina for services rendered to Cortés. Between large tracts of woodlands, charming plains fill the island's open space, which is home to lovely looking deer and pheasants. Cattle feed on grass that grows tall above their heads. The residents let their animals graze indiscriminately and no one objects in the least to this system. In the clearings every once and a while I caught sight of a *rancho* or a milpa where a hut with a conical thatched roof of palm leaves stood. But towering trees, with glistening, varied foliage are what dominated this landscape. The tallest of these are the fanned-out palm trees and coconut trees, whose brilliant aigrettes sway elegantly above the rest.

An ever-changing scenic panorama of varied greenery quickly passes before us. At every turn, the river offers a new sight. Towards noon, the boat stops briefly across from the village of Hidalgotitlán, which is also known as Los Almagres, located twenty miles from Minatitlán on the right bank of the river. The thatched cottages of this pueblo, shaded by handsome orange and coconut trees with their slender trunks, are pleasantly grouped together on the hillside along the river. It comes as a welcomed change from the splendid monotony of woodlands that have passed before us for the last three hours. Through the foliage, I catch sight of a woman standing on the banks, waiting for goods to be unloaded from the steamer. She had European features and her pale, melancholic face naturally elicited my curiosity. I asked Murphy if he knew anything about her and he told me that she was a French woman named Madame Raimond, the widow of one of the first colonists to settle this area with the disastrous expedition of Laîsné de La-Ville-l'Évêque. She and her husband had both suffered terribly and their adventures had the makings of an epic novel. Mr. Raimond overcame hardship and died just a few years ago after having accumulated a great deal of wealth and leaving his family comfortably well off. The tall beautiful girl next to his wife was his daughter, who had recently married an American.

The steamer continued upstream. A few miles beyond Los Almagres we reached La Horqueta, where the two branches of the Coatzacoalcos reunite once passed the island of Tacamichapa. I looked out over exceedingly charming views of the water and woods. There were crystalline lakes interspersed with enchanting gardens, where nature's hand had brought together an abundance of towering plants and the most beautiful brilliant flowers. Some thatched cottages, with their pointed roofs, could be seen in the distance on either side of the river, but as we advanced, our solitude became greater and more tangible. Having lost the last vestiges of human life, the woods took on an atmosphere that was both more majestic and monumental. The banks disappeared entirely under the foliage, but the enormous branches arching over the river, often concealed muddy swamps, where their roots, tangled with vines and aquatic plants, were the perfect refuge for reptiles and most notably for caimans, which often sunned themselves, sleeping languidly on the warm mud or swimming like tree trunks floating on the water.

When they heard the clamor of the steamer they lifted their hideous heads and quickly retreat to their hiding places in the swamp's dark recesses. I saw one of these monsters that must have been twenty-five or thirty feet long. What a horrible sight, with his gaping jaws and the slits of his tiny red eyes half-opened as if he was concealing something! Apparently more brazen than the others, this creature remained in plain sight, stretched out on a thick tree branch jutting out above the water. As soon as they saw him in the distance, some of my fellow passengers took aim with their guns. They were all Americans or had been Americanized and therefore, it would have been a wonder if there were a single one of them without a firearm, rifle, or revolver. One man, who went by the name "Doctor," a former filibuster with William Walker and associates, in Nicaragua, seized his Colt[B19] and shot the monster in the abdomen. The dreadful amphibian spun around in agony and fell from his branch into the water, rolling over dead after a final ghastly convulsion, tingeing the surface of the river with a great circle of blood.

As I said, once we had passed Tacamichapa island our isolation was all the more real. We continued for another ten or twelve miles before reaching the first Coatzacoalcos rapids, located at the base of the clayish Loro Hills. The river squeezes though rocks and rages over the shallow waters, making this section treacherous to navigate. The previously calm waters became turbulent, loudly roaring as they churned, and consequently the steamer advanced slowly and cautiously. It is at this point that I first saw the approaching mountains. Along sharp turns in the river, the water violently broke against the sheer banks that pressed the flow as if between two walls. Here, accumulating alluvial deposits wreak havoc upon the superb forests that collapse like ramparts of a citadel in ruins along its banks. The night that soon descended and the evening sky began to add yet another element to this expressive scenery. From the river, which was already enveloped in darkness, I saw the last rays of sunlight, gilding the tops of the tall trees, while the moon rose with its luminous wreath shining through the clearings in the forest. The hot, fragrant humidity that hangs in the air after sunset eventually yielded to a light breeze fluttering through the trees. This was the time of day when the river was suddenly solemn, while never losing its mysteriously thrilling charm. Lit by flickering stars and moonlight, the beautiful play of light and shadows on the water was indescribable. I fell completely under its spell, mesmerized by

---

B19. Colt is the name of the creator of the first revolvers in New York. He still manufactures the most sought-after revolvers, which bear his name.

the force of the swaying waters, overcome by the forest scenery, and spellbound by the palpable solitude of the tropics after dark. Even the deliberate speed of the steamer intensified the fantastic turn that this nocturnal spectacle had taken. At times, we were engulfed in an uncertain dusk that covered the river and allowed only the faintest glimpse at the endless distant landscape along its bends. At times, when the moon penetrated the dark forest, there was a gentle, misty splendor like a summer's dream. As moonlight flooded this dormant countryside making everything clearly visible, it reminded me of the elaborate staging of some sort of theatrical extravaganza.

I was lost in contemplation before this captivating setting for so long that it was very late by the time I finally returned to my cabin to get some sleep. The next day, at around seven in the morning, we passed the site of Abasolo-titlán, formerly the center of the French concession of the Guazacoalco. A mile from there, the steamer stopped in front of a hillock that rose on the right side of the river, with a small house perched on top.

This was called Brewer's, named after an industrious American, who had decided that until something better came along, this was as good a place as any to set up shop. The captain of the *Suchil* announced that we had to disembark here, explaining that the water had become increasingly shallow over the last two days and consequently his steamer could go no further.

From Brewer's to Suchil was a long stretch of uninhabited land. Before the Americans started work along this river, the only settlements passed Abasolo-titlán, were the Indian villages of San Juan Guichicovi and Santa María Chimalapa or the Mal Paso Rancho at the confluence of the Sarabia River and a little further upstream the hacienda San Gabriel Boca del Monte. The Americans who established Suchil, which is the starting point for all navigation on the river, also set up other posts along the way as relay stations for carriages transporting passengers from Suchil towards Tehuantepec and La Ventosa. We were now attempting to get to Suchil, which was about eighteen miles away by boat but, in fact, much closer by land. Murphy had already made arrangements for his associates to continue upstream on *bongos*, or pirogues, with our luggage.

Meanwhile, John Hargous and he had horses waiting for them at Brewer's house, and they were kind enough to offer me a third one. I was delighted. The prospect of going the rest of the way in a canoe was not particularly appealing to me, especially since given this unexpected turn of events, no one had had time to get leaves that were commonly used as protection to shade passengers from the heat. The sun was already up and soon enough we could all expect its full force, which would have been all the more unbearable when reflected off the surface of the water. Pirogues are boats carved out of enormous tree trunks, usually from mahogany trees commonly found in the forests surrounding the Coatzacoalcos River. They can be quite large and I have seen some as long as sixty feet and as wide as eight or ten feet. Indians and mestizos handle them with skill and speed, but since they don't have a keel, they have to be carefully ballasted and passengers must remain extremely still so as not to capsize. Depending on their size and their load they need two to six rowers. If two are enough, which usually is the case for a bongo, one sits in the back propelling the boat forward, while the second sits in front steering the rudderless canoe with his paddle.

While the luggage was being unloaded, I went up to the house with Murphy and Hargous, where they gave us slices of pineapple to refresh us. At ten o'clock, we were on horseback. Immediately after leaving Brewer's property, we forded the Chalchijapa River and entered the thick forest. To get to Suchil we had to follow a very poorly marked path. But Murphy had gone this way so often he couldn't possibly get lost. We were at the end of the so-called summer season and although the river had already swollen once or twice from the mountain rains, there was no sign that the rainy season had begun in this great expanse of woodlands. The ground was hard and cracked, the streams dry, and the liana—whose long arms wrapped around the branches of the trees—looked like dead vines. As a result of the American presence, the forest had lost its virginal beauty. The sun was now able to penetrate the growing number of clearings, thereby absorbing the humidity that otherwise flourishes in the luxuriant foliage. However, there were still areas where the vegetation stood tall and solemnly untouched by light. We passed from exposed paths, subjected to harsh scorching sun, to sections where we rode beneath archways studded with brilliantly colored flowers and wild orchids that led to even thicker woods. We passed under a massive vault through which rays of light filtered almost imperceptibly. In these impenetrable thickets—these lairs for jaguars and wildcats, which can be so dangerous when they are hungry—my inquisitive exuberance ebbed and gave way to apprehension. At times I imagined that I saw the ferocious eyes of an ocelot in the darkness, but the next moment all my fears subsided. These animals flee human contact and during the day it is rare to see them along well-traveled paths.

When we returned to sunlight, we encountered arid brush and woody vines choking branches and trunks like snakes and often the lifeless debris of fallen trees in dusty decay blocked our way. I can't say that it was particularly pleasant to ride through such a tangled mess of branches. Granted, it was hardly the first time I had traveled in this way, but after two years away from this region, I felt like a novice. Murphy had a good laugh when he noticed my hesitant pace. Luckily, Mexican horses are accustomed to this sort of obstacle course and as wanting as my mount had seemed to me at first glance, he was performing feats that would have made me the envy of the acrobatic equestrians in Franconi's circus.[42] In fact, once, when I became unexpectedly entangled in a vine that got caught around my waist, he made such a leap that he almost disappeared from between my legs. Fortunately the vine broke off when I was forcefully pulled along; otherwise I would have remained suspended from a tree, dangling not by my hair like Absalom, but by my waist.

We made good time, despite these difficulties, and in the end, we managed to ignore them. Every once and a while, however, one of my companions would stop short either to shoot at a flock of brightly colored parrots or macaws, flying above cawing like crows, or to laugh at the grimacing monkeys frolicking in the high branches of amate or mahogany trees. Emerging from a dense stretch of forest, Hargous caught sight of a royal pheasant, perched on one of the tallest trees in the forest. It was a magnificent bird with black and white feathers with highlights of copper and blue and a crest like a superb crashing wave. We were able to get close enough to admire him, but when Hargous was about to pull the trigger, this forest king majestically spread his wings, landing on the branch of a nearby tree.

We didn't have time to go on a wild pheasant chase because it was important to reach Suchil before nightfall. We had arrived at the edge of the river after four hours on the trail. We descended onto the sandy banks along the river, riding for a half an hour. Then we entered the forest once more. Unfortunately, the path that lay ahead was completely exposed and the hurdles formed by the tangles of liana, wild vines, dead branches, and fallen tree trunks were more abundant. In the heat, our horses were panting from all the fits and stops of our steeplechase. We had trouble pushing forward. This stretch went on for another hour at which point the river reappeared before us, wide and majestic, like a fork whose immense points disappeared to our right and to our left, deep into the woods. We were at the confluence of the Jaltepec and Coatzacoalcos Rivers. For approximately one mile, we continued along the south side of the riverbank, across from the wooded hills that rose between the two rivers and where I eventually saw three or four extremely unattractive large wood-board constructions. These were the Louisiana Tehuantepec Company's depots—a pompous title for such unprepossessing buildings. Although such audacity was quickly surpassed when I saw the neighboring building that they had the gall to call a "hotel." Welcome to Suchil.

The location seemed pleasant and well chosen. The Jaltepec and the upper-Coatzacoalcos, which unite at this point, are two great rivers of more or less equal size. The former has its source in the mountains near Lachixila and Quetzaltepec in the state of Oaxaca and flows through these mountains onto the hilly savannas of Tuxtla, linking a handful of hamlets to the sea. The upper-Coatzacoalcos, which is sometimes called the Río del Corte, del Paso, or Suchil, emerges from the uncharted mountains of the Zoque people which rise to the east of Santa María Chimalapa. It swells in size along the way with the waters of several other sizable tributaries. Standing in Suchil at the company's station, the river is an imposing sight, pleasantly snaking between the hills like a great shimmering ribbon in a charming distant land of woods and pastures.

When we arrived across the river from Suchil, we got down onto the bank, and I tried to recover from the fatigue of a first day on horseback by rolling on the sand. It was four in the afternoon. Someone had already noticed us from across the way and a pirogue with two strong Indians was on its way to fetch us. One of the Indians, who was completely naked, dove into the water when the boat had almost reached us and carried us, one by one, to the canoe that immediately set back to the other shore. He deposited us on the company's side of the river in the same way. The depot's administrators greeted Murphy like an old friend. Murphy introduced me and there was the usual unending round of American-style handshakes all around. We all entered the main depot together. It was a vast room, where everything was kept in messy piles. There was no ceiling or floor to speak of. At one end, a partition separated a space into two small rooms, each with a trestle bed and mosquito netting. Otherwise, there was no furniture. The rest of the space was filled with equipment, trunks, cases of wine and liquor—some still full and neatly stacked, others empty and turned upside down to be used as tables and chairs. There were old cigar boxes and bottles of all shapes and sizes everywhere. In fact, the first thing they offered us was a cigar and a drink. But Murphy and Hargous were as hungry as I was. After a few minutes of conversation we moved on to the hotel to see our rooms and to order dinner.

CHAPTER IV

The Suchil Hotel. Paso de la Puerta and the Plains of Sarabia.

Like the depot, the hotel was no more than a large shed. It was divided into three sections, the largest of which was the dormitory, with twenty trestle beds, no mosquito netting, and less than a foot between each bed. Because of the hot climate the owner could get away with not providing mattresses, so the only bedding available was a pillow and sheet. In this land of liberty, Americans, who are generally such prudes at home, undressed without giving a second thought about offending their neighbor. Here, imitating the natives, they slept like Jacques Rennepont, the debauched drunk from Eugène Sue's[43] novel, *The Wandering Jew*, who went by the name Sleeps-In-The-Nude. But when in Mexico, anything goes! Or at least, so they say. There were two other separate rooms in the shed: one the master of the house's bed chamber and the other the entry hall and barroom—an amenity that no hotel in the United States is without. A dozen or so people were gathered around the bar when we came in. Murphy's arrival was greeted with cheers and handshakes and all manner of toddies. I was introduced as a "scholar," traveling in pursuit of science and a crowd of new friends suddenly started calling me "doctor" and shaking my hand to the point that I thought it might be dislocated. It seemed that a title—captain, colonel, or doctor—was conferred on everyone in this place. Even Murphy was greeted as colonel upon his arrival and Mr. Chamberlain, our innkeeper, was addressed as captain. After a few words from Murphy, Mr. Chamberlain was on his best behavior and as polite as an American of his class could be towards me. He was quite proud of his establishment in this foreign land. He showed me to my room, in other words, my bed and then led us to the dining hall. This was another shed at the end of a filthy muddy yard, where Capitan Chamberlain's pigs, chickens, and dogs ran free. Dinner consisted of half-rancid sardines, fried eggs, and salt pork, served with a plate of rice prepared in water and a cup of coffee the likes of which I have only ever had in Belize in Miss Waldron's hotel. Instead of bread we were given stale sea biscuits. This succulent meal was replicated every evening and was preceded by exactly the same for lunch. And it was thus for the three days and nights that my lucky star led me to stay in the Chamberlain Hotel, for a fee of two and a half piasters a day for room and board, in other words a bit more than fourteen francs.

You might object that such persnickety comments regarding the fare provided by poor Capitan Chamberlain in such a wild and remote location are completely uncalled for. How could he be expected to obtain fresh supplies? However, your objections would be invalid. Far from being isolated, Suchil was in regular contact with the United States. Chamberlain received shipments of flour that he sent on to the town of Barrio and elsewhere. The captain had a yard full of sheep and poultry. He could have obtained milk in the neighboring ranchos. But Americans are not very particular. As long as there is liquor, they are happy. As for Chamberlain, even if his guests left with a low opinion of his hotel, he undoubtedly took comfort in knowing that he would likely never see them again and in the end they had no alternative. As for me, I have traveled extensively throughout the Americas and have often stayed among Indians, who lacked for many, many things but with whom I never had to put up with such abysmal food as when I was among the citizens of this so-called *civilized nation par excellence*,[44] whose citizens actually brag about their disdain for decent food, countering that in their country at least everyone can read, write, and do math.

Throughout the Isthmus of Tehuantepec, in the areas that had been taken over by the Americans, in other words, by the Louisiana Tehuantepec Company, everyone I met, to a man, was attempting to acquire the biggest possible piece of the pie. Some justified their actions by saying that they were just trying to recoup the money they had spent getting to Mexico. Some saw it as a way of making up for their poorly compensated work and still others were just trying to stay busy. As a result, everyone was up to something slightly unscrupulous, and when opportunity knocked, they all reached their hand for the till. Meanwhile the company and more specifically its silent partners were under the impression that that everything was moving along smoothly and therefore continued paying all the bills. The company was represented by William Sidell, the chief engineer; Mr. Rieken, his secretary; and other high-ranking employees, who were charged with completing the remaining work on the isthmus. And I certainly don't want to tar these fine gentlemen with the same brush as those shameless types that I mentioned earlier. These men were responsible for the boats and carriages used for transporting travelers from the port of La Ventosa to New Orleans. Unfortunately, Mr. Sidell had brought with him four or five nephews along with a dozen or so flunkies and entrusted them with too much authority. During my trip the situation had become critical. While Sidell had established his headquarters in Chivela, the highest point on the route, the construction workers, most of whom were Indians or mestizos from the villages of El Barrio de La Soledad and Petapa, were spread out all along the route in places that they called *camps*.[45]

The treaty signed with Juárez's government meant that the company was exempt from paying custom fees on any imports related to its work, food, or clothing but it was responsible for feeding all of its workers and employees. All supplies, clothing, equipment, and tools were therefore brought in from the United States, and the depot in Suchil was the main storage facility. This provided a cover for smuggling in large quantities of merchandise onto the isthmus. What—in the hands of honest administrators, honorable officials, and friends of law and order—could have yielded big profits, in this case was a constant source of losses due to scandalous misappropriation. Each camp was headed by an engineer or at least someone who went by that title. He ordered the supplies and equipment that he needed from Suchil. He received these supplies depending on whether the engineer in question was on good terms with the depot managers in Suchil, because the latter distributed their cache as they saw fit. They might refuse a request on a whim, alleging that the items were out of stock and that they had to wait until a shipment came from New Orleans with the order. But in the meanwhile, they were planning for a rainy day by selling what they could, cash in hand and well below cost, to natives who were purchasing things for their own personal use. As far as keeping records, it was much more convenient not to have any. In fact, you could have searched long and hard for account books in their offices. It would have been in vain. All you would have found were empty or opened bottles.

It was all too common for work to come to a halt because of a lack of tools. In the camps the laborers kept themselves entertained. Some slept, others danced. The engineers spent their time hunting rabbits but mostly drinking. Suchil's depot was the site of overindulgence, if not debauchery: Maryland hams, salt pork, Cincinnati sausages, and sardines in cans vanished into thin air somewhere among all those bottles. And yet the backers continued paying the bills believing that all was well. Mr. La Sére, the company's president, kept assuring them profits were right around the corner. In reality, the Tehuantepec route was an unfathomable money pit. The disorganization was such that even before the route was completed they realized that the whole line would need to be reinforced. However, with the rainy season soon approaching, everything would soon get bogged down in the mud and sludge that would emerge between stretches of virgin forest. Soon it would be impossible to ford rivers. And instead of building stone bridges at a reasonable cost like the natives do, the company's engineers, who were busy lining their own pockets, chose to build wooden ones at twice if not three times the cost only to see them promptly swept away by rising waters in winter.[B20] Instead of buying horses and mules to pull the company's stagecoaches they decided to rent them, thereby entering into expensive contracts. Then the company representatives on the isthmus claimed that all contracts had already been paid through New Orleans, which was not the case. Out of sheer carelessness they neglected to build sheds for storing carriages, which were left outside exposed to the hostile tropical sun. Instead of finding pastures where their horses could graze, the animals were allowed to wander. Workers and contractors were not being paid, and the day I arrived in Suchil, we learned that judicial authorities in Tehuantepec had just taken possession of horses and carriages in order to pay the company's debts.

The people who suffered the most from this disgracefully chaotic state of affairs were the small creditors and of course the workers. And then there were the travelers, who had paid for their trips in New Orleans or San Francisco never imagining the hardships that awaited them in crossing the isthmus. Despite the claims that appeared in the American newspapers, the reality was quite different. The truth was that passengers embarked for Minatitlán, from which they traveled on to Suchil. A lucky few reached Suchil

---

B20. It isn't that wooden bridges are more costly than those made of stone but rather that the Americans brought in carpenters from the United States to build them, whereas they could have used natives to build stone bridges and had much cheaper labor costs.

by river steamer. But when this was impossible, they went by bongo. A small number of privileged travelers made the journey, along with the mail, in a large canoe with robust rowers. But the rest painstakingly made their way upstream in much smaller boats. When they arrived in Suchil, they dashed off to Chivela and then directly on to La Ventosa. The Pacific steamship, which the company had contracted to stop on an appointed day, took the mail and set off immediately. However, those who had not traveled with the mail might arrive in Tehuantepec just a few hours later to find the ship had sailed. As a result, they had to wait two weeks and in some cases a month, staying in two-bit hotels, often depleting their resources. Sometimes, in the confusion, even the mail arrived too late and the boat left without waiting for it. The same scenario played out in the other direction. I met travelers who had paid exorbitant rates for their passage and then were abandoned on the isthmus, forced to sell their personal belongings, clothes, and jewelry to pay their hotel bill and continue their trip. This is the sad truth about the Tehuantepec interoceanic route. I discovered much of this by speaking to hundreds of witnesses and of course I was a first-hand observer. But it was only when I arrived in Suchil that I really started to understand what was going on.

This explains why I was compelled to stay for three days at Capitan Chamberlain's hotel. I couldn't wait to leave that dreadful place, but no matter how much I tried to persuade Murphy that we were losing precious time, he didn't yet dare openly discuss the collapse and ruin of this company—after all, he was one of their high-ranking representatives. There were no horses to take us to El Barrio, and as far as carriages were concerned, they were sequestered in Tehuantepec, where the creditors had allowed only those that were strictly necessary to transport the travelers who had taken our places on the Coatzacoalcos back towards Minatitlán.

Finally on Sunday, May 22, at around 3 PM, they brought us a few pathetic-looking nags more raw-boned than Don Quixote's horse and harnessed in an even more pitiful manner. We had to accept our fate. Murphy, Hargous, and I mounted the sturdiest of the lot but after about ten minutes on the trail my horse refused to go any further. I was too heavy for her. Murphy had a good laugh at my predicament and then suggested that we return to the hotel. I accepted because it was better to have to spend another night in that shed than to see my horse fall from exhaustion as we rode through the woods and then have to walk five or six leagues through deserted countryside in the baking afternoon sun. Later I couldn't help but wonder whether Murphy had suggested that I mount that miserable creature in the hopes of preventing us from leaving. Mr. Rieken, the chief engineer's secretary, had arrived the previous night to find out whether Murphy had brought cash from the United States. We were introduced and he had invited us all to join him and a few of his friends for a dinner. I had refused in order to be able to leave Suchil as soon as possible. As for Murphy, he seemed to regret leaving and he was beaming when we walked back into the hotel. He immediately barked out orders for a new mount for me and promised that we would set out again without delay after dinner.

This dinner was purportedly going to be a showcase of gourmet masterworks from the kitchen of Chamberlain's chef. I was somewhat optimistic at first, but then cruelly disappointed when the omnipresent omelet with rancid ham appeared, with rice in water, and the usual coffee. All this was accompanied by a pudding, created by the chef for just this occasion, but which even the worst Parisian or London hole-in-the-wall wouldn't dare serve. With the exception of Hargous and me, everyone devoured it with delight, washing it down with copious amounts of strong liquor, which—like the guests at Chamberlain's hotel—bore pompously overblown titles, in this case: sherry, madeira, and champagne. They ate and drank from nine in the evening until one in the morning, and when it was time to set out on the trail, they were almost all drunk. But this was life as usual on the isthmus. While most of the guests were deep in sleep, Rieken and Murphy unsteadily straddled their small bidet horses. Hargous and I also got in the saddle, and at around one thirty we were finally riding along on the American trail.

Immediately after Suchil we entered the forest and followed a trail called La Picadura for several miles. This replaced a former Spanish mule trail that went as far as the hacienda of Boca del

Monte. According to my companions, it is quite picturesque with great views. But it was dark and despite the brilliant starlight, I could only vaguely make out the surrounding countryside. In fact, I could only judge the height of the trees on either side of the trail by the dark shadows that they cast upon us. There was another reason that that I wasn't able to fully appreciate the beauty around me. Rieken and Hargous were more than a mile ahead, and I had stayed behind with Murphy. He had come out of his drunken stupor but now, in the forest's fragrant air his head drooped as he started to nod off. Each time he slumped over onto his saddle's pommel his horse stopped, which made it even easier for the rider to sleep. I tried in vain to poke him and yell in his ear. I tried to point out the dangers of being in such a position. I didn't want to abandon him especially since these forests are full of tigers, and he and his horse would have certainly become their prey if they had crossed paths on the trail. After two or three hours of this slow and halting pace, he admitted that he was in no state to keep going so he begged me to let him sleep for just a moment under a tree. I agreed, in the hopes that once he had slept he would be able to shake off this torpor. He slept for a half hour and since dawn was approaching, I woke him by placing a wet towel in his hand and he doused his face and hair. We got back onto our horses at once.

The path we were on followed along the slopes of hills that rose up to the south of the Jaltepec River and joined the foothills of the Cordillera to the southwest. All around there were signs that the forest had been despoiled and destroyed by the American's construction. Nevertheless, it was majestic especially in the tranquil silence that precedes sunrise. The morning star, that passing sun, as it is known by the Indians, who still worship it as a divine being, rose in the sky so bright and unlike anything that we see in our countries that I have often mistaken it for the moon. As it rose, its intensity made the other stars relinquish their place, and I started to notice the cool air that comes with the tropical morning dew. Murphy finally woke up. The brightening sky was tinged by rose hues in the east. At that exact moment we were descending from the top of the hills from which the Amate Creek flows. Below us lay a series of cool, humid valleys where perfect calm reigned. Soon the first rays of sunlight penetrated from above the distant mountaintops around Santa María Chimalapa, and their exhilarating action stirred the breeze, filling the forest with murmurs and soon sounds of life could be heard. With the increasing intensity of the sun, smoky mist drifted up from the ground and water. A vaporous fog wafted up from the rivers and the depths of the damp woods, enveloping the landscape in a light veil that made it resemble an immense lake, where the forests jutted up at acute angles like promontories or islands covered in foliage. Soon the valley echoed with the thousands of morning sounds that bring life to the remote tropics. There were cries, warbling birds, and the tinny rustling of insects with their piercing calls, which gave the impression that human beings inhabited the forest. Nature was greeting the return of the rising star that the Indians once worshiped as the supreme master of heaven and earth. As the sun climbed higher, the white veil of fog, torn asunder by the wind, tumbled down the hillside like snowdrifts, eventually melting away in the warming sun.

As we gazed out over this fantastically altering landscape, we arrived at an American post, called Camp XV Miles, a stop for carriages on the Tehuantepec line. It was 7 AM. A large shed, which was on pilings and completely opened to the wind and elements, sat at the bottom of a gloomy and isolated valley. This was what remained of a camp, now almost in ruins, established by the company's employees while working on the route. Racks built with crude sticks and on posts four feet above the ground were meant to be used as beds, benches, and couches in this dwelling that donned the name hotel. The hotel in Suchil was a palace in comparison to this place! The only furniture was a cast-iron stove and two or three miserable boards placed on top of empty Bordeaux wine crates. A battered old pot with frijoles, or Mexican beans, was cooking on the stove along with a coffee pot, which had seen better days, since it lacked both a handle and lid. We were exchanging our "Capitan" Chamberlain for a "doctor"—Dr. Chandler, the resident innkeeper. He was a man of approximately thirty-five years, who was tall, thin, and dirty with unkempt hair. He only wore a shirt, which had once been white, with linen pants torn at the knee. On one foot he wore a turned-down boot of a completely indeterminate color and on the other an old-styled yellow shoe with red morocco trim. The only other living souls to be seen were a young fifteen- or sixteen-year-old Zapotec Indian, who was wearing even less than the doctor, and a ram in lieu of a family dog.

When we entered the shed, I noticed Rieken and Hargous lying on the couch, snoring like two village trombones. Nearby, also asleep, was a sweet Italian boy, born in Rome, who went by the name Hector. He was from a wealthy family but had run away from home and found his way to the isthmus with Murphy, to whom he had been highly recommended. While we had been dining in Suchil, he had mounted one of the nags reaching the Hotel Chandler a few hours before us, where he promptly took to a so-called bed to await our arrival. He was fast asleep and Murphy wasted no time following his example. As for me, my desire for sleep had disappeared with the sunrise; so, I merely sat on a board and observed the house and its inhabitants. Dr. Chandler lingered attentively about—the picture of grace and charm with his boot and yellow shoe. He spoke of his hotel in the way one might expect from the owner of the Metropolitan or Astor House in New York. He complained about an unending list of thankless tasks and the company's complete lack of appreciation for his work. As he presented his grievances, I couldn't help but yawn because I was very hungry. In my previous travels, I had always made sure to pack plenty of my own food supplies, and when traveling through Indian lands I had always been able to find eggs or chicken. Here, unfortunately, I had put too much faith in Yankee civilization and my traveling companions' reassurances. I was caught completely off guard without even a biscuit to eat. The only thing this warm-hearted doctor could offer was a cup of bean broth for which he kindly charged me six Spanish reals.

Just before nine o'clock, Murphy and the others woke up. They also had a cup of bean broth, we shook hands with the doctor, who—along with his ram—graciously bid us farewell, and we got back on our horses. The road leading away from Camp XV Miles is fairly unremarkable. Plains pierced through the forest and the wide, lovely road offered up rich woodland on either side reminding me of those old bridle paths found on our castle grounds. After several hours, at around noon, we arrived at the edge of a wide stream. This was the Tortuguero Creek, a tributary of the Jumuapá River, which was right below where we stood, rolling rapidly, deep down in a gully shaded by lush foliage. We found a camp of American carpenters, who were building a ferry to transport carriages and passengers across the water. Since they were about to have lunch they cordially invited us to share some biscuits and coffee with them. Moments later we were back in the saddle and forded the stream. We hadn't gone more than fifty paces when we came to the Jumuapá River with an unfinished wooden bridge stretching across it.

This river bursts from the Guichicovi Mountains in the form of thundering waterfalls and flows into the Coatzacoalcos a few miles passed Suchil. It was quite wide at that point, although not particularly deep. Its waters were surprisingly clear, moving slowly between piled-up black rocks and fallen trees and over a bed of fine sand strewn with pebbles. Superb forests formed archways of green above the silent water to our left in a long expanse of shade and light for as far as the eye could see. On the other side of the river, there was no hamlet or village to be seen, just a few huts with palm leaf roofs. One of these was a recently built American hotel known as Ladd's, named for the establishment's owner, a strapping lad who appeared to be both gentle and honest. Despite the fact that his was a fledgling business, it was much cleaner and more comfortable than what we had experienced in Suchil and after a two-hour wait, Mr. Ladd served us a perfectly acceptable lunch, to which we did great justice.

We were in a place called Paso Puerta. It is on the same latitude as Mal Paso, a location ten or twelve miles away that owes its name to the fact that in the past it was the site for many an armed robbery. There are two trails leading to the plains of the Sarabia, which are renowned in the region for being a wide and naked expanse that stand in stark contrast to the surrounding luxuriant fertile lands. One trail goes through Mal Paso to reach San Gabriel Boca del Monte and traverses a continuous stretch of dark forest suspended high above the hills that separate the Sarabia River from the upper-Coatzacoalcos. The other trail, through Paso Puerta, leaves the Jumuapá River behind to enter plains that extend all the way to the foot of the Sarabia Mountains that stand out against the Guichicovi Mountains.

We got back into our saddles at around 4 PM and continued on our way. We still had nine or ten miles to go before reaching the American station known as Sanderson, named for the woman who owned the house that was being used as a hotel there. Murphy assured me that there was only a single, straight path through the plain and that it was impossible to get lost. Since I was eager to see the landscape in daylight, I set off with Hector and we rode ahead confident that we would arrive at our destination before sunset. The savanna that we cut through was just as I had heard it described—an extensive undulating plain that continues over quite a large area until eventually joining the high canopy of the forests that surround it. The red sandy soil provides only the thinnest layer of humus upon which a short scraggy grass grows. The feeble flowing streams that irrigate the land grow dry once the rainy season has passed. The only trees and arable land are found deep in the gullies that have been carved out by the rain.

Hector was as eager as I to arrive at our inn. Unfortunately, we foolishly took for granted that our guide had given us accurate information. We had already ridden for two solid hours without stopping. The sun had set suddenly behind the high western mountains that were casting long shadows over the plain. Dusk had quickly come and gone, leaving only the feeble light of the stars to guide us. In the woods it is easy enough to make out a trail, using only the slightest clues. But in this immense savanna that until recently had been relatively untraveled, the path was far less clear for inexperienced visitors like ourselves. We found tracks from wagon wheels, a sign that perhaps we were on the right path, and so continued moving forward. Finally we saw light ahead. Obviously, we thought, this must be Sanderson's inn. We joyfully headed straight in that direction. This race towards the light went on for another half hour, but as we made our way our certainty slowly eroded. The light, which was still before us, grew in intensity, over a long stretch of land to our right and it soon became vexingly clear that what we were seeing were the flames from a forest fire, which had apparently been set in order to clear the land for a cornfield. To cap all this off, we arrived at a fork in the trail. We had the choice between going to the right where I could just barely make out a deeply rutted path that led in the direction of the burning forest or to the left onto a path, completely shrouded by the dark night. Perplexed we dismounted to better survey the situation. This only added to our confusion. Hector claimed that we should go to the right, but I was of the opinion that we must go left. I suggested that he call out in the hopes that Rieken and Murphy, who should have been behind us would hear his voice. But to no avail. Not even an echo responded.

"Let's wait here," I told him, "and wait until they arrive. They'll catch up to us soon enough."

However, I was afraid that we had taken a wrong path and that and we might have to spend the entire night on the plain. Not that I was concerned about sleeping under the stars in the open air. The night air was warm; the sky was so luminous and clear that it would have been a great pleasure to be outside in such conditions. Nevertheless, we were near the forest, with a fire burning just four or five miles away, and wild animals frightened away by the flames could very well be drawn to the plains and the scent of human flesh. I had no weapons and Hector had only a few percussion caps for his revolver. He was perfectly unaware of the dangers that these uninhabited regions presented. Consequently, I did my utmost not to share my fears with him. Suddenly, I saw him loading his pistol. He told me that he was going to shoot it off to let our companions, who were behind us, know where we were. I wanted to prevent him from doing this, fearing that the sound could just as well attract a tiger or lion. But how could I break it to him? The shot was fired. I strained my ears, listening attentively. I scanned the blazing forest with a fixed gaze. I listened some more. It seemed I heard a far-off sigh with a muffled roar in the distant plain. Our horses pawed the ground with their hooves, and I had the distinct impression that they were sniffing the air with concern. I admit that I was afraid.

A terrible shiver went through my veins. That's a tiger, I thought to myself, and it can't be far away. For his part, Hector was completely unconcerned. But he also heard the noise.

"What was that?" he called out.

I was going to respond when a new sound could be heard. I took a deep breath. It was the sound of a steady pace, soft but regular like ambling horses.

"It is Murphy and Rieken," cried Hector.

He was quite right. A few moments later they had joined us. I explained to them that we were uncertain about the route.

"It is straight in front of you," was their response. "The trail that goes off to the right leads into the forest to link up with trails further up that go to San Juan Guichicovi."

Who could ask for a clearer explanation? Without speaking a word of the terror that had struck me as they arrived, I got back on my horse and along with Hector, followed them the rest of the way. One hour later, we could once again make out lights. This time it was the Sanderson Hotel, where we shortly arrived. Like the place in Suchil, it was a long wood-board shed, divided up into several sections, with a bar at the entrance, followed by a dining hall where the Tillmann brothers, who ran the place, immediately served us dinner. We had eggs with chicken and rice and for dessert a cup of coffee with milk. All this was the sort of luxury not experienced since I had left Mr. Allen's hospitable table in Minatitlán. Next to the dining hall were the sleeping quarters and the beds, which were arranged in the same way as in Suchil. Right after dinner, I retired for the evening, but Murphy, who was suffering from a violent migraine—an after effect from the little orgy from the night before—was up and about all night keeping the rest of us from sleeping. Moreover, the barroom was transformed into gambling den where the hosts and guests played until dawn, yelling and swearing loud enough to keep the marmots all the way in the French Alps up all night!

Since it was impossible to sleep, I got up early in order to contemplate the beauty of the surrounding mountains at sunrise. It was the same plain as the day before, with its thirsting wooded gullies. But above Sanderson's, the plain dwindles between the two secondary mountain ranges that separate it from the forests of Boca del Monte in the east and from the Sarabia and the Malatengo Rivers in the south. I was hoping that we might be on our way early, but it was useless to try to hurry Murphy along with the argument that we should take advantage of the cool temperatures as we make our way towards the interior. Although I was touched by the solicitude shown to me by my travel companions, especially Hargous and Murphy, whom I will never forget, I was tired of this Yankee-style adventurer's life, which I had been leading for the last week and which deprived me completely of my personal freedom. I was anxious to arrive in Barrio de la Soledad, so that I could regain my independence and return to Spanish civility and to the Indians, whose simple and unpretentious hospitality I preferred to these dreadful and sophomoric American inns. But poor Murphy had a migraine for most of the day. Therefore, it was with great difficulty that we were finally able to get onto our horses towards four in the afternoon. Once we were in the saddle, he completely recovered from his headache and was his old gay self again.

After crossing the Sarabia River, we continued for several miles through the sometimes-undulating and sometimes-wooded savanna. To the left we passed by the hacienda of Boca del Monte, which is located less than a mile and a half from the American route. At this point the woods thicken with clusters of trees and the rolling prairies turn into veritable hills, whose slopes are saturated with shade and where crystal clear streams flow towards the nearby Mogañe Creek, which is itself a tributary to the Malatengo River. In the dark depths of these streams I discover a mysterious beauty that goes beyond the merely scenic charm of its landscape. Unfortunately, the night was already projecting its shadows on the mountain paths along which we had just started to ride. And at the exact moment I was ardently invoking the light to illuminate the details of this landscape, the last splendors of sun were being extinguished in golden and purple waves of light above the neighboring mountaintops. It had been a half an hour since we had passed the Mogañe. There was just enough of that brief dusk, which is a prelude to night in the tropics, for me to be able to make out several overgrown tumuli and the pyramid-shaped foundation of a teocalli in ruins hidden under a thick mantle of vegetation that Murphy pointed out to me. This was the first trace of the region's ancient indigenous civilization that I had seen since returning to America. I wanted to examine them, despite the oncoming darkness under the already shadowy forest canopy, and I showed my companion that there were remains of ancient fortifications surrounding these remnants. The Pachiñe River, which flows towards the Malatengo from the southwest, rolls through a deep, wide ravine bathing the base around this curious site, which once served as circumvallation. As soon as we crossed the narrow Pachiñe, we had entered the territory of San Juan Guichicovi, and these ruins were a reminder of this area's former days of glory. They made me think back to the Mixe people, a valiant nation who long resisted waves of attacks first from the Chiapanec, then the Mixtec, the Zapotec, and finally the Mexicans. Even today, in the wake of the Spanish conquest, they still have managed to maintain their independence and kept their people almost perfectly intact.

 From the promontory where this pyramid was located, we descended deep into the ravine and continued following the twisting banks of the Malatengo River that we crossed now and again. They say the landscape in this area is quite remarkable, but it was night and the fact that we were making our way between two rampart-like walls of stone and earth, whose color I could not even discern, made it seem even darker. We rode for one or two miles in the pitch-black, and it was only when we climbed out of this ravine to the plain that I saw, not a single light, but millions of points of light dangling in space, colliding, crashing, and crisscrossing from every direction in the trees not far from where we stood. They created an indescribably fantastical illumination. It was as if thousands of ghosts were chasing about but only the flames from their torches were visible. It took me a few minutes before I fully grasped what I was seeing. As I drew nearer, I realized that myriad fireflies were wafting about the trees along the ravine, which at this particular moment looked more like enchanted groves in Armida's[46] gardens. I had never seen so many of these brightly lit insects in one place, and as everyone knows they are particularly large and brilliant in Mexico.

They soon disappeared along with the thicket of trees atop the Malatengo ravine as we continued on our way. Moments later we arrived at a dreary rancho bearing the name hotel. It was in the same mold of what we had seen in Suchil, at Sanderson's, and in our doctor's shack. This place was run by an American that everyone called Nash, who was one of Walker's former soldiers in Nicaragua.[47] He decided that he was better off deserting the ranks of the filibusters, concluding instead that joining the enemy was more worthwhile. After the war, he spent time in Guatemala, where he plied many a trade, and when his travels led him to Mexico, he rented this rancho and transformed it into a hotel. When we arrived, Nash was in his shirtsleeves, and his shoe selection was reminiscent of Dr. Chandler's. He was just as attentive to his guests, however, and he provided an infinitively superior meal. Americans regarded him in general as a traitor and couldn't bear to be around him. Murphy, who was my source for all this information, just laughed the whole thing off. In fact, as soon as we came into his place, Murphy gave him as cordial a handshake as he had given Capitan Chamberlain. Everyone in the rancho was busily preparing dinner. John Hargous and a few others, who had preceded us, had told Nash to expect more company. Several Zapotec Indian women, who made up this Yankee sultan's harem, were grinding the corn on the *metlatl*, or grinding stone. Some were kneading the tortillas that they were cooking on a large *comal*, or Mexican griddle mounted on three stones, being used in lieu of a stove. Others still were frying eggs and chicken. Meanwhile Nash was busily preparing soup as if restoring his tarnished deserter's reputation depended on it. The dinner table was made of boards propped up on empty crates. And although the table was less than impressive, his soup was admittedly by far the best I had tasted since leaving Minatitlán. Most of Murphy's associates arrived at around the same time we had, some on foot others on horseback, and they all took part in the feast cheerfully. Some sat indoors with us, others were outside, but none seemed to be giving much thought to the innkeeper's minor act of betrayal.

At eleven o'clock, the rancho started to empty out. Everyone retired for the evening, choosing to sleep out in the open air. I remained alone with Murphy and Hargous, who attempted to make themselves comfortable in their beds. But in the end, they too left to escape the increasingly stifling atmosphere in the sleeping quarters. Less sensitive to the discomfort, I was in fact quite pleased to have the place to myself. I started to dose off on a bed made from the boards that only two hours earlier had been our dinner table. But I was suddenly awoken by two or three grunting pigs and as many dogs who had crept into the room and were now sleeping just three paces away. If you add to that a swarm of mosquitoes turbulently buzzing around my head, then you will have a clear idea of the restful night's sleep to be expected in this rancho. After an hour of this, I had had enough. I grabbed my sheet and mosquito netting and headed outside, just as Hargous and Murphy had done. One of our travel companions, who wasn't yet asleep, found my befuddlement amusing. He brought me four poles and helped me set up my lodge. I folded up a large hammock made from native cloth to use it as a mattress. I wrapped myself in my sheet, with my travel bag as a pillow. The night was tranquil and serene beyond words. Sweet cool air with the scent of the distant forest filled my senses with a delightful drowsiness. This was quite a contrast from the sweltering and foul conditions inside.

Above, thousands of surprisingly big golden stars stood out against the canopy of the heavens, whose infinite depths appeared to be awash in a luminous powder. Captivated, I searched the sky for new constellations. This magnificent spectacle, to which nothing in our cold regions of Europe can compare, set my mind reeling. I was transported into an ideal world. I imagined ancient times when the fathers of the human race founded the science of astronomy in Chaldea. Through the gauze of my mosquito netting my eyes went from sky to earth, eventually getting lost in the uncertain twilight that made the dark night seem transparent and allowed my thoughts free rein. As I contemplated this delightful scene, little by little I forgot the heavens, the earth, mosquitoes, and Nash's rancho. My eyelids grew heavy and closed. I soon was in a profound sleep.

CHAPTER V

Petapa and the Mixe People. The Causes of the Mexican Revolution. The Caves of Guie-xila.

I awoke to hear voices calling me. It was bright daylight. The sun was rising on the horizon, piercing through a sea of clouds streaked with pink and orange. It cast its fiery light over the tall hills of Cabeza de Tigre, Guie-vixia, and Xochiapa. While Nash prepared breakfast, I quickly washed up, and at the same time, I tried to survey the surroundings to see what I had missed the night before. By six, we had finished our coffee and we got into our saddles. But first we shook hands with Walker's deserter even more cordially than we had upon our arrival. From the valley, where Nash had made his home, the road twists up along the side of the foothills of Mount Guie-xila and follows the upstream course of the Xuchiapa Creek,[48] one of the main tributaries of the Malatengo River. We were now leaving behind the steep banks of the Pachiñe River, the tall Mixe tumuli, as well as the last traces of a landscape with an exuberant wealth of tropical vegetation and abundant rivers and streams flowing down from the mountains to pay tribute to the Coatzacoalcos valley. From that point on, everything changed. The climate, soil, vegetation, and mountains all took on a more distinctive and pronounced character as we approached the higher plateaus of the Cordillera. It was now hot and dry. Flaking chalk-white rock was strewn on the rugged slate-colored soil, with patches of withering tall grasses that the long months of the rainy season couldn't quite sustain. It was a startling transformation. But despite the comparative sterility, from the perspective of the European traveler, this region had one enormous advantage that compensated for everything: there were no mosquitoes! Nor were there those insects called *rodadores*,[B21] midges that thrive in great number and are such a nuisance during the rainy season. Emerging from the Malatengo gorge onto the

---

B21. *Rodadores*, meaning "roamers" or "prowlers," are midges the size of the head of a pin, which are a great nuisance since they fly into your mouth, eyes, and ears. The Americans absolutely dread them and they call them sand flies.

Xochiapa plateau, we were completely liberated from these foes as well as the mosquitoes that became rare, only to be found in a few humid valleys.

From this vantage point we dominated the immensity of the plains undulating far below. We could see woods, verdant hills, and frantically jagged mountains in every direction. To our backs, to the west, there stood the menacing San Juan Guichicovi, whose barren summit would be a melancholy sight, if it weren't so imposingly framed by the splendid blue horizon. Its magnificent silhouette joins gracefully with the Petapa Mountains that suddenly sloped down to the south forming the valley that cuts this end of the Isthmus of Tehuantepec. These mountains link to the towering mountains on the border of the isthmus and Chiapas through a series of secondary mountain ranges and foothills. The Guacamaya and Masahua are the principal mountain ranges, and their highest peaks, rich with shady pine forests, reach no more than fifteen hundred meters above the level of the Pacific Ocean. Below these mountains the Xochiapa plain stretches out at our feet, interrupted a few miles away by the Majada and Mesilla ranges. The headsprings of the Xuchiapa Creek are found in this desert basin, with its steep rocky hills and intermittent swampy bogs. These hills were strewn with avocado trees and copses of stunted green oak trees—showing no sign of life unless they were fortunate enough to be on the banks of a stream—as were the intervening plains, where the livestock from a nearby farm, called Hacienda Antigua, grazed. As we passed by, I saw the ruins of some sort of Spanish building and pyramid-shaped burial mounds, which appeared to have been the foundations of indigenous structures from the past.

We had been traveling for several hours on the road built by the Americans leading directly to Tehuantepec. We then left it by going to the right at a fork onto another American trail that led to Barrio de la Soledad, a small Mixe town, where my travels with Murphy and his group would come to an end. We entered the Petapa River basin, ascending by way of the foothills of Mount Guie-xila that eventually lead to the Majada range. The meandering path climbed from a shallow gorge onto the slopes of a high hill to which my companions gave the ungrammatical name Niza-Conejo. The Malatengo River flowed through the ravine below on its way to the Petapa River and its tributaries. The mountain's arid slopes were sparsely covered by dry grasses with a scattering of oak trees making the arduous attempt to thrive in the gray rocky soil, as they awaited sustenance in vain. Long ago, this area swarmed with a multitude of nations, who had developed ways to make these mountains fertile and who also often opposed Spanish rule. There were still signs of their previous labors. Their large-scale landscaping, reported by authors during the conquest period, are still evident in the red soil, where horizontal furrows on the slopes of these towering foothills were dug by industrious natives in order to moderate the flow of water and retain the soil in these walled terraces that are reminiscent of those built by the Israelites in Palestine.

As we continued, the landscape became increasingly arid and sterile. No vegetation grows on these fully exposed mountain slopes, only shriveled scrub. We rode on the naked, sun-struck rock, which burned beneath our horses' hooves reverberating the midday sun. We arrived at the top of these hills at the hottest moment of the day. And then, undeterred, we proceeded to descend towards the Petapa River basin. There were only one or two miles before reaching Barrio. The valley opened up before us and Murphy pointed to a series of hills covered with cassia trees and other thorn bushes, a quarter of a league away. This was the pueblo. Rising strikingly above the town against the cloudless sky, were the implausibly craggy peaks of Banderilla and Almoloya, which are part of a range that cut across the basin from west to south. When I saw the greenery that graced the valley, it gave me hope that we might soon find some cooler temperatures. But the heat was even more stifling in the valley. The heavy, parched air gripped me when we reached the scrubland below. A few streams with stagnant and foul water struggled to flow beneath the bushes whose meager leaves and big brown pods let the sun through, intensifying the heat. However, I was immediately comforted when, as we arrived, I heard the village's church bell announcing Angelus. Its silvery tone proclaimed that I had finally reached my destination and that I was now in a Christian land. It is hard to imagine the extent to which the simple sound of a bell—a sound that was such a comforting part of my bygone childhood—could bring back a flood of memories and feelings, as I emerged from the savage terrain through which I had just traveled.

A few minutes later I could see the pueblo's first shacks and the slender portal of the modest white church that dominated the town. The dwellings were grouped on a small hill covered in green brush. What good this scene did my sun-damaged eyes! I urged my horse on towards the top of the hill, which he climbed quickly. I crossed a narrow street through ranchitos separated by haphazardous rows of gleaming cacti of all shapes and sizes. Murphy and I stopped before a well-appointed house, known as the French Hotel. It was clean and sturdily built of stone and cob. The exterior was roughcast and whitewashed. The interior offered more comfort than any of the American hotels that I had stayed in so far. The place was run by a Mexican Creole named Mr. Blanco, and Mr. Belcher, who was a Frenchman. Two or three of my compatriots graciously greeted me as I entered. After a bit of polite conversation we went into the dining hall with Murphy, Hargous, and Rieken and heartily ate a satisfying dinner, served in the European style. In the afternoon, another Frenchman, Adrien Laffont, from the Bordeaux region, called on me. He had come to find fortune in Mexico and set up as a planter and trader in Barrio de la Soledad, where he married the daughter of Don Luis Calderon, the richest man in the area. Laffont was in his late twenties, but despite his youth, he knew the region quite well, having worked for the Louisiana Tehuantepec Company at the time that they were tracing their route. After a brief conversation, we walked to his house, one of the most comfortable in Barrio, and he cordially invited me to stay with him, while in town. I accepted his hospitality without hesitation, especially since it provided a good excuse for breaking away from my travel companions and letting them move on to Tehuantepec without me.

El Barrio de la Soledad, Santo Domingo, and Santa María de Petapa are three small villages in the foothills of Mount Guie-xila, all within three miles of one another. All told they have a population of fewer than three thousand souls, three-quarters of which are Indians. Fifty or sixty years ago, the single big town of Petapa embraced the other two within its boundaries. Back then, Petapa was home to more than ten thousand residents of the same origins as the inhabitants of Guichicovi. But in fact, the people of these towns were descendants of those who originally came from the ancient indigenous cities of Guie-xila, Guie-vixia, and Guichilona whose ruins can be found along the daunting precipices of the surrounding mountains, near the villages or haciendas that still bear their names. This entire region belonged to a single nation, with a reputation for unsurpassed bravery, known as the Mixes. Their territory encompassed the region from the mountains of the Sierra Macuilapa that tower over today's city of Zanatepec in the east, to those in the south that extend towards Lachixila from which the Tehuantepec River flows, and in the north, from the Villa Alta range all the way to the savanna where the tributaries of the Alvarado and the Coatzacoalcos Rivers flow. They were already occupying this entire territory from sea to sea, when the Wabi or Huaves, fleeing a distant land that some say was Peru, came by sea to Tehuantepec and seized control of that area away from them. During fourteenth and fifteenth centuries, the Zapotec kings progressively took control of their most prized territories, and in order to maintain their independence they were reduced to settling in some of the harshest, most bitterly cold mountain regions. The exploits of their last king, known as Condoy, brought back some measure of the dying nation's prestige. Legend has it—of course legends are always well disposed to the fantastic—that he had neither father nor mother. He emerged one day from the caves at the foot of Mount Zempoaltepec,[49] leading a powerful army and in just a few months he drove out their enemies briefly restoring his people's former glory.

    Condoy, a prince of unwavering courage, was omnipresent. He fought against the Mixtec, Zapotec, Chiapanec, and the Zoque, without ever losing a battle. However, his good fortune was short lived. The neighboring princes, concerned by Condoy's string of victories, understood the danger of allowing him to consolidate his power. They joined forces to invade the Mixe provinces, and as a result the towns under Condoy's control were decimated. Most notably, their capital, Xaltepec—located on the tributary of the Coatzacoalcos River and renowned for being one of the region's most thriving cities—was captured and burned to the ground after a long siege. Condoy managed to escape the flames with the last remnants of his army. His enemies hunted him down like a wild beast, wreaking havoc and in their pursuit, demolishing towns and villages along the way.

The Mixes desperately sought refuge in the most remote forests where, dispossessed of their homes, they looked longingly at the lairs of wild animals. As they faced these dire conditions, they heard the news that Condoy had disappeared. In the hopes of providing respite for his people and drained by his unending battles, Condoy and his soldiers, carrying the remains of their dead, all returned to the cave from which he had emerge only a few years earlier. He was never seen again. They say that he obstructed the entrance of the cave with a large bolder and then escaped through another passage. They also claim that he planned to conquer another far-off region and then one day return to reign over his people. In any case, the defeated Mixes were henceforth under the rule of Mixtec and Zapotec kings, with the exception of a small number who, until the Spanish conquest, continued their resistance in the harsh lands surrounding Mount Zempoaltepec.

Today, the descendants of these people on the Tehuantepec isthmus have been disseminated throughout several villages in the mountain region, where I had just arrived. The largest number live in Guichicovi, a town that was off to our right when we came from the plains of Xochiapa to Barrio. Even if they accepted the Spanish yoke and—in their own way—the Gospel, they have nonetheless maintained their independent spirit. They are still Mixe through and through. Despite the Dominican priests, who inculcated them with the teachings of the Catholic faith, they have maintained a great many of their ancient pagan rites and they continue, as do most of the indigenous populations of Chiapas and Guatemala, to perform sacrifices in sacred sites, as was once done in Israel. They have even added new superstitions to their ancient beliefs. One example comes from the introduction of livestock to their region.

In the fertile valleys below their mountains, their herds can graze in green pastures all year long. But of all the animals imported from Europe, mules found the greatest favor with the Indians of Guichicovi. They built a considerable trade selling them to the people of Oaxaca, Chiapas, and Tehuantepec. As is the case in most towns in Mexico and Central America, each year on the day of the feast of Saint John, their church's patron saint, there is a fair in Guichicovi. People come from far and wide to attend. On that day, all you see are mules. On the mountain paths and in the pueblo's streets—everywhere you look—there are mule drivers, rancheros, and Indians driving or pushing long mule trains. As always, the feast starts at the church. The majordomos from the various brotherhoods meet at the cabildo, or town hall, wearing their finest clothes before heading to the church. Meanwhile, the village's finest mule, festooned with flowers and ribbons, is brought to them. The leader of the brotherhood of Saint John makes a speech in the Mixe language, addressing the animal as if it represented the supernatural spirit of its hybrid race. I couldn't say whether the animal answers back. What I do know is that, after this ceremony, everyone goes to the church, respectfully leading the mule along with them. The priest, dressed in surplice and stole meets them at the door of the church and blesses the animal with holy water. Whether it likes it or not, the beast is then led inside by the majordomos and attends mass. This is a sine qua non condition imposed on the priest when he is installed and to which he must submit along with other such things, if he wants to be the priest of San Juan Guichicovi.

The night after our arrival in Barrio, Murphy and Hargous came to Laffont's house to say goodbye. They planned to leave early the next day. And yet, to my great surprise, that next morning I saw them at the hotel, where they were staying. News had come from Tehuantepec and none of it was good. The political situation in Mexico, both then and now, is common knowledge. Two parties split this beautiful country apart. On the one hand there were the supposed defenders of the Catholic Church, who occupied the capital city, parts of the federal district, and the states of Jalisco, Guanajuato, Querétaro, Puebla, and Veracruz. This group was headed by General Miramón, a young, enterprising, energetic, and brave officer, who was perhaps too militaristic and too Spanish to make the fouled wheels of this government turn. On the other hand, in the remaining states of the Mexican confederation, there was the president of the so-called Liberal Party. Benito Juárez's authority was nominally recognized. However, as a result of poor communication throughout the territory that he controlled, the reality was that there were as many presidents as there were commanders in chief or supreme governors. Juárez, driven from the capital, was entrenched in the port town of Veracruz, with the knowledge that he could escape to the fortified castle on the island of San Juan de Ulúa or onto an American ship off shore.[B22]

Benito Juárez is a Zapotec Indian from the mountains near the Isthmus of Tehuantepec. He studied with a priest, who, after having taught him grammar and a bit of Latin, sent him off to continue his education in a school in Oaxaca. The indigenous people whom I have had the opportunity to get to know in several provinces of Mexico and Central America are not only quite intelligent but also have an exceptional capacity to learn, despite the fact that they often give the impression of being hypocritical. In particular, Zapotec Indians stand out among other indigenous groups and Juárez is considered by most people to be a man of remarkable talent and integrity. He was a lawyer and later became the governor of his native state of Oaxaca. When he was dismissed from that office, he retired empty-handed, not having accumulated any wealth from his position—a rather remarkable occurrence in a country where an intentional lack of self-interest is practically unheard of. He was elected minister and then named chief justice of the Supreme Court, the equivalent of the vice-presidency in Mexico. Thus, when President Ignacio Comonfort resigned, according to Juárez's interpretation of the law, he was the president's legal successor. The pro-Church camp waged a counterrevolution and Juárez, who lost the ensuing power

---

B22. This text was completed by November 1860. [No doubt, Brasseur points this out because the civil war, known as the War of Reform, ended with the victory of Juárez's Liberal Party in 1861.]

struggle, took refuge in the city of Veracruz, where he formed his own government. Unfortunately, today this statesman's fundamental and sincere steadfastness, with which he has confronted so many obstacles, has become a liability to him and his country. He is surrounded by advisers who push him to take extreme positions, and regretfully, he has confused stubbornness for strength. He is convinced that it would be a great dishonor to back down from any of these actions, given the overall justice of his cause. Juárez was in an excellent position to judge the extent of the clergy's misdeeds and their abuse of power in more prosperous times. Therefore, in his eyes, past misconduct mitigates the wrongs perpetrated by the so-called liberals. Instead of leading, he is unduly influenced by this liberal faction and the generals, who pledge their allegiance to him and pompously call themselves the country's liberators. As a result, he tolerates their violent and criminal acts. But at the same time, he protests against the malfeasance of Miramón's party, which he also attributes indiscriminately to the Church.

European readers, who have tried to follow these troubling and tumultuous events from abroad, have seen each camp accuse the other of all sorts of crimes. And for most, it has been reduced to an unbridled struggle between Liberals and the Church. Although there is some truth to this perspective, it would be a mistake to attribute the root causes of the current war to that alone. Of course, the warring parties in Mexico are not interested in making this clear to foreigner observers. When the Hispanic-American states declared their independence, a conflict immediately flared up based on resentment on the part of the Creole population—in other words, the sons of Spaniards born in America—for those who came directly from Spain. The Creoles were barred—as is still the case today in Cuba—from administrative or government positions and were naturally envious of those born in Spain, who had exclusive hold on these offices. Following independence, the pure blood creoles, or those who considered themselves such, formed a sort of aristocracy and attempted to take over the government. In turn, the mestizos, who were born from the association of the conquering races with Indians and blacks, and who had been instrumental in helping the more privileged classes overthrow the Spanish, became envious. Consequently, they worked to supplant the Creoles. More recently, the Indians in certain provinces have been exposed to this intellectual movement and are joining the struggle, which they hope will lead to complete freedom for their race.

Thus, those who claim to be defending either the Church or liberalism in Mexico are merely masking the real issues. One group is masking the machinations of those holding on to the last shreds of privilege of the conquering race. For a brief moment this minority triumphed over its motherland, from which it violently separated in 1821, only to quickly extend a beseeching hand when it became the victim of its own victory. As for the second group, their modern European clothes divert attention from the fact that they are striving on behalf of mixed and indigenous races, who for too long suffered humiliation throughout Spanish America. This group outnumbers the other, six to one, and it is fighting to regain its rights. Consequently, there are a great many red-skinned, yellow-skinned, olive-skinned, and swarthy individuals in this party, with only a few pure whites. They certainly have nothing against the Church. They are all Catholics and more so than we might imagine. Rather, they are attempting to eradicate a form of foreign domination, which—it must be said, unfortunately—too often found a great deal of support from high-ranking clergy. Thus, it should come as no surprise that as a result of such a clash in which all sorts of human passions are at play—greed, avarice, and self-interest in all their various guises—some have cloaked themselves in liberalism as a pretext for stripping the Church of its holdings and banishing its representatives. Contemporary history offers a host of such examples. And I certainly won't attempt to justify them. But in the case of Mexico, I can simply report what I saw. I will add that, in my opinion, in spite of the disastrous consequences of this dispute, I firmly believe that the Hispanic-American races, having learned a great deal from their painful past, have every prospect for a peaceful and prosperous future. Their association with Latin and Catholic peoples has allowed them, almost instinctively, to understand what freedom represents. But if this freedom translates into absolute equality for all before the law, they will have to accept that in order to preserve their rights they will need to united and obey those in power. The best for all concerned would be for Mexico's government to be strong, stable, and independent from foreign influence—and, of course, that no single race have primacy over another. Equal rights will never prevail under this current crop of weak, lawless oligarchs who have sapped the country's vitality for so many years. The indigenous people of Mexico have always had a profound respect for authority. This is due, no doubt, to their deep-seated memories of their own royalty and even of their conqueror's royalty. But all Mexicans, no matter their race, are naturally religious. Thus, they have every hope that with a strong government, they will obtain both equal rights and see the Catholic Church exercise justified and legitimate influence in their land.

This was the situation at the time of my last visit to Mexico and it continues to be the current state of affairs. The state of Oaxaca, which includes the district of Tehuantepec, was under Liberal control, as were the neighboring states of Chiapas and Tabasco. In all the provinces, especially those with well-traveled roads, there were all sorts of incidents of arson and looting. Armed bands, supporting one faction or another, were laying waste to cities and causing disturbances throughout the countryside. Throughout the isthmus, bandits, alternatively known as *Patricios* or *Juchitecos*[B23] robbed and murdered travelers with impunity, depending on which party the victims were deemed to belong to.

Along with the other news that Murphy had received in Barrio was news that Manzano,[50] one of the Patricios' most feared leaders, had arrived in the vicinity of Tehuantepec. Murphy didn't seem particularly concerned. Since arriving on the *Coatzacoalcos*, he had been accompanied by a large number of Americans, who

---

B23. In Mexico, they call Irish deserters from the United States Army's invading forces, Patricios because Saint Patrick is their patron saint. In several provinces, the name was later attributed to the soldiers, who supported Miramón. Juchitecos, or the "residents of Juchitán," refers to an Indian town near Tehuantepec that has almost always supported the Liberals.

were all well armed. Their reputation on the isthmus was firmly established and they had no doubt that they could stand up against Manzano's gang. However, there was another piece of news that did give them cause for concern—namely that the poor management of the Louisiana Tehuantepec Company was starting to have serious repercussions. Everyone seemed to have turned against them and even their supporters were troubled by the situation. High-ranking employees were complaining about not receiving their wages. Moreover the laborers, who were doing the digging, and poor Indians, employed to do all sorts of odd jobs, were not any better off, since they were owed a great deal of back pay. The rainy season was quickly upon us. The Indians working for the company had not been able to plant crops, because the alcaldes[51] had forced them from their fields and into these jobs. And now, they didn't have a single *medio* to give their wives to buy much needed corn. Moreover, the brutal arrogance of certain American representatives and the incompetence of a whole host of others had disgusted almost everyone. Complaints were pouring in from every direction. But no one was taking any heed. Even the judge of Juchitán, a mestizo, with a reputation from one end of the isthmus to the other for having committed many murders, and who was perceived as friendly to American interests, finally sided against them. Of course, it turns out that his motivations were self-serving. He and a group of Juchitecos had just arrived in Barrio on their way to Chivela, where the company had established their headquarters. Their intent was to force the company's chief engineer, Sidell, to adjust their interest rates. Should Sidell fail to comply with this request, the judge was threatening to impose an embargo on any commercial activity with the company and if he met with any opposition his next step would be to burn the place down. The good judge was on the best of terms with Murphy and Laffont. The latter invited him to dine with us at his house, where I was introduced to him. There was no way of avoiding the custom of shaking his hand, although I did it with great regret. I must admit that as I felt his grip I was filled with horror, imagining the blood of the twenty-nine victims he loudly proclaims to have killed.

The next day, Murphy left with his travel companions. I took advantage of my new-found peace and quiet to visit the village and its surroundings with Mr. Laffont. Santa María de Petapa, with no more than thirteen or fourteen hundred inhabitants, is the biggest of the three pueblos that previously composed the city of Petapa. It is said to be the oldest Spanish settlement on the Isthmus of Tehuantepec. Santo Domingo is even smaller, with about nine hundred residents, who farm a considerable quantity of vanilla, indigo, and sarsaparilla. The village church, which is in rather poor condition, is notable only for its extremely solid walls. There is an adjacent *convento*, or presbytery, which is the home of a young and friendly priest of the Dominican Order. El Barrio de la Soledad has a larger population, mostly due to the number of recent newcomers, mainly from the United States. Its stone huts, covered in clay and thatched with palm leaves, are strewn across a rugged hill, where a stream flows into the Malatengo River. The town's best and most comfortable house was the one in which I was staying. Built in the shade of several splendidly leafy orange and amate trees, it stood at the end of a small hill, looking out over the mountain range that bounds the Petapa River basin on three sides. From this vantage point, my eyes went from the forests that covered the valley floor to the magnificent cliffs of this amphitheater, whose tiered layers rose till they were lost in the clouds.

The following day was Sunday. The previous day I had met the priest of Petapa and during our visit Laffont had suggest that he might be able to help us organize us on a trip to Santo Domingo's caves, which were famous throughout the region. The priest promised to find us guides. Immediately after mass, Laffont served lunch, and in no time at all, we were on way to meet the priest at his presbytery, joined by Charles Belcher and Mr. Blanco from the French hotel. We quickly made our way through the thorny bogs around these three towns and had soon arrived at the convento. The priest was waiting there with half a dozen Mixe Indians, sitting by the door of the presbytery, each armed with his machete, ocote,[52] and candles. We started off through the woods, going west, traveling upstream along a tributary of the Malatengo River. This is where the road towards Mazatlán and Oaxaca begins, taking a path that dives down into one of the gorges carved out between the foothills of Mount Guie-xila. This ravine has been shred to pieces. Along with the bench gravel and the piles of stone that were strewn about where the river once dug out its bed, there stood enormous boulders, fallen from the mountain above, that had become small islands of greenery. Some of these blocks of stone were a hundred feet in diameter and overgrown with brilliant vegetation that had taken root wherever possible. At the very top flowers, cacti, and elegant clusters of trees grew. Atop one, there was even a thatched cottage, with a pointed palm leaf roof, which could be reached by crude steps that had been dug into the stone. On either side of the ravine, the mountain abruptly jutted out with immense strata of limestone and vegetation at heights that elude the naked eye. They looked like promontories placed there by Titans and set only half a league apart, on either side of the river, which soon disappeared beyond the mountainous forests into the dark and narrowing precipice.

We followed this treacherous route for an hour. The entrance to the caves, dug into the sides of the foothills at an altitude of more than eight hundred feet above the valley, was to our right. It was time to start climbing. We left our horses with a servant. And each of us did our best to cling to vines and shrubs that grew interlaced along the rock wall as we made our way up a perpendicular path. This arduous ascent, undertaken in incredibly hot temperatures, lasted more than an hour. I was out of breath and drenched in sweat. My clothes were soaked, as if I had fallen into a hot bath.

In front of the cave there was like an esplanade or immense balcony. Thorny shrubs and large trees that had taken root in crevasses acted as the enigmatic guards of its entrance. After such a climb, the idea of stretching out for a moment beneath their shady foliage was appealing. This was the hottest moment of the day. The sun was right above our heads. Elsewhere it flooded the countryside with light, but here it gently filtered through a green dome. Two or three leagues away, Mount Almoloya rose through the clouds. Mount Portillo, which stands between Almoloya's peak and another mountain that is almost as high in the Banderilla range, is a perpendicular abyss from which both the Barrio River and a trail to Tehuantepec descend. From this vantage point you can see the entire Petapa basin rippling with silvery glints reflecting off the rich woodlands and in the hazy distance, the hills of Chivela, with the bluish summits of Chimalapa beyond to the east.

The landscape at this time of day was particularly brilliant. For that reason, I have to admit that it was with some regret that I turned away. Before me was a natural landscape resplendent with life and light, behind me, the gaping mouth of a dark cavern as gloomy as the tombs that lay within it. The opening, an arch eighty feet long and twenty feet high, led to a steep path that penetrated under the limestone rock and immediately struck our guides with a superstitious terror. Their fears were intensified at the sight of several tiger prints in the dirt as we entered. To reassure them, I gave out a loud cry under this vaulted ceiling and the only response was an echo. Moreover, my companions had firearms, so comforted in that knowledge, I slid down the sloping path that led to the first cave, one hundred feet below. The rest of the group followed me into the depths. A few flickering rays of sunlight came to perish along the ledges of this vaulted archway, coloring it with tints of blue. Certain Indians, with vivid imaginations, have transformed these into supernatural beings that act as the guardians of the dark cave. Suddenly twenty torches were lit, projecting their light on the surroundings. We were in a vast natural sitting room, decorated with a profusion of alluvial cones, serrated drapery, aigrettes, and brilliantly multifaceted stalactites refracting all the colors of the prism. Alabaster grew like plants of all sizes and in the strangest of shapes, encrusted with small crystal blades shining like diamonds. Adding to the dazzling play of light, a sheet of crystal-clear water stretched out over one hundred feet to the right of the chamber, before disappearing beneath the arches of this grandiose dome. In the torchlight, this peaceful pool that had never been disturbed by the breezy outside air, reflected perfectly the mysterious splendor of this isolated cave.

At the edge of the water, like a broken column whose base was still intact, was a split alabaster block used as an altar, hidden from prying eyes, where the Indians sometimes came to worship deities from a past, which they no longer truly understand. They had hollowed out the top and I found remains of coal and copal with a bouquet of wilted flowers that must have been there for several days. Shards of pottery scattered about suggested that they made offerings other than incense. Elsewhere, next to fantastically shaped stalagmites that looked like living beings, I noticed that someone had left copal and flowers. This led me to believe that, in their simplicity, these dear indigenous people imagined that these stalagmites, arbitrarily created by acts of nature, represented their lost gods or the cave's spirits. One day, in one of the many caves that riddle Oaxaca, a Dominican priest discovered the preparations for a ceremonial sacrifice that the Indians of his village were going to offer to the goddess Pinopiaa,[53] whom they identified with the sister of the last king of Tehuantepec. This princess died without having married, only a few years before the arrival of the Spaniards. Her priests, who for more than two centuries passed down their teachings from father to son, continued to worship her in the form of alabaster that nature had created at the edge of a subterranean stream.

Beyond this great chamber, there were long galleries that led to other caves, carved into the depths of the mountain. We climbed over strange collections of rocks. We went passed precipices where hidden waters flowed so deep below us that we could barely make out their muffled murmurings. Drearily lit by our line of torches, we moved along escarpments with the remnants of snow-white columns and frontispieces in a sublimely chaotic state that made me think of Dante's funereal descriptions. These passageways sometimes present dangers. You can easily slip on these alabaster stones, dripping from humidity. Sometimes, there was the unexpected sound of a massive slab that had come loose and fell to the bottom of an abyss, unseen and yet with thundering echoes in all directions.

At the far end of one of the last caves, they pointed out to me traces of various crudely executed figures drawn in ocher on the walls along with several black handprints. They reminded me of what John Lloyd Stephens[54] described seeing on the walls of a great many ruins in Uxmal and elsewhere. The handprint obviously represented some sort of superstitious belief. As for the figures, they perhaps had a deeper meaning, because right across from them on the ground there was a small opening, just big enough to for a person to fit through. Laffont told me that it was a passage to a cave below and that some Americans had gone down there using ropes and said that they had found human remains with obsidian arrowheads and shards of ancient pottery.[55] I wanted to see this for myself and to explore where this cave could lead. Our Indian guides quickly started to try to dissuade me, saying that it was sometimes dangerous at those depths. This was exactly the sort of argument that would prompt me to want to go. But given their apparent distress and especially the anxious looks they shot in the direction of the priest I gave in to their concerns. They seemed quite relieved. Since then, I have learned that the network of caves of Santo Domingo leads to secret passageways going to other important caves, which in the past were the burial grounds for the royal family of Petapa. Reputedly in ancient times, the people of the area put a great deal of work went into making it a magnificent space. In the past, this was where superstitious rituals were performed, the traces of which are still practiced among the Indians of Guichicovi. In a related subject, an *arriero*, or muleteer, from Juchitán told the story of having gotten lost one day while looking for his mules in the mountains and entering one of these sepulchral caves. He says that he counted more than one hundred strangely shaped painted urns neatly arranged in recesses around the cave. Seized with terror at this strange sight, he quickly left and since that day he had not been able to find the entrance again.

After five long hours of walking back and forth in this labyrinth, I decided that it was time to leave, to the great relief of our guides. Once we were back in the first chamber, we rapidly climbed the steep slope at the entrance. It was a great pleasure to see daylight once more. The fresh warm air, the blue sky with the fiery ball of the setting sun, distant mountains on the horizon, the green valley below, Almoloya's peak above—all this helped revive my senses as I emerged from the dark sepulchers of Zapotec idolatry. I was chilled to the bone from the penetrating humidity of the frigid cave. To remedy the situation, Laffont offered me a flask of *mezcal*, a distilled alcohol made from aloe. That, and the rapid descent back to our horses, successfully warmed my bones.

We mounted our horses and galloped back towards Santo Domingo, where we said good-bye to the priest and thanked him for his kind help. When we got back to Barrio, we heard some alarming news. Everyone was saying that Oaxaca had been taken by General José María Cobos, one of Miramón's lieutenants and that Manzano was present in the Tehuantepec area. There was also news that General José Santos Degollado, a commander of the Liberal army had advanced as far as Tacubaya but was defeated by Miramón outside Mexico City. In the wake of his rout, a great deal of his matériel fell into enemy hands. Along with the young José Justo Álvarez and several other high-ranking officers, he hastily crossed Michoacán towards Acapulco. He boarded a Louisiana Tehuantepec Company steamboat for La Ventosa and then made his way to Tehuantepec, where he stayed just long enough to receive condolences from his supporters. According to the rumors, he had passed through Chivela incognito, on his way to Minatitlán where he hoped to meet with Juárez and his companions in Veracruz.

All this news convinced me that I shouldn't put off my departure from El Barrio, despite Mr. Laffont's insistence that I should extend my stay with him. I was still not sure where I would go after Tehuantepec. I was wavering between traveling through either Oaxaca or Chiapas. I would only be able to reach a final decision once I had more information that would allow me to determine where I could travel in the greatest safety given the civil war. I had another reason to hasten my departure. It was the first day of June and the rainy season had already made its presence felt with one or two heavy and somewhat alarming storms. I was concerned because I knew that once the rains began, the isthmus trails would be more or less impassable, despite American efforts to improve them. It would be equally as difficult and often even quite dangerous to try to ford overflowing rivers. Rieken came by to repeat a previous invitation to spend a few days in Chivela. I took that opportunity to urge Laffont to get me two mules for my belongings and a horse, as well as a mozo de camino[B24] for the next day. Since there were fewer than twelve miles between El Barrio and Chivela, my host told me that this would be no problem and promised to arrange everything immediately.

CHAPTER VI

Chivela. The Plain of Tehuantepec. The History of Tehuantepec's Last King.

The next day, on June 2, everything was ready. Laffont and another Frenchman decided to join me as my guides to Chivela. At around noon, while we had our lunch, our horses were saddled and our mules prepared. I requested that my mule driver go ahead without waiting for me since I was concerned about the possibility of rain. Coming from the northwest, huge, dark, copper-tinged clouds were rapidly banking up in the sky above the valley. The air, thick with intoxicating odors, quickly became stifling and there wasn't the slightest breeze. Laffont, who predicted that a storm was coming, tried to convince me to prolong my stay by a day and Niña Magdalena, his wife, gently scolded me, saying that it was dangerous for me to set off in these conditions. But I had made up my mind to leave no matter what. Instead of listening to their advice, I quickly finished my meal and a few moments later all three of us were on our horses. The trail out of Barrio headed southeast, and after two leagues it met up with the main American route. It continued through the undulating plains that are at the far end of the Petapa Basin.

Three miles from Barrio, we arrived at the top of a sparsely wooded hill from which we could take in the view of the entire plains of Chivela with the blue outlines of Mount Tarifa and Masahuita towering in the distance. To the left, Laffont pointed out other, much taller mountains—the summits of Atravesado in the Macuilapa

---

B24. The mozo de camino acts as a servant for travelers and helps the mule driver on the trail.

range and the Gineta Pass, well known in the region as the way to cross from the state of Chiapas to Tehuantepec. The character of the landscape changed completely from that point. The vegetation was scarce, the soil rocky, red, and sparsely covered in grass. The ground was deeply rutted by winter waters. For the most part, we moved along hollowed-out paths with the bare hills on either side of us concealing from view the mountains at which we had just been gazing.

The storm threatened to strike at any moment. Thunder rumbled in the distance and dazzling lightening crisscrossed the overcast sky above. Laffont assured me that we would arrive in Chivela before the storm hit with nothing more than a scare. At the halfway point, the landscape became a bit hillier. Between the palm trees, spread out in graceful bunches along the road, I could glimpse a long, ugly shed made of tree trunks, from which some half-drunk Americans emerged, singing and greeting us with *good-byes*.[56] Meanwhile, a slovenly old man came into view. Perhaps for lack of brandy or perhaps in an attempt to sober up, he was kneeling like an animal by the stream that cut across the road, lapping up the water in great gulps. We were at one of the main stations for the Louisiana Tehuantepec Company carriages, that they called the Almoloya station. It was a revolting spectacle and I continued to ride on without replying to their calls, as did my companions, who followed behind. We soon arrived to the woods of Chivela where I met up with my muleteer slowly walking in front of us.

The sky was growing increasingly dark and threatening. There was a driving wind from the northwest and its gusts whipped our faces with large drops of steady rain. For the last hour, the sun had been obscured behind a thick veil of clouds with their harsh mix of copper and violet hues. It now began to set and dusk quickly yielded to the dark of night. It was now quite urgent that we get to our destination. Fortunately, Chivela's Casa Grande was not far. We quickened our pace, and following a path that cut through the thicket, we emerged into a vast exposed space in the center of which was a crudely built, square-shaped shack, which adhered to no particular architectural plan. This was the company headquarters and office for the chief engineer of the Tehuantepec route. We arrived just in the nick of time. As we stepped under a covered walkway, the storm broke and torrential rain started to pour down all around us. Upon my arrival, I was greeted by Mr. Rieken, who was in charge in the absence of his superior, Mr. Sidell, who had left for Minatitlán the day before. He led me to the room for the high-ranking employees of the company and I spent an enjoyable evening with these gentlemen, followed by a pleasant night's sleep in Mr. Sidell's room that was left at my disposal.

The next morning, while I was still in bed, Laffont came to say his good-byes, and left immediately, without waiting for me to get up. Everyone was anxiously awaiting the mail that should have left New Orleans two weeks after our departure. The fact that it was so late was starting to worry the people in Chivela, especially since Casa Grande had completely run out of funds. There was talk that Mr. La Sére himself would bring the needed money. Urgent requests for payment were streaming in and it was obvious that some creditors were prepared to resort to coercion. Rieken was not sure how to deal with the situation, and for that reason Sidell had decided to go to Minatitlán in the hopes of finding the company president there. I was waiting for the mail coach to pass through but for a different reason. My hope was to ride with it to Tehuantepec. However, three days passed without any news at all.

Before the arrival of the Louisiana Tehuantepec Company, Chivela was nothing more than a hacienda, owned by Mr. Maqueo,[57] a Milanese merchant who has been living in the state of Oaxaca for the last thirty years, having found both his fortune and a wife there. His farmhouse, known as Casa Blanca, is in every way superior to the neighboring Casa Grande, a masterpiece of bad taste and Yankee ineptitude. Maqueo's house, built on a plateau, located at 780 feet above sea level, is at the most elevated section of the American route. This is precisely where the route crosses the Chivela Pass and where the foothills of the Cordillera slope down. The blustery winds blowing unobstructed through these gorges and over the plateau are said to make this a healthy spot. It is certainly a factor in making it extremely cool, relative to its altitude. There are few mosquitoes and the temperature is almost always quite pleasant. On the morning after my arrival to Casa Grande, when I went outside, the full force of the wind suddenly battered me. The air was humid, the sky cloudy, and the valley below was bathed in a hazy mist. Above the haze, three rows of hills were staggered like in an amphitheater, creating an enchanting scene. It resembled certain parts of the Apennines, not where they are severe and grow dark from the pine trees, but on the warm and laughing slopes along the Arno, near Florence. Other hills, shaded by thick forests, branch out into the jagged mountains, where the Uspanapa River has its source in the tall mountain range from which the Atravesado and Macuilapa Mountains rise.

Since the long-overdue mail had still not made an appearance, I announced my intention of leaving for Tehuantepec. Rieken, who was losing hope that it would arrive, was kind enough to propose that I travel in one of the company's carriages that had remained at the Almoloya station. Thus, on Monday, June 6 at noon, I left Chivela. The plateau ends approximately one hundred feet from Casa Grande, at the foot of steep hills covered in greenery, above which I could see the summits of Mounts Prieto and Guacamaya, where the unequally distributed waters that flow towards the two oceans originate. Mr. Webster, my driver, spurred the horses forward and the carriage climbed the tortuous path that had been dug out through the stone cliffs. From the heights just above us, thousands of crystalline rivulets flowed into the Almoloya River. Plants, liana, and shrubs—the rich tropical flora that I had not seen since I had crossed the Malatengo River—all reappeared, abundant and vibrant, due to these sustaining waters. It was a magnificent day and the sun highlighted every beautiful detail of this springtime scene. We quickly reached the Chivela Pass and began our descent along the southern slope of the mountain. At that point, the landscape changed as if by magic. I could see forests, distant hills, valleys covered in woodlands as well as precipitous cliffs, donned in their warmest colors. As we descended towards the plain, all these scenes became intertwined and merged into one. The diverse features of the surrounding landscape vanished and reemerged anew with each change in perspective. These isolated valleys—with their leafy shade and lively waters that appear at times dangling as waterfalls along greened sheer cliffs or at times plunging into deep recesses—exert an irresistible force. How I would like to travel each one of those dark gorges and explore those chasms, whose depths appear to be at once so terrifying and so delightful.

My driver pointed out a ravine hemmed in by tremendous cliffs, from which grew a host of tall, intertwined aquatic plants and tree ferns. Between the elegant serrations of their plentiful leaves, deep within this wondrous recess, I could just barely make out a crystal clear sheet of water, which was gleaming in the reflected sunlight like at the bottom of a glass. This spring, which was partially concealed beneath the rocks, at times flowed hot, warm, or icy cold, depending on the season, and is reputed to cure any ailment that afflicts man. Just a few steps from where I had contemplated this wonder, we crossed paths with five or six señoritas on horseback with as many servants, each with a child sitting in the saddle in front of them. Ten or twelve Mixe Indians followed behind, carrying enormous loads, and as is usual here, bearing the entire weight on their heads. They slowly made their way up the hill, in single file. A few moments later, at another bend in the road, we came face to face with three or four other people on horseback, escorting a strong and stout mestizo, whom I recognized as being a clergyman from the blue and yellow pearls around his neck. Webster, who appeared to know him, greeted him in passing and told me that he was the priest of San Juan Guichicovi, who had just bathed in this extraordinary spring in order to recover from some illness. Nearby there was a rustic house, large enough for many people to stay, and the priest, so as not to be alone, had brought along his entire family—brothers, sisters, nieces, nephews, etc.—who made up the procession that we had just passed on the road.[58]

We continued to descend quickly. As we went around a cliff, my driver stopped his horses suddenly and called out: "Look!" The plain of Tehuantepec was at my feet. To my right were three or four staggered bluffs, covered in a dark lush green, above which rose tall jagged mountains with brightly tinted peaks and black patches along their distant, deeply scarred slopes that suggested greenery. This is the Guiengola mountain range, to the northwest of the city of Tehuantepec stretching towards the road to Oaxaca. I stood facing these inaccessible ridges that abruptly unfurl onto the plain, alternately carved into by blinding light or deeply dark recesses. On the plain below, the villages, prairies, swamps, and rivers that surround the fourteen districts of Tehuantepec stretched out like a verdant latticework. It was a poetic hodgepodge of steep cliffs and hill tops, Moorish domes and white church towers, and woodlands and gardens, all flooded in the unforgiving sunlight that revealed the slightest ripple in this enchanting panorama. Morro Hill, the final headland of the Zapotec mountains, puts an abrupt end to this grandiose backdrop to the city. It comes up to the very edge of the Pacific, with the hazy sky above and the ocean's blue waves breaking against it below. This magnificent vision is indelibly engraved in my mind, however, I must admit that while traveling through these Mexican Alps I saw so many striking and unforgettable sites that I would be hard pressed to choose which was the most memorable.

An hour later, we had completed our descent onto the plain. From that moment on, the charm disappeared along with the soaring landscape of the high mountains. My carriage drove along a straight path, rather like something you would find on the grounds of a large estate, among the mimosas and the other thorny bushes that cover Tehuantepec's outskirts, with its alternatively sandy and swampy terrain. We had passed the village of Iztáltepec[59] on our left without even noticing it. However, from less than a league away, looming above the woods, I could see the solitary knoll with rough white limestone crevices shimmering in the light of the setting sun from which the village derives its name.[60] After having descended from the mountains and as we approached Tehuantepec, the boggy plain that we rode through soon yielded to sandy soil, drenched by a vast system of irrigation that fed into milpas and gardens that offered cool alternatives to the arid surroundings. This section of the American route, which has since been abandoned,[B25] led you through the

---

B25. When the rainy season began, this route turned into a quagmire that was impossible to negotiate even for those on foot or horseback. The Americans were forced to use the former Spanish route. Of course, the locals had warned them beforehand that this would be the case.

outskirts until, quite unexpectedly, you suddenly found yourself in the center of the city. We drove down several streets, lined with garden hedges of great cacti or banana trees. The elegant heads of coconut trees with dentate leaves towered above them all, standing out against the already darkening blue sky. The sun had set. During the fleeting moments of this region's brief dusk I was just barely able to glimpse ruins of old Spanish homes and huts that stood side by side with newer houses within enclosures of bamboo and reeds. I could also make out a church or two. However, their dilapidated state was a clear sign that I was entering a city that had seen better days. The carriage continued to drive down the only paved road of Tehuantepec, layered thick with sand. It reached its destination at around seven in the evening, stopping across from a large square, in front of the Oriental Hotel, one of the biggest hotels of the city.

It was a lovely building in the old Spanish colonial style, which had a ground floor at least three feet above street level, with a long flight of stairs leading up to it. Despite its dated and neglected appearance it had an air of grandeur that suggested Tehuantepec's prosperous past. There were spacious rooms each with one or two tall windows, bulging with large-grilled balconies and with two enormous shutters instead of glass, which is unnecessary in this climate. The doors opened through serrated archways onto a long gallery through a spacious courtyard with two or three coconut trees, whose large, jagged openwork leaves dangled from one hundred feet above over a large pool of crystal clear water. The hotel had a *table d'hôte* in the "French style" as they said, where all the guests dined together in the dining room. After what I considered a rather good dinner, mostly because of the sad meals that I had had in Chivela, the manservant led me to my room. It was as big as a church, which is a positive feature in such a warm country. The walls were painted in tempera and the only furniture were two chairs, a table with an ewer, and a trestle bed. Over the bed lay a single sheet, which was actually more than was necessary for a night's sleep given the sweltering temperatures. It was extremely hot and since the rainy season was late this year, the atmosphere was inordinately dry and torrid.

Before the fall of the Toltec empire, in the eleventh century, the

Mixe people occupied the entire territory of the Isthmus of Tehuantepec, from ocean to ocean. However, we don't know whether they founded the city that the Mexicans called Tehuantepec. As I mentioned earlier, what we do know, is that the Huaves or Wabi, fleeing an unknown region in the south, traveled up the Pacific coast until coming ashore along the lagoons that extend between Tehuantepec and Tonalá, where they still live today as hardworking fishermen. At the time of their arrival, they took control of the surrounding area from the coast to the foot of the mountains by force of arms. Two or three centuries later, they were subdued by Ahuitzotl, the Mexican ruler and uncle of his successor Montezuma II. Soon Zapotec forces, under their king, Cocijoeza, took advantage of the Mexican withdrawal from the territory of Tehuantepec, to bring it under their control. The Mexicans tried in vain to regain control of this prized possession but in the end, Cocijoeza's arms and bravery shone brighter than his adversary's. As a result of his losses on the battlefield, Ahuitzotl signed a treaty with the Zapotec king and married him to his niece, Snowflake. They had a son Cocijopij, whom his father placed on the throne of Tehuantepec. He was in the prime of his life when the news of Cortés's march on Mexico City sounded the alarm throughout out all of America's kingdoms. Both Cocijopij and his father presented their crowns to the king of Spain as tribute and the son welcomed Pedro de Alvarado when the Spanish warrior passed through his territory on his way to conquer Guatemala. Cortés arrived in Tehuantepec a few years after his lieutenant's visit. He stayed in the port city of La Ventosa long enough to build the brigantines that he sailed on the journey that led him to California. The indigenous prince received Cortés with the highest honors. Cortés, in turn, compelled the prince to be baptized, despite his obvious reluctance and the opposition of his royal court. Thus Cocijopij was baptized with the name Don Juan Cortés de Montezuma, but deep in his heart he preserved his absolute devotion to the faith of his forefathers, which he continued to practice in secret for many years.

His reticence notwithstanding he proceeded to build a superb convent for the Dominicans, who had been entrusted with the missions in the provinces of Oaxaca and Tehuantepec. But his benevolence and generosity, which the Dominicans fondly remembered for years to come, was a clever ploy in his attempt to hide his true beliefs. Of all the indigenous kings who had survived the conquest, Cocijopij had managed to retain the facade of sovereignty most ostentatiously. His monumental palace was always teeming with throngs of people eager to pay tribute to him, and he never appeared in public without all the majestic trappings of royalty. Despite his largesse and outward signs of piety and although he attended mass every day, the Dominicans regretfully realized that his devotion was completely feigned. One night, a Spaniard slipped into the palace, and returned to the Dominicans with information that confirmed their suspicions. Father Bernardino de Santa María, vicar-general of Tehuantepec, shared the information with a much-trusted Zapotec nobleman, who was the fiscal in his church. The nobleman appeared surprised by the revelation, but at the clergyman's instigation, he promised—not without a sigh—to inquire into his master the king's conduct. A few days later, he informed the vicar-general that the following evening a ceremonial sacrifice would be performed in Cocijopij's palace. The vicar hastened to summon the appropriate legal authorities and at midnight, accompanied by the alcalde mayor,[61] he silently proceeded to the scene of the crime—the royal residence.

No measures had been taken to safeguard the palace. Nothing prevented the intruders from easily entering since, apparently, everyone was attending the sacrifice. They passed through courtyards and galleries until they reached the chamber that the idolaters used as their temple. Inside the chamber, fires burned releasing fragrant smoke into the air. Images of the ancient gods of the cities of Mictlan and Tehuantepec were placed atop a magnificent altar lit with the altar candles. The king, dressed in a white robe and gold miter adorned with quetzal feathers, stood surrounded by priests from Yopaa,[B26] who were fulfilling their pontifical roles. The sudden

---

B26. Yopaa or sometimes "Lyobaa," which means "the place of sepulchers." These are the Zapotec names for the city of Mictlan, today known as Mitla, approximately seven leagues from the city of Oaxaca.

presence of the vicar brought the sacrifice to a standstill and the distraught spectators fled in terror. "Your Highness is my prisoner by order of the Most Reverend Bishop" Father Bernardino said gently to Cocijopij, as he took him by the arm. Dumbfounded, the prince could not muster a response. He understood that any resistance was futile. Silently, he removed his priestly robes and followed his captor calmly to the monastery, while the priests who had assisted him were brought to the local jail.

Bringing the king back to the monastery, instead of locking him up in the city jail, turned out to be a fortunate decision by the Dominicans. It was common knowledge that there was no prison in the convent. And the entire population of Tehuantepec would have risen up against the Spaniards and their clergy had they thrown the king in jail. Out of respect for the favors that they had received from the deposed monarch, the authorities had prepared adequate accommodations and treated him in a manner befitting his status. Despite all these precautions, the next morning the entire city awoke in a volatile state. News of Cocijopij's arrest had spread like wildfire. From the mountains to the coast, a furious mass rushed towards the monastery demanding the return of their beloved king. Too few in number to disperse the crowds by force, the Spaniards feared the worst from the outraged mob. Consequently, the Dominicans turned to the prince. They pointed out that they had merely been doing their duty by arresting him for his apostasy and explained that as soon as the bishop's orders arrived, absolving Cocijopij of his sin, he would be freed. Unfortunately, they told him, it was impossible to release him until that time. They suggested that it would be in his best interest to order his people to go back to their homes and they made clear that any attempt to incite violence would only make his situation worse.

Cocijopij had lived far too long under Spanish domination not to understand the strength of these arguments. He responded by saying: "Father, my vassals are my children and I have always treated them as such. They would be unworthy of me if they were not aggrieved. After all, until yesterday I was their leader and king and now I am reduced to this miserable state. But if you allow me to speak to them, I am certain that they will obey my orders." The crowd was already amassed all around the monastery, when their king appeared on the front steps of the church. His people fell to the ground, prostrate and in tears, moaning and crying in a way that would have softened even the hardest heart. With merely a hand gesture, complete silence was restored. "I knew," he exclaimed "that you were all loyal and faithful subjects, who were thankful for the kindness with which I have always treated you. Some time ago, I had already declared that our kingdom and its domains must pass into foreign hands. This has come to pass and there is nothing we could do to escape our fate. The priests, who are surrounding me here, love and treat me with the greatest respect. Return to your homes and put an end to this disturbance, which has only added to my pain. Don't make my situation or your own any worse with futile protests that expose you to persecution."

This was the language of reason, understood by all. His people retreated. They also shed tears, which although silent were no less bitter. A few days later, commissioners, advising the bishop of Oaxaca, arrived in Tehuantepec to investigate the king's apostasy. Cocijopij answered firmly that although he considered the bishop a friend, he was certainly not superior in rank to the king and therefore had no jurisdiction in this case. Cocijopij had subjugated himself to the Spanish court without losing any of his sovereign rights and consequently he would appeal to the viceroy in Mexico City. The commissioners did their best to assure him on behalf of the bishop that this was purely a spiritual matter and did not impugn his temporal rights. Cocijopij remained resolute. The news was conveyed to the royal audience, and this highest royal court issued an order for the king to appear before them in Mexico City, without stripping him of any of the honors that were due to him. After so many years and so many incidents related to American royalty, this was unprecedented. It was the first time that an indigenous sovereign appeared with such pomp and circumstance before the populace. From Tehuantepec to Mexico City, his trip was a triumphant run. People came from near and far to line his route. With tears of joy and of despair in their eyes, young and old contemplated this prince, a descendant of so many kings and the nephew of the unfortunate Montezuma, whose death had signaled the beginning of their oppression at foreign hands.

Upon his arrival, Cocijopij was received with full honors in the capital. But apparently, during his stay Visitador[62] Valderrama, also known as the "torturer of the Indians," arrived in Mexico. Consequently, instead of seeing his case dealt with as he had hoped by Viceroy Vélasco, whom he felt would be more open and sympathetic to his plea, it dragged on for more than a year. Ultimately, the court decided against him. His punishment was the loss of his states and domains along with all sovereignty and his title. What made this sentence all the more unjust was that it was contrary to the will of the crown. However, there was no possibility of appeal. The king of Tehuantepec, who had gone into debt due to the enormous expense of his trip and the stay in Mexico City, returned to his capital in a state of dejection. There, his people, who were aware of the turn in events, awaited him with increasing impatience, determined, despite the news, to celebrate his return. However, when the broken hearted king arrived in Nejapa, he was suddenly struck dead by an attack of apoplexy.[63]

CHAPTER VII

Overview of the City of Tehuantepec. The Rayudeja Witch.

The city of Tehuantepec, which the Spanish called Guadalcázar, was densely populated at the time of the conquest and the names of its fourteen districts, preserved to this day, attest to its ancient history. The plain surrounding the city, which today is practically deserted, had once been expertly farmed and irrigated. It boasted rich, heavily populated towns, and for more than a century, the plains of Tehuantepec were considered some of the most fertile and productive lands in Mexico. The Dominicans, who controlled the area, considered it an earthly paradise. It was an important commercial center, and the port, where Cortés built his ships, was one of New Spain's main depots. In the seventeenth century, the Dominican monk Thomas Gage wrote:

> This port of Tehuantepec is the chief for fishing in all that country. We met here in the ways sometimes fifty, sometimes a hundred mules together laden with nothing but salt fish for Oaxaca, Puebla, and Mexico. There dwell in it some very rich merchants, who trade with Mexico, Peru, and the Philippines, sending their small vessels out from port to port, and these come home richly laden with the commodities of all the southern or eastern parts.[64]

During the three centuries of Spanish domination, Tehuantepec's prosperity along with its population has diminished and although currently Oaxaca's second city, it has been reduced to thirteen thousand residents. Its population is one of Mexico's most diverse, comprised mostly of Zapotec Indians and mestizos. The Spanish families—along with a few German, French, and American residents—are very few in number. The city's decline, far from being reversed with the arrival of the federal government, was accelerated. The turmoil of civil war was more detrimental to this city than to others in the republic. Most of all, it suffered from the violent struggles that broke out with its neighboring town, Juchitán. These rivalries that are so common between different indigenous groups and which the Spaniards exploited so effectively in conquering this region, had been more or less suppressed under foreign rule. But old antagonisms reemerged following independence. Instinctive racial pride mixed with their natural resentments ignited a fire, which has continued to consume one of the most beautiful provinces of Mexico for the last thirty years. Juchitán, with its mostly Zapotec and Mixe residents, could not bear to be controlled by Tehuantepec, where the majority mestizo and Creole population had a stranglehold on power.

Juchitán began the war. José Gregorio Meléndez, a mestizo born in this small town, was angered when he sought to become governor of Tehuantepec but was denied. He blamed the state leaders living in the city of Oaxaca and harbored a great deal of resentment against them. This was in 1850. A new tax on salt extracted from the isthmus's salt flats had just been levied while, at the same time, cholera was ravaging the province. Since his fellow citizens were as superstitious as he was deceitful and cunning, Meléndez was able to persuade them that the Creoles were responsible for both plagues. Moreover, he added, the plan was to first take all their money and then eradicate them entirely. This was enough to inflame the people of Juchitán, whom he easily convinced to march on Tehuantepec. With their newly minted leader guiding them, they advanced en masse against the enemy city. Rebuffed in their first attack, federal troops, in hot pursuit, chased them back to their homes in Juchitán. But the sight of their wives and children renewed their courage. They soon drove back the soldiers who had given them chase and the federal troops were forced to retreat, having suffered heavy losses. Then the Juchitecos decided to return to Tehuantepec. They took control of a first district, setting it afire. The forces moved on to besiege the governor, who had taken refuge in the main square within the thick walls of the monastery of Santo Domingo. Meanwhile the insurrection spread throughout the countryside, with Indians from Huilotepec, San Gerónimo, and Iztáltepec joining the Juchitecos. Meléndez's victory was secured. The city surrendered and the rebels maintained control of most of the sector. The outskirts of Tehuantepec had already been ravaged by fire, and now the center of the city was robbed and pillaged. The Juchitecos tortured or killed residents of the city, focusing their abuse on those who had fought against them, or in the case of the Creole population, singling out people based solely on their origins. As a result many residents went into hiding or fled to the city of Oaxaca.

Tehuantepec remained under insurgent control for an entire year. In the end, the government was forced to deal with them. They abolished the salt tax as well as land registry. And the cholera epidemic, which had subsided, was forgotten. Meléndez, who was amply rewarded for his efforts, wisely chose to retire to the Guatemala border. During the presidency of Santa Anna, the Creole faction endeavored to regain its former predominance and Tehuantepec sought to avenge itself by oppressing Juchitán. But the revolt led by General Juan Álvarez,[65] quickly brought about the dictator Santa Anna's abdication and leveled the playing field. Civil war reignited in Tehuantepec, more intensely and cruelly than before. The fall of Ignacio Comonfort, to whom Álvarez had handed over the presidency, only worsened the situation. Conflicts broke out immediately all over Mexico and as everyone is aware, these struggles have continued to rage on with unimaginable ferocity. Motivated purely by its hatred for Spanish blood, Juchitán and the Indian population of the region, in general, as well as the dark-skinned mestizos, all embraced the cause of the so-called Liberal Party, which is the party that most foreigners that are not of Spanish extraction support as well.

The Creoles—or those who claim to be—were Miramón's natural constituency and were known as the Patricios in Tehuantepec, the group who made the unwarranted claim to be defending ecclesiastical immunity and the church property. Nevertheless, as I believe I have shown in my previous comments, the Catholic faith is not really a factor in this bloody game. Instead it is a question of holding on to the last vestiges of Spanish influence. In the state of Oaxaca, priests had actually taken up arms and were fighting, some for one side, some for the other, depending on their complexion. In Tehuantepec, the prior of the Convent of Santo Domingo, Father Mauricio López, the sole Dominican that his decrepit order could manage to send to Oaxaca, was one of the most active Liberal Party leaders. At the time of my stay, he and the governor Don Porfirio Díaz were the absolute masters of the province. They were at the head of the bold Juchitecos, who once more, controlled Tehuantepec and held all the key positions in the city. In all honesty, I must point out, once more, that neither faction in these clashes that have brought such suffering to Mexico is beyond reproach. Both the Patricios and the Liberals perpetrate acts of cruelty and treachery. Systematic pillaging and murder are their guiding principles. With a shared callousness, they rob, ravage, and burn. Everyone in the area spoke of the priest from Juchitán who had participated in the sack of Tehuantepec and mercilessly engaged in the most horrific acts of war. Not long afterwards, he was ambushed by the Patricios and killed in a skirmish.

The Liberals hung his portrait in the church of Juchitán and worship him as if he were a saint.

This was the situation in this unfortunate country when I arrived in Tehuantepec. The first night that I spent there was extremely uncomfortable. A dry overwhelming heat kept me from sleeping and it was only towards the morning that the air, cooled by a fine rain that fell from a cloudless sky, afforded me a few moments of slumber. When the first rays of sunlight entered my room, I jumped from my trestle bed. I quickly washed up at a nearby fountain, whose constant gurgling had unfortunately not helped send me off to sleep. Leaving the hotel, I went straight to the large main square, where along two sides there are unremarkable buildings with arcades. The most striking structure is the house of Don Juan Avendaño, to whom I had a letter of introduction. Since I knew no one in Tehuantepec, I called on him unceremoniously even though it was only six in the morning. He greeted me in a large room. He had just come from the river, where he had just been bathing—a practice that was common among both men and women from all social classes. Don Juan Avendaño was a Zapotec merchant, originally from Oaxaca, from a comfortably well-off and honorable family. He was a short man with an honest face, in his thirties and he seemed both open minded and courteous. In Tehuantepec, this well-connected man, was considered one of the most powerful supporters of the Liberal Party. He was also known to be very sympathetic to foreigners. He was the banker and general contractor for the Americans, who held him in high regard and sang his praises, while simultaneously taking advantage of him.

When I presented my letter, Avendaño welcomed me warmly. He insisted that I should consider his home as my own. These were not merely empty words of politeness. He immediately sent one of his servants to collect my bags at the Oriental Hotel saying that this establishment would not be suitable for me. I had reason to believe he might be right. But nonetheless, I am certain that during the three weeks while I enjoyed his hospitality he was a most attentive and thoughtful host. I had a cup of coffee with him and soon after he offered to introduce me to the prior of Santo Domingo and the governor. I accepted enthusiastically.

We left his house and crossed the street called calle del Comercio, where the hotel where I had been staying was located. Before us there was a second square, which was not as big as the first one I described. On the right was the town hall. In front of both this building and the former government palace, nearby, I noticed arrogant-looking, half-naked soldiers from Juchitán standing guard under the arcades. Several partially destroyed houses lined the left side of the square. At the far end, on two levels, rising up like a large esplanade ten or twelve feet above street level, was the monastery and church of Santo Domingo, whose proud, monumental appearance was more reminiscent of a fortress than a religious structure. Of course, given the period and circumstances under which it was built, I immediately understood that the Dominicans, here as elsewhere in New Spain, must have considered those high walls as a refuge against the constant threat of insurrection by their flock. That certainly turned out to be the case when they imprisoned Cocijopij. The first thing that struck me was that everything—the staircase, terrepleins, and walls—all showed signs of decay. The church that was visible from the terrace had regrettably deteriorated both inside and out. It has a tall front gate built of red brick, without ornamentation and built in a style that would be difficult to identify, if it weren't for a vaguely Moorish dome, crowning the top of the main body of the edifice, just before the apse, where a few narrow windows projected light into its single nave. The entire place is sad and gloomy. The high altar, like the others that were set up along the walls had been stripped of the precious metals that once adorned them. Their only distinguishing characteristics, besides their dismal condition, were the crude wooden images that even the vandals had not deigned to loot when they ransacked the place.

Of the buildings that were once located to the right of the church only ruins remained, but to its left, the monastery still stood. The entrance was through a low, cramped porch. Like the rest, it was unadorned. There were no salient architectural features, no windows other than narrow slits. What distinguished it from other buildings in Tehuantepec was that it had a second floor above the ground level. Inside, it was designed like most convents with vaulted ceilings and square cloisters on both the first and second floor surrounded by galleries along which were located cells and rooms. You reached the second floor by way of a large brick staircase, as dilapidated as the rest of the building, and which was in even worse condition than the church. And yet, what I had seen so far was nothing in comparison to the revolting conditions I found on the second floor. The half-naked soldiers garrisoned in town had taken up residence there. I had never seen anything more vile. They were there with their concubines, wives, and children. When I entered with Avendaño, the soldiers, who were not on guard duty, were sprawled out in every imaginable position, screaming and hollering while gambling on mats. Beneath the gallery that led from the sacristy to the church soldiers were on the floor with women, indecently pressed up against one another—and right at the sanctuary's door. It turned my stomach. And yet, you can imagine how thrilled I was to visit this monastery, which had been so horribly desecrated. I thought of its founder, the wretched Cocijopij and how he was forcibly brought to these cells, which today house the brutish descendants of his subjects. What a lesson this could have been for Spain! If only back then, Spain could have imagined the scenes I was witnessing! God was avenging the last king of Tehuantepec.

I was eager for a change of scenery. As we left, I went with Avendaño to visit the prior, who lived in temporary housing next to his convent. He welcomed me very politely and had the most wonderful manners. Father Mauricio was a man in his forties or fifties, with Indian blood in his veins and a level of education far superior to most priests that I knew in this part of Mexico. He wore his order's habit, looking quite dignified. After a short conversation, he brought me to meet the governor, Porfirio Díaz, who lived close by, and whose welcome was equally as gracious. His appearance and demeanor were striking. He was a pure-blooded Zapotec Indian and of all the indigenous people whom I had met in my travels he was the most perfect specimen that I had ever seen. I felt I was in the presence of a youthful Cocijopij, or of Guatimozín,[66] as I had so often imagined him. He was tall, good looking, and remarkably distinguished. His noble, pleasantly bronzed face seemed the embodiment of ancient Mexican aristocracy. Díaz was actually still quite young. Preoccupied by his studies in Oaxaca, he had not yet completed his degree when the civil war propelled him into a military career. He owed his nomination as Tehuantepec's governor to Juárez, who knew him personally. Following this meeting, I saw him almost every day. Along with two or three of the officers in the garrison, he ate his meals at my host's house. I was therefore in an excellent position to study his character and his behavior. Leaving aside any discussion of politics at this point, I can say that the qualities that I observed in that private setting only confirmed the good opinion I formed of him on that very first day. Moreover, it could only benefit Mexico to be governed by men of his character.

After dinner Avendaño proposed a stroll up the Dani-Guivedchi, also known as Tiger Mountain. I accepted enthusiastically, especially since I hoped I might discover remnants of Cocijopij's former palace, whose location I was eager to ascertain. I had spoken about this to no effect with the prior of Santo Domingo, who was incapable of giving me any information on this topic. Sunset was an hour away, but that was more than enough time to climb the hill that rises up abruptly right behind the town square. The city's main neighborhoods are bound in between its steep slopes and the river that divides the city in two. The S-shaped hill uncoils from north to south, and its sheer rock face casts shadows across the outskirts of town that are inhabited by Indians. On the hillside above the main square, there are adobe shacks and bamboo huts alongside little gardens that form a maze of narrow streets, which zigzag up and down. All of this made climbing the hill particularly tricky. Don Juan led me along quite blithely, without taking into consideration that beyond this neighborhood that was suspended in the heights there wasn't even a path to be found traced along the white rock.

Soon however, we had reached the top, panting and soaked in perspiration. But the wonderful panoramic view was worth the effort. It provided a vantage point from which to see the city and all its surroundings, those neighborhoods that the S-shaped hill wraps around with their Moorish churches, their white crenelated houses shaded by magnificent palm trees as well as those parts of the city across the Tehuantepec River at the foot of Mount Dani-Lieza,[67] which rose up before us. The plain all around us appeared to ripple with steep hills. Each one of these hills had its ruins and each recalled a memory from the past or legend related to the kings of Tehuantepec. Farther, in one direction there was the Pacific Ocean's azure surface, illuminated by the setting sun and in the other the vast semicircle of the Cordillera, whose deep crevices coalesced in the blanketing shadows of the night. To the east, my companion pointed out the promontories and small islands that dot the lagoons that infiltrated inland as far as twelve miles from the coast.

Pointing he said, "The Wabi fishermen go there as they did at the time of Cocijopij, to offer mysterious sacrifices to the *Heart of the Kingdom*, one of Quetzalcoatl's many titles. They do this in underground temples on the enchanted island called Monopostiac."[68] To one side stretching out over the plain like a long steely ribbon reflecting the last light of day, the Tehuantepec River snaked majestically through on its way to the sea, bringing life and providing a cooling presence along the way. To the other side, less than a league away, the river poured out of the deeply cut gorges of Mounts Guiengola and Mizitiguie, whose splendid peaks loomed behind me menacingly.

From these aeries the Zapotec king defied the full force of Mexico's power for an entire year. Seen from the city, which is five to six leagues away from the site, the fortress of Guiengola looks like a cone with a flattened top. With its terrifying precipices often veiled by clouds, it takes a day of hard climbing to reach this plateau. The size and architectural grandeur of the magnificent ashlar ruins, with its palaces, temples, and fortifications have left visitors in admiration. Cocijoeza was not satisfied with the abundance of natural springs, which still today feed plentiful groves of banana trees. He had large ponds dug and then relocated fish from the rivers there. Three times the Mexican king dispatched troops with the intent of flushing out his enemy from this fearsome site. Three times the troops were shred to pieces along the way, or decimated on the plain. Finally, the great Ahuitzotl was forced to sue for peace.

The Tehuantepec River becomes tranquil after leaving the Guiengola gorges. It's reviving flow cuts across the plain, covering the sandy outskirts of the city with verdant crops and splitting up into thousands of little streams that fertilize the gardens that are found tucked into even the most arid corners of the Guivedchi. Sitting at the base of the cross crowning the hilltop, I was quietly contemplating the sublime landscape that encircled me as we rapidly plunged into the dark of night.

"It is time to turn back and return home," my host said to me, lightly touching me on the shoulder. "This place is not safe after sunset and Tehuantepec is swarming with bandits."

Alas! In my bliss I had forgotten the civil war, Juárez and Miramón, the Patricios and the Juchitecos, who through their cruel conflicts had turned this earthly paradise into a living hell. The sun had disappeared behind Guiengola and its jagged peaks had, one by one, lost their halos of light. Suddenly, all the church and chapel bells from the neighborhoods below set off, sending their harmonious sounds echoing off the mountains.

"*La oración de la noche!*" said don Juan, as he removed his hat. "The Angelus." After a few moments of solemn contemplation, he offered me the customary good wishes.

We descended from the hilltop and in a few minutes had crossed the sandy expanse of the city square that separated us from his house. In the evening, every family, rich or poor, sat out on their wide-grilled balconies or at their doorsteps, taking in the fresh night air. In the starlit night, they discussed the events of the day or the weather. They talked party politics, while keeping an eye on late-night passers-by of both sexes, who—either by necessity or because of a taste for adventure—were walking down the streets of fine sand. Under that admirable sky, the nights were so cool and dazzling, that it was tempting to sleep under the stars, laying out one's bedding or *petate*[B27] outside as was done in the past. Unfortunately, civil war has changed age-old customs and the tranquil pleasures of tropical

---

B27. Petate, from the Mexican word *petlatl*, is a mat commonly used in this country.

living have had to yield to a state of siege that although undeclared, terrorizes this land. My host was right. At nightfall, it was dangerous to be out. Common criminals were not to be feared as much as bandits in military uniform. Like jackals, they roamed the narrow streets, lurking around houses. Today they were called Juchitecos, but tomorrow they could be Patricios. They stalk their prey, whom they rob and kill with impunity.

At eight in the evening, the sound of drums resonated from under the high galleries of the palace and monastery. The bugler's protracted notes announcing retreat sadly echoed off the Guivedchi and Dani-Lieza. You might assume that it was time to return to barracks. Not for these bandits, who went by the lofty name of soldiers! They stayed out, with or without authorization and carried out their raids. In actuality, retreat was being sounded for the city residents and visitors. It was a signal that it was time to go in and to be vigilant. Meanwhile, armed sentries took to their posts. You would think that this was a guarantee of security but it was quite the contrary. A passer-by who had the misfortune of venturing out onto the square, just a hundred feet from the ragged sentry, immediately heard the menacing bellow: *quien vive!* That "who goes there?" which is used throughout all of Spanish America, is the most idiotic thing known to man. Everybody knows that you are supposed to respond immediately with the watchword *la Patria*. This is quickly followed by a second question and response that are equally ridiculous. If you don't respond immediately, they shoot you point blank in the head or back. Too bad if you are a foreigner, who has not yet learned to say these absurd phrases, known to opponents and supporters alike! Commit these phrases to memory or pay the consequences! Too bad if you are hard of hearing or if you are distracted! They are free to shoot you down like an enemy or a wild animal. Three unfortunate women were killed in this way, during my stay in Tehuantepec and the Juchitecos callously treated it as a laughing matter. Sometimes these scenes veered from the tragic to the absurdly comic. One dark night, a few days before my departure, the sentry, who was pacing up and down, glimpsed something passing just a few steps from the palace. He screamed out his usual quien vive loud enough to make the walls shake. No one responded. The object of his attention kept moving. So, the Juchiteco fired randomly and killed... Who was the victim, you may ask? A cow that had broken its ties and was running about looking for its calf.

Don Juan Avendaño was a merchant and like most native or foreign merchants in Central American cities, he ran a shop on the square down the street from his house. Along with the shop, he had a bar and in the large waiting area there was a billiard table. My compatriots introduced this game to the area and unfortunately Hispanic Americans, who already had a tendency to gamble too much, took a liking to the game. Each evening all the notable local residents, including the governor and the prior of Santo Domingo, gathered around the billiard table at Avendaño's. It was an odd affair especially in such turbulent times. There was a great deal of conversation and it certainly provided me with new observations on a daily basis. Although the women of Tehuantepec, with the exception of the Creoles, were among the least reserved that I had seen in America, they still had enough decency not to frequent public places like this. I only ever saw one woman there and she mingled with the men with seemly no sense of impropriety. She brazenly challenged them in billiards—a game she played with incomparable skill and tact. She was a Zapotec Indian, with bronzed skin. She was young, svelte, elegant, and so beautiful that—much like Cortés's mistress had done long ago—she stole the heart of every white man there. I could not find her name in my notes. So I either forgot it or I never knew it. But I remember some people laughingly called her Didjaza in front of me, which means "Zapotec woman" in that language. I remember that the first time I saw her I was struck by how superb and proud she looked in her lavish indigenous dress. She was so reminiscent of the way artists have represented Egyptian goddesses that I thought I was seeing Isis or perhaps Cleopatra before my very eyes. That first evening she was wearing a striped skirt, which was sea green and wrapped simply and tightly around her body from her hips to just above her ankle, and a crimson huipil of silky gauze, with gold trim, which was like a short sleeved camisole, draped over her shoulders and chest, upon which she wore a gold woven-link necklace. Her hair was parted in the middle and braided into two splendid plaits with big blue ribbons. She also wore another brocaded huipil of white muslin worn as a headdress that framed her face, exactly like the Egyptian calantica.[69] Let me repeat, never before had I seen such a striking image of Isis or Cleopatra.

I will not speak at length about her reputation. It was not much different than that of most of the women of Tehuantepec at every level of society. In fact because of a general lack of morality in the city, due to its hedonistic nature and the current political situation, Avendaño decided to temporarily separate from his wife and send her and his young daughter to stay with family in the neighboring state of Chiapas. From what I observed, this Indian woman was considered a seductive beauty by most, and yet she terrified others in a perplexing way. According to some she was crazy, but most, especially from the lower classes, said that they feared her because they thought she was a witch able to communicate with the *naguals* or spirits of Mount Rayudeja. She had a deep understanding of medicinal plants and their secrets, and people maintained that she used her extensive knowledge of plants and a host of other things for good or evil, depending on whether or not she liked someone. Even her skill at billiards was attributed to her magical arts. The Indians respected her like a queen. And no matter when she ventured passed the guard posts, the sentries seemed to recognize her instantly and withheld their quien vive.

As for me, although I was skeptical of her supernatural powers, I was rather pleased for the opportunity to see what the people of Tehuantepec called a witch. When Pancho Portocarrero, one of Avendaño's friends, pulled me aside, for the first time in the billiard room, to point out this extraordinary creature, it occurred to me that her personal power of seduction was far more formidable than any spell or magic potion could have been. Nevertheless, I couldn't help but notice something strange in her eyes. They were the darkest and most brilliant that I had ever seen, especially when she was focused on playing. But there were times when she stopped suddenly. She leaned on the edge of the table or against the wall and stared with a fixed and subdued gaze like a corpse. A moment later she closed her eyes and from beneath her long ebony lashes shot a flash of light that made the person she was gazing at shudder.

"*Es loca.* She is crazy!" Don Abram, Avendaño's chief employee said to me once.

Was it madness, as he claimed? Or was it as others thought, an absence during which her spirit became completely absorbed, transporting her along with her nagual to an unknown world? I will let the reader be the judge. I never had the opportunity of speaking directly to this woman. I was content just to observe her and listen to what she and those around her said. She spoke Castilian as well as any señora from the highest classes of Tehuantepec. However, there was nothing as melodious as her voice when she was speaking that beautiful Zapotec language, which rings so sweetly in the ear and that could be considered the Italian of the Americas.

CHAPTER VIII

Naguals and Nagualism. The Hermit of Guacamaya.

After a few days of rest, I had planned a trip to Mount Guiengola in order to visit the remarkable ruins that I discussed earlier. Murphy had just arrived back in Tehuantepec from his expedition to Huatulco, returning with a number of idols and other ancient artifacts that he had found in the ruins of the ancient city of that same name. They landed there from the coast, and found it practically deserted, which meant that he and his companions had found no food or potable water. However, he returned rather pleased with the results of his trip. He had drawn a map of the port of Huatulco, indicating the results of his soundings. According to his report, this harbor, which had a great capacity, would be as good and convenient as the port of Acapulco. It was easy to enter and ships of considerable tonnage could cast anchor there in complete safety. Thanks to the information that I had given him when we were in Barrio, he discovered the ruins of a vast fortified city just two leagues away from the current town of Huatulco, which he assumed was the ancient site of the same name. The ruins were located on a plateau surrounded by steep precipices that extend out towards the sea. The area residents confirmed the legends that I told him about the place. Murphy explained that they had assured him that in the remote past, boats had often come from far-off lands in the west, in other words from China and Japan, to trade with the merchant-princes of Huatulco. Unfortunately his expedition ended tragically. A young and talented artist, the same man, who had helped him draw up maps of the port and make drawings of the surrounding landscape, fell to sea while making sketches of the promontory of Huatulco from a rowboat. He disappeared, but within seconds blood rose to the surface, leading them to believe that a shark had immediately dragged him down into the depths of the ocean.

When he learned that I intended to visit Guiengola, he offered to join me with several of his friends. I couldn't be happier. Going with them would make the trip more secure given that I had been told that bandits had infested the area along the road to Oaxaca. Also, this would mean having one or two artists, who would be able to draw sketches of the main ruins. Since it wouldn't be possible to return to Tehuantepec on the same day, despite the mountain's proximity, we had to make arrangements to have plenty of food on the summit as well as shelter against the rain if needed. Murphy promised to take care of all this and we agreed to start our trip in two days.

Time was of the essence, if we wanted to undertake this venture before the start of the rains. It was June 13 and so far no precipitation had fallen on the Tehuantepec plain. The rains were obviously long overdue and as a result it was extremely hot and dry. In the morning, the sun was already intense and at night the sand on the streets continued to burn underfoot. Everyone's throat was parched from an unquenchable thirst. That day the few thick white clouds, which I had observed the night before, started to accumulate. The air that at first was stifling, as if I were steaming under a leaden cover, eventually became less sultry and I could breathe again. At sunset, a light breeze came in from the north. The tops of the trees began to quiver as large, yellow leaves detached from their branches and fell making a dry, melancholic sound. I was starting to feel the ill effects of this prolonged dry spell, so I went to bed early, asking the servant, who attended to me, to bring something refreshing to my room. Meanwhile, as I got into bed, I felt my skin ache and burn.

A few minutes later, the servant entered the room holding a pitcher of lemonade. He poured me a glass and seeing that I didn't seem sleepy, he sat by my bed in case I needed anything or wanted to engage in a bit of conversation. This boy was called Eusebio. He was an intelligent young Zapotec of about twelve or fifteen years old, with bronzed skin, and a gleam in his eye. He was part of Avendaño's household staff and I had taken him on to serve me, giving him one or two medios from time to time to compensate him for his attentive service.

Earlier, I had started packing for my trip to Guiengola and my bags were opened and sitting on top of a trunk. Eusebio looked over at them and seemed concerned.

"Sir, are you leaving?" he asked with a vague smile.

"Why do you ask, Eusebio?"

"It's just that I see that Your Lordship has packed his bags."

"Of course, in two days we are going to go visit Guiengola."

"Guiengola! Sir, you won't be going to Guiengola. I am sure of it."

"And why is that, Eusebio?"

"*Quien sabe*?[70] They say that it is dangerous to go up there."

"But others have gone before me, Eusebio. And it won't be dangerous. The Americans are coming with me . . . Even if the Patricios wanted to, they wouldn't dare attack us."

"I am not talking about the Patricios."

"So, then, who would prevent me from going there, Eusebio?"

"I don't know . . . but I know, sir, that you won't go . . ."

I listened, surprised that this child's was so adamant about whether I would go on this trip. As we talked, thunder started rumbling in the distance. With a strong gust, the north wind blew opened my shutters, noisily knocking down some of my things. The impending storm was announcing its presence. Eusebio smiled, looking at me with a singular expression that I had noticed before on the faces of certain young Indians. He got up to close the window and sat back down by my side.

He continued: "You see, sir, you won't be going to Guiengola now." And then he added with a weighty tone that seemed quite solemn for a child, "Anyway, Didjaza told me so . . . the Americans won't go there again."

I was flabbergasted! In my astonishment at hearing the name of that strange creature associated to my plans for an excursion, I sat up. I looked at my young servant directly in the eyes and asked: "What does Didjaza have to do with this?"

"Nothing, sir, nothing at all," exclaimed Eusebio, who was taken aback by my sharp response.

"Now, now, don't be upset my boy," I said giving him a medio in order to gain his confidence. "I just want to know why the Americans wouldn't be able to go up there any more."

"It's because everyone says the Americans are infidels, who disturb the dead in their tombs. The dead must rest in peace where they are."

I could hardly argue with such a sound argument. Since Major Barnard's expedition, several groups had gone to Guiengola and other historical sites. Tumuli had been dug up. They removed remains from some and, from others, idols and vases of various sizes that were brought back to the United States and Mexico City. The travelers, who visited these regions, know that the Indians respectfully, in fact jealously, guard the ancient buildings and sepulchers of their forefathers. They have seen the admirable discretion with which the natives conceal cave entrances—caves where the remains of their princes lay—from the profane and probing eyes of foreigners. Consequently, it is easy to imagine what our expeditions to Guiengola, or elsewhere, looked like from their perspective. As for Didjaza, my guess was that even if she wasn't a witch, she was undoubtedly more than happy to be considered one if it enhanced her influence over her compatriots. Moreover, with all the foreigners who were starting to flock to Tehuantepec since the Americans had built the road, it must have seemed to this Zapotec Indian—a descendant of the former lords of this region, as I would later learn—that it was paramount to safeguard her ancestors' remains from disrespect. Eusebio's words had got me thinking. While Didjaza might want others to take her for a madwoman or a witch, she was far from crazy. For example, at first it might seem strange that she always came to play billiards. But the mostly American foreigners and notable local citizens all gathered to drink at Avendaño's bar in the evening. She heard everything, without ever seeming to be paying attention. With her charms and eccentricities she inspired love in some and struck fear in the hearts of others, all of which helped her maintain her reputation and her influence over the people that she exploited.

While these thoughts were going through my mind, the storm broke. I heard the rain beating violently against the sandy street and the cobblestones in the courtyard.

"Well, it is obvious to me that we won't be able to go to Guiengola," I said to my young servant.

"Oh, no señor . . . You hear the storm. Tomorrow it will be even worse. I told you so."

"We'll see. But tell me something Eusebio, in order to know all these things Didjaza must be a witch."

"Oh, no señor . . ."

"Of course, she is. In any case, whether she is one or not is none of my business, and I don't want to cause her any trouble. It's just that I have to tell you that I have heard stories about Mounts Rayudeja and Guiengola that say that her nagual, and perhaps yours as well, dwell there. Aren't you really afraid that if the Americans go hunting for tigers or wild cats they might shoot them and then you would die along with them?"

Eusebio's bronze skin grew pale and he was struck dumb with terror to hear me speak so lightly of such an esoteric subject. These are mysteries that indigenous people here usually carefully conceal from foreigners and even from compatriots who are not of their race. Having read the Dominican Francisco Burgoa's rare and curious work, I knew how deeply rooted the powerful superstitions surrounding Nagualism were even to this day in the minds of the aboriginal people of the states of Oaxaca and Chiapas. This was actually one of the reasons that I had chosen to travel in this area. I wanted to discover the truth about all this Indian witchcraft. I was hoping to penetrate the mystery surrounding this subject. I wondered whether there was any basis for the extraordinary spells that are mentioned in their chronicles and which are attributed for the most part to the royal princes of Guatemala.

Was it true, as the most reliable and sincere Spanish authors had claimed, that Indians were capable of transforming themselves into all sorts of animals? Was it possible that they could be transported instantaneously from one place to another, so as to be an invisible presence at their enemies' council meetings? Can we give any credence to Sahagún[71] when he says that before the eyes of spectators they could make rivers, springs, forests, or palaces appear where just minutes before there had been nothing, and then could make them disappear a moment later. Can we believe him when he says that they could slit open their stomachs, cut off the arm or leg of a neighbor or even kill him and then heal or resuscitate him immediately afterwards without any trace of a wound? And all this, in front of a crowd of people assembled to witness this fantastical spectacle! These things are scrupulously reported, and perhaps what makes them all the more astonishing is that they are reported by serious-minded men writing in a time that is not so distant from our own. Were these all just the result of strange hallucinations, produced by unknown causes? I myself had witnessed the skill with which modern-day witches, called *Curanderos* or *Zahoris*, used magnetism and ventriloquy, as I believe that they do, or—as Sahagún and Torquemada[72] suggest—potions and smoke to attempt to disturb spectators' minds, making them see all sorts of ghosts, with the aim of imposing their will on viewers and gaining complete control over them.

Even if we assume that they were not able to communicate with the forces of an invisible world, it is beyond dispute that in the years following the conquest of Mexico, indigenous priests and noblemen, who had managed to survive, used these formidable techniques to turn their people away from the teachings of the Catholic clergy. Thus, they incited their followers to gather in secret councils held to celebrate their forbidden cult's rites and clandestinely conspire against their conquerors. Just like King Cocijopij, they ostensibly obeyed the new laws that were imposed on them and followed with feigned diligence the main principles of the Catholic Church. Meanwhile, they assembled at night in some remote palace, in the woods, or in caves. Among the rare accounts that were handed down about this fascinating period, history has retained the astonishing number of caves in the state of Oaxaca where, despite the great vigilance of the Dominicans, Indians continued to celebrate their ancient solemn rites. These caves were the final refuge for the religion preached by Quetzalcoatl. In these sanctuaries the last remaining indigenous priests attempted to maintain the power that had all but completely slipped away from them. It was in this context that the formidable secret society known as Nagualism operated for almost two centuries throughout all of Mexico and Central America. Most commonly, Nagualism harkens back to practices under ancient Toltec law such as drawing up horoscopes for newborns and giving them a name that is in phase with their calendar. As an offering to Chalchiuhtlicue,[73] the water goddess and protectress of infants, blood was drawn from a child's ear or from under his or her tongue as a purification ceremony comparable to a baptism. It should come as no surprise that this rite continued among those who preserved an attachment to their forefathers' beliefs. But I would like to draw attention to the great skill with which these idolatrous priests surreptitiously contrived ceremonies, based on their ancient rites, to counterbalance Catholic ceremonies in the hopes of reducing the Church's appeal to their population.

The leaders of the ancient religion secretly resumed their roles, especially in areas where there were less than zealous or inattentive Catholic pastors. They reestablished their hierarchy or modeled their organization on the Catholic Church, an easy enough task given the striking similarities between the two groups. Although we lack details on the resurgence of Mexican idolatry, we know that its stronghold in Guatemala was in Samayac, a large town in the province of Suchitepéquez.[74] The pontiff there had a large number of ministers of lower rank under his jurisdiction. The last high priest, who was imprisoned in 1703 by the Franciscan, Father Antonio Margil de Jésus, died at the monastery of Cristo-Crucificado in

Antigua, Guatemala. According to the report of the proceedings against him, he claimed to have transported himself several times to European kingdoms, where he had even attended papal consistories in the Vatican as an invisible presence. The high priestess of the underground temple in Huehuetán, which was founded by Votan, in the province of Soconusco, Chiapas, the birthplace of American civilization, was prohibited from practicing her functions in 1697. That is when Nuñez de la Vega, the bishop of Chiapas, learned of her existence during a pastoral visit. He immediately ended this female pontificate and in a solemn ceremony set the archives and divinities of this ancient sanctuary aflame.[75] In Tehuantepec, where Cocijopij had been the priest of Mitla, his illegitimate son Coquitela held the position for more than fifty years after his father's death, despite the Dominicans.

In smaller towns, low-level sacrificers continued to practice their rites, just like the priests and clergymen whom they wanted to supplant in the hearts and minds of their flock. When a child was born, the father called on the Nagual priest to offer the infant to the gods before his Christian baptism. At the age of seven or eight the child was confirmed in Nagualism and if he had a calling, he would commence initiation to the sect's mysteries. Then and now, weddings were performed in church only after an indigenous ceremony. Even at the end of life every precaution was taken. As soon as the priest had left the deathbed, having given his blessing, the Nagualist appeared and thoroughly washed the parts of the body that had received the extreme unction.

This mysterious sect did not limit itself to clandestinely eradicating or imitating the sacraments of the Church. Its greater goal was to silently undermine Spanish domination and reestablish, not only the altars of the ancient religion, but the native princes' rule. In pursuit of this goal, an abundance of Castilian blood was shed and its primary victims were almost always Catholic clergymen, sent to administer small indigenous towns. These cruel scenes most often played out in the fertile valleys of Chiapas and Oaxaca, as well as majestic Yucatán. Before the end of the sixteenth century, the Zapotec Indians twice rose up in the hopes of regaining their independence. In the insurrection of 1550, surprisingly enough, their leader took the name Quetzalcoatl. In 1713, the Tzendal Rebellion, which went on for an entire year in the state of Chiapas, brought Spanish rule to the brink. Insurgents, led by a twenty-year-old witch, killed priests in Cancuc and Oxchuc in front of their church altars.[76] It was astonishing to see that the august temples of Palenque and Ocosingo reemerged as sites for religious ceremonies just as they had been in ancient times. The situation was urgent and the governor general of Guatemala came to Ciudad Real in person to find a way to stifle this triumphant rebellion. In fact, to this day, an annual mass is celebrated in the cathedral of this city to give thanks to God for having saved the colony from such a threat. The Spanish landed in Yucatán in 1517 but they were only able to bring it under their control sometime between 1537 and 1540. Three times during that interval the Maya chased them from their land. Later, the Maya rose up several times against their oppressors, with a widespread insurrection in 1763. In the last twenty-five years these rebellions have reignited and still the violence continues to rage. Mérida, the state's capital, was the site of a lengthy siege. The cities of Valladolid and Bacalar were both taken over and horribly pillaged in recent times. As a result, two-thirds of the peninsula is now in the hands of the triumphant Maya people. Today the indigenous people of Mexico, whether religious or idolatrous, are fully engaged in a shared struggle, driven by an animosity to destroy any and all remnants of the conquest.

There is no denying that Nagualism still exists and is a vast political and religious organization. However, in comparison to their ancestors, today's practitioners are not as knowledgeable. The decimation of native cultural wisdom resulted in a great loss of the knowledge, which was key to their ancient superstitions. Those who wanted to learn had no choice but to seek their education among the Christians. However, there are still priests who on certain days don great white pontifical robes and a miter and offer solemn rites of sacrifice in caves or on mountaintops. Christian beliefs have been incorporated into their ceremonies and have crept into their invocations. Crudely sculpted images in their churches represent both their forefathers' gods and the conquistadors' saints. The very essence of modern Nagualism is that mixture of ceremony with political and religious animosity manifested in so many different and curious forms. In my research and in my own personal observations while traveling and during my stays among the Indians, I found convincing evidence of associations akin to freemasonry or secret societies, where leaders and followers had formed strong bonds to one another through fearsome rites. Do they all have the same blind faith in these rites? This is something I cannot say. But what is indisputable is that several of these leaders were well-educated men, who studied in Spanish universities in their countries.

We know that some of the high-ranking followers are responsible for performing secret rites, like those mentioned earlier related to newborns, who all have their nagual. Unlike Christians, mestizos, or Spaniards, they have been given the name of a bird or animal based on their birthday. In general, they deny it, if you ask them about it. They believe that their witches or true Nagualists, who were confirmed in their superstitious rites at the age of seven or eight, can communicate directly with this bird or animal and therefore they exercise considerable supernatural powers. They can transform themselves at will into their nagual, transport themselves instantaneously from one place to another and a host of other extraordinary miracles. There is a counterweight to these mysterious powers. If the animal or bird that is their nagual falls ill or is wounded, they will immediately feel the same wound or the same disease in the corresponding part of the body. If their nagual dies, the person dies as well within the hour.

There are many examples of this mysterious sympathy found in texts written about Mexico and Central America. I wouldn't dare speak of this topic here, if I had not heard these accounts borne out by a great many people from a variety of linguistic and cultural backgrounds. There are books and manuscripts full of these narratives. The Dominican or Franciscan brothers, who often claimed to have witnessed them, didn't know how to explain these wonders and therefore attributed them naturally enough to the work of the devil. Were they hallucinations? Were the witnesses under a spell? I have no idea. The reader can believe what he or she likes, but I will admit that more than once, I witnessed strange occurrences, for which, to this day, I cannot find a rational explanation. In fact, I will discuss one such event a little later. It is therefore easy to understand the great interest that I had in learning anything I could about the Zapotec witch in my conversations with Eusebio. After this long digression, let me return to that conversation.

The evasive answers of this young Indian and his blanching face when I mentioned his nagual, were sufficient proof to me that I was not far from the truth. For several minutes he dared not answer me or even look me in the eye. But from between the long eyelashes veiling his dark eyes, I discerned the same flashes of light that I had seen in Didjaza's eyes. I watched with great curiosity trying to think of what I could say to best gain his trust.

"Eusebio," I said, after a long silence, "I am neither your nor Didjaza's enemy. I know that she has her nagual and you have yours."

"No señor," cried out the boy, staring at me with his fiery eyes shining with both resentment and fear.

"Let me finish, my friend. I know this because I know more about these things than you do and than she does. I, too, have my nagual. In fact I have more than one. I will show you one."

"No, *no quiero*. I don't want to see," he repeated with terror in his voice. And since he tried to leave the room, I took hold of his shirt, which was the only item of clothing that he was wearing in this blessed climate.

Meanwhile I pulled from my pocket a small metal box containing a compass that I had bought when passing through New York. There was nothing frightening about it. Reassured he sat down again and stared at it with great interest.

"This is my nagual," I said to him. Look at this needle. It always points to the same side. At sea or in the woods, during the darkest nights, it shows me my way. It shows me where the sun will rise and set. If I want to go up to Guiengola, with this nagual I can do it with no problem. You can see that I know as much as Didjaza, even if my nagual is different from hers.

However, my little speech did not exactly have the effect I was expecting. The look of distrust in Eusebio's eyes had dissipated a bit, but as he stared attentively at the magnetized needle there was as much incredulity as there was curiosity. It was clear that he had never seen a compass before. But although he seemed to believe that there was something magical in that little box, he was hardly inclined to accept the idea that it was a nagual. I have to admit that he had a point; he knew quite well that no Indian would imprison his nagual in a box. He was also probably persuaded, despite my claims to the contrary, that a foreigner, no matter how knowledgeable, was still no match for a nagualist. And, once again, I had to admit he might be right. For that matter, I have to confess that I have often tried to impress Indians with my compass, but I can't say that I have ever had much success. On that day, Eusebio was no exception.

Eusebio, who was no doubt anxious about where this line of questioning might lead, found an excuse to stand up, offer me a cup of lemonade and slip out unnoticed while I was drinking it. The storm, which had started to rumble, continued throughout a good part of the night. I was quite uncomfortable. My limbs were burning, and to make matters worse, for the last two or three days I had been experiencing the symptoms of dysentery.

The next day, for the first time the weather was dark and gray, with a cold, almost icy, north wind. Despite the change, I still felt like I was suffocating, as if it were still unbearably hot. I was impatiently awaiting the *aguacero*[77] convinced that it would calm my restless nerves. However, I was sorely disappointed. The clouds finally burst open all of a sudden towards eleven o'clock and a rain shower was furiously unleashed on the city. In an instant, the street disappeared under water as impetuous as a mountain stream flowing over the bed of sand. Standing at the balcony of Avendaño's room, I watched this muddy torrent pass by. For some reason, at that moment, I had the crazy idea that I would feel better if I could bathe. The storm had passed, so I packed a few raggedy clothes and I made my way down towards the river. I got undressed between two large stones and dove into the water. A half hour later I was back home and told my host what I had just done.

"That was quite ill-advised," he told me. "Here we only bathe in cold water in the morning or at night. Let's pray to God that you won't regret it."

He had hardly finished his sentence when I was suddenly overcome, feeling worse than I had before. At once my teeth were chattering and icy shivers went up and down my spine. I felt terribly anxious. Those shivers might have been the sign of one of those tropical lowlands fevers that I inherently feared. Inconsolably, I took to my bed, reproaching myself for my careless behavior and wrapping myself in a heavy woolen blanket. The spell of high fever lasted two hours, followed by chills. I was horribly thirsty. My whole body felt like it was burning up and my bowels were inflamed. I had succumbed to the two most alarming diseases in this menacing climate. When my fever broke, I was drenched with sweat but thought my suffering had come to an end. I felt that I had come back to life. But when I tried to get out of bed, a few hours later, I was still extremely weak. I returned to bed downcast and dejected, grumbling to myself. I started to accept the possibility of having to give up my hopes of going to Mount Guiengola. In my fever dreams, I saw Eusebio blocking my way and pointing to Didjaza standing on a cliff holding a magic wand.

I had an agitated and uncomfortable night. However, the next day I woke with no fever. The sun was shining. The rain had cooled the air, purifying it of the oppressive humidity. Although I was still quite weak, I felt a great relief and by evening I thought that I was well enough to go for a walk and climb up to the top of the Guivedchi to contemplate the view of Tehuantepec. Don Juan lent me a horse and one of his servants, also on horseback, to accompany me. He was a strapping *Zambo*[B28] who was robust and seemingly more inclined to talk than the young Eusebio. He led me to the Vijana neighborhood, where the path was not as steep as the one I had previously taken from the main square. From the base of the cross, I pointed to all the neighborhoods of Tehuantepec, hills and cliffs as well as the mountains surrounding the city and the plain, asking him their names as well as any legends that might be associated with

---

B28. Zambo, a person born of a black man and an Indian woman. [Term used in the Spanish colonies to identify individuals in the Americas of mixed African and Amerindian ancestry.]

them. When I showed him Rayudeja, he stopped a moment, as if he were afraid of saying too much.

I continued: "Rayudeja is where the witches of Tehuantepec meet with their nagual."

"Do you believe in naguals, sir?" he responded shrewdly. "I have heard that foreigners don't believe in any of that nonsense."

"Nonsense! Chico, I am sure that you don't think that it is all nonsense. Well, neither do I. People perhaps exaggerate here and there, but there is some truth to the matter. As for foreigners, like the Americans, who make fun of such things, I can assure you that in their countries there are people who believe in things that are equally absurd."

"So, you believe that naguals exist, *mi señor*?"

"All I can say is that I have read books written by educated and rational men, who believed in them, and I would like to learn more about them. What is your opinion of Didjaza, Chico?"

Chico seemed momentarily flustered and appeared to be trying to come up with a response while I waited. "She is a strange woman. Some people say she is crazy."

"What about you? Do you think she is a madwoman or a witch, Chico?"

"Quien sabe?"

"What are her financial resources, Chico? It seems to me that she is always very well dressed."

"Oh, she has everything she needs. Some people say that those city gentlemen give her money, but I don't believe it."

"And so?"

"Well, Rayudeja..."

"Is that where she gets her money?"

"Either there or on Guiengola... at least that's what people say. They claim that she knows the location of the cave where the great Rey Condoy disappeared with his army and his treasure and that she can get to it by way of Rayudeja. Others say that a nagual gives it to her."

"Is that why she tried to prevent me from going there with the Americans?"

"I don't think so. The Americans wouldn't have found anything. They say that she alone knows the underground passages that connect all the ancient Indian caves and she only goes there with her friends."

"Who are Didjaza's friends?"

"All Indians are her friends. But any Ladino who tries to harm her will regret it!"

"But why is she so respected?"

"They say that she is a descendant of the former rulers..."

"But what kind of harm could she do someone if she wanted to take revenge?"

"Oh a great deal of things..."

"So she is quite powerful or perhaps very cunning?"

"Everyone here thinks so. My mother saw her make a rosebud bloom by saying only three words..."

"I would love to see such a rose!"

"For your sake, sir, I hope you don't."

"Why not, Chico?"

"Witches cast that evil spell so that the man they desire will share their passion. The man who smells such a flower will regret it! He will fall in love with her, even if she is ugly and grizzled and he will think that he is seeing the most beautiful girl of all."

"And you think that is possible, Chico?"

"No one doubts it, sir. There are many examples. But roses that bloom because of evil spells have another singular property," he added, seeing that I was interested in his explanations. "If the woman who made it bloom has the misfortune of smelling it herself, or if by accident someone places it under her pillow, she will lose her mind and go crazy. For several months, as if in a dream, she will call out for the man she had intended to smell the flower."

As we spoke, we had descended the Guivedchi. I am not sure how I started talking to him about macaws, which were worshiped by the ancient people of this area. He interrupted me once more to say: "Sir, do you know why the mountain that rises up over the Chivela plateau was given the name Guacamaya?"[B29]

B29. Guacamaya—a large parrot known as the "macaw"—is a name that has its origins in the ancient language of Santo Domingo and was adopted by the Spanish.

"No, Chico, but I would love to hear the story."

"As you know, sir, there are many caves in all these mountains, like Condoy's cave and the underground passages of Rayudeja. Sixty years ago, when the Dominican fathers were still sending priests to all the pueblos, Father Alonso, who had a great reputation for saintliness, was going to the hacienda of Guichilona one day. Someone told him that there was a cave at the top of the mountain where the Indians went in pilgrimage to consult an old man who had the reputation for being one of their great magicians. The priest was incensed at the idea that there were still such idolaters in the province and was determined to climb up there to see for himself. Accompanied by loyal servants, he arrived at his destination after almost an entire day of walking along a treacherous mountain path. The entrance to the cave was hidden in a thick forest and the father had to be extremely vigilant not to get lost in this labyrinth. He took a few steps into the cave and what did he see? A splendid gallery, swept perfectly clean, with mats on which several Indians lay prostrate, each holding a censer filled with copal. Try to guess in adoration of what?"

"Most likely before a guacamaya, Chico?"

"Exactly, *mi señor*. Within the cave, on an altar covered with candles and flowers, was this pagan animal that these poor unquestioning people were worshiping as if he were our divine Master in the flesh. Father Alonso entered so quietly that no one noticed his presence. But the nasty creature started screeching as soon as it saw him in the distance, as if it was truly possessed by the devil. The old magician, who was in a nearby chamber, ran in, letting out awful cries of his own at the sight of this man of God who had wandered into his satanic hermitage. You see this dreadful pagan was completely naked and bloody from having pricked himself all over with thorns so that he could feed his own bloody meat to this accursed bird. He performed all sorts of acts of penance like that to honor this animal. Before Father Alonso could get any closer, the hermit ran to the foot of the hellish altar, rolling to the ground. As he kissed and caressed the creature, he cried out that no one should dare touch the bird, who was his god and his whole existence. Of course, what the old pagan was saying was true. Despite the old devil's efforts to resist—going as far as actually biting the priest—Father Alonso grabbed the bird from the old man. He then made the sign of the cross and wrung its neck. At that same moment, the sorcerer let out an awful groan and reached for his own neck that seemed to be twisted in pain. Satan, himself, must have taken mercy on him as he was leaving the body of the guacamaya, which was the magician's nagual. The blessed father took the opportunity to address a poignant exhortation to the wretched idolaters, who had witnessed the scene transfixed with fear. And to this day the mountain is known as Mount Guacamaya."

CHAPTER IX

Traditions of Tehuantepec. Fever. Bankruptcy of the Louisiana Tehuantepec Company. Departure.

The day after Chico told me the story of Mount Guacamaya, I had chills and another bout of fever that were worse than the first time. Instead of going away, my intestinal pain became more intense and I was getting weaker. I was starting to worry and desperately wanted the fever to subside so that I could leave Tehuantepec, which, frankly, I could no longer stomach. The following day was Saturday. Since it seemed that my chills came every other day, I realized that I would be fine until Sunday. Too sick to consider a long excursion, but in need of some sort of diversion, I sat on the stoop of Avendaño's shop, across from the city's main market. This market consists of two or three wooden sheds with tiled roofs and is not particularly interesting. There are a few stalls that sell goods imported from abroad. In the past this market had a reputation for selling expensive luxury items from all over. But Tehuantepec's square has slowly been abandoned. It is now just a shadow of what it once was, due to a dwindling population and now, the civil war.

Under the tiled roofs, merchandise produced in Mexico was displayed on the ground. It's a veritable hodgepodge of goods: rope and thread made of maguey and pita, cotton cloth, silk belts, black or yellow buckskin shoes, straw or palm-leaf hats, and mats that run the gamut from refined and brilliantly colored to the most run-of-the-mill. These are found alongside fruits, vegetables, sausages, sun-dried meats that are cut into thin strips (and sold by the foot), tobacco, jams, eggs, and cheese, as well as iguanas that are hung from bamboo sticks and, despite looking quite gruesome, are a favorite delicacy of Tehuantepec's finest gourmets. Nonetheless, this odd mix with all its confusion has its charms. With the exception of a small number of Indians who come from rather far away, the market is run almost exclusively by women. Some stand, others kneel. But they are always busy preparing their corn dough on their *metate* and cooking the tortillas that they sell piping hot to tortilla enthusiasts. Most are sitting with legs crossed, like when they are in church, with their skirts spread out about them. Young and old, Indian and mestiza, these women are gathered next to their merchandise, chattering, laughing, talking, screaming, and arguing with incredible liveliness. They openly poke fun at their customers, whom they tease indiscriminately in either Spanish or Zapotec and with a brazenness equal to any of the women peddling their wares in Parisian markets. Dogs, pigs, chickens, and turkeys grunt and shriek in the midst of this hustle and bustle. And of course, making the picture complete are the children ranging from ages two to ten, wearing nothing more than straw hats and their innocent smiles, and constantly knocking up against the animals and vegetables. This market doesn't sell any valuable items. The silver and gold trade, for which Tehuantepec was once renowned, is now done in a handful of shops, where you have to go to see finely worked saddles and harnesses. These are sought-after in the region and the residents of this city still enjoy a deserved reputation for the quality of their work.

    They dress in a way that resembles more or less what one sees throughout Central America. Only Indian clothing differs from one region to another. I have already said enough about how indigenous women dress in the most vivid example that I came across—the Zapotec witch. The only difference is that Ladinas, mestizas, or Creoles wear petticoats that tend to be full and supple like those of European women. High-neck dresses are quite rare. In general, they wear embroidered muslin or tulle huipils, which are much better suited to the hot climate. They also either wear *rebozos*, which are types of long and wide scarf that they drape over their heads and chests with inimitable elegance. In some cases, they have a wool or silk shawl, imported from France or England. There is nothing particularly colorful in the way the men dress. For the most part, they wear cotton pants of varying lengths with a red or yellow belt around their waist and a palm leaf hat to complete the outfit. Some Indians and most Ladinos of the lower classes, add a shirt that they tuck in or let out like a smock, depending on the season; they are almost all barefooted. Those in the upper classes dress in the European style, with the exception of frock coats and paletots that many of them have replaced with a linen or woolen morning coat. Since the arrival of the Americans, who have imported a great deal of ready-made apparel, European-style clothing has become more prevalent and everyone is starting to wear shoes as well.

While I was occupied watching what was happening in the market, I noticed that there was a substantial movement of troops on the square. The Juchitecos emptied out of their palace barracks and paraded in the street beating their drums. Don Abram explained to me that for the last two or three days, Patricios led by Manzano had been sighted in the area. The Juchitecos were concerned that if they didn't get organized, enemy forces might attempt an attack on Tehuantepec, where moreover, the Patricios had a certain number of devoted followers. Consequently, the governor, after consulting his officers and supporters had decided to make a show of force, marching alongside the soldiers, with the intention of flushing out the enemy from the road to Oaxaca, where they were reportedly lying in ambush behind the cliffs.

During the afternoon, since I was feeling a bit stronger, I got on a horse and with Chico by my side, I went in the direction of Santa Cruz, an Indian district on the other side of the river. I crossed the river across from Mount Dani-Lieza. Having told Chico my destination, he led me down a path with two rows of huts made of reeds and bamboo. They resembled openwork cages, through which the breeze blew freely, and frankly the indiscreet gaze of passersby could penetrate just as easily. But what did they care? In this blessed land, the indigenous people need nothing more than a roof over their head to protect them from water, two petates that act as screens around their bed, if they have one, and a third one to sleep or eat on. If he has three banana trees, a coconut tree or two, and his milpa of corn and frijoles outside his hut, then he has more than he needs to subsist. He can nonchalantly while away his life in peace and quiet. And yet, large beautiful houses used to stand on these streets where now I was seeing such miserable dwellings. At every step of the way, I found the remnants of brick or stone walls, half buried beneath sand or vegetation, and the road that I traveled seemed to be littered with debris.

    I rode along for a rather long stretch, after having left behind the last of Santa Cruz's huts and the neighborhood, known as Taqulaba. After another half a league along the same road, we started to ascend to a higher elevation. But it was still the same soil—arid and sandy—although now partially shaded by a forest of mimosa and other thorny bushes. As Chico and I entered these woods, which extended over a rather considerable distance, other types of ruins caught my eye. There were tumuli and foundations that implied perhaps that this was the site of ancient sanctuaries or sizable homes. But the ravages of time had done their work with a great zest. Thus it was difficult to detect these vestiges under the delicate and dentate foliage of the overgrowth. Were these the remains of the ancient city of Tehuantepec? Was this the site of the palace where Cocijopij was taken while officiating in the vestment of an idolatrous priest and offering sacrifices to his forefather's horrific gods? I had every reason to believe all this could be plausible. But I got no satisfaction for my many questions. The only response I received from either my guide or later the prior of Santo Domingo was a frustrating quien sabe. For two hours, I vainly crisscrossed the area, up one trail and then another. I didn't find a single edifice that could shed light on my investigation. I concluded that if this was the location of the last king of Tehuantepec's palace, then the dark political hand of the colonial government had done its best—and more successfully here than elsewhere—to erase its memory from the minds of his former subjects.

As I returned to town in the cool evening air, I felt so much better, so refreshed and reinvigorated, despite my two bouts of fever in the preceding days, that I was already thinking again of Guiengola, whose beautiful ruins I so wanted to visit before leaving Tehuantepec. On my way, I went by the Hotel San Francisco where Murphy was staying with his companions. It was one of the finer establishments in the city: well run and tolerably well furnished, with a lovely court yard, where the elegant fan-shaped leaves of coconut trees swayed gently above the crenelated walls. I brought up my plans with Murphy, and we agreed that if the fever gave me two or three days of rest, we would take advantage of the good weather to go up to the mountain.

The next day, unfortunately just when I least expected it, I suddenly felt a chill run through my veins. It was almost noon. The sky was alight and the heat was as unbearable as before the recent storms. And yet, at that moment I felt the cold cut through me like a knife, as if it were one of those dismal days of frigid European winter. I also had an upset stomach that gave me cause for concern. I took to my bed dejected. When Avendaño saw that I was so demoralized, he came to my bedside, trying to raise my spirits with words of kindness and sympathy. My distress was based more on the trouble I was causing him than from my situation. He guessed this, and being the decent man that he was, he did his best, by his attentiveness, to show that his hospitality was quite sincere. This bout lasted longer than the others. When this chill had passed I suffered terribly in the intervening two hours until I broke my first sweat. My skin was dry and burning and I was parched with thirst. Unfortunately, the servant that Don Juan had left by my side after his departure felt compelled to refuse my requests for water until I started to sweat. These had been the doctor's orders. A horrible pain gripped my stomach. Unable to resist any longer, I took advantage of the fact that the servant had his back turned for a brief moment, seized a pitcher full of fresh water, and I drank it avidly without giving it a second thought. The effect was as I might have hoped. My skin became humid. I drank again, and the sweat started to roll down my forehead. Relieved, I was soon asleep.

I have no idea how long I slept. When I opened my eyes, it was almost dark and I could barely make out a few blurred shadows. I could hear a sweet song that I thought I recognized as an aria from an opera that I had heard long ago in Paris. It was as if it was being repeated in two parts from the courtyard and close to my room. I sat up in my bed, in disbelief and cried out: "*Quien es?*" (Who is there?)

"*Soy yo*" (It is me), was the response in a soft voice. It was Eusebio, whom I had not seen since the night when we had spoken about his nagual.

He was sitting the threshold to my room, but he immediately got up and came closer.

"How are you, sir?" he asked. "Is monsieur still sick?"

"Thank you, I am better, my friend. But tell me, Eusebio, were you the person who was singing a moment ago?"

"I hope I didn't disturb your sleep, sir. I wasn't the only one singing, in any case. There are people in the chapel, because it is Sunday. I was singing along softly with the others."

"In Zapotec, Eusebio?"

"Yes, sir, in Zapotec."

I remembered that I had in fact noticed a small chapel right next to Avendaño's house across from the market. From the arcades one could see the sanctuary beneath the coconut trees in the adjoining courtyard. It was a pious tradition to assemble there from time to time on Sunday night. I had the vague recollection that the slow and sweet melody that they had been singing was a cantilena in honor of Our Lady of Guadeloupe, the patron saint of the indigenous people of Mexico, which was also reminiscent of that aria that I had heard long ago. Now that I was completely awake I could no longer hear the child's sweet voice and the song seemed less clear to me. It only came in waves when it wasn't drowned out by the melancholic harmony of trembling palm trees in the wind.

Once again, Eusebio sat at my bedside, after lighting a candle that he had set on the table.

"May I bring you anything, sir?" he asked after a few moments.

"Yes, give me something to drink. I am thirsty."

"Would you prefer lemonade or the *atole* that has been prepared for you, sir?"

"What do you mean? What atole?"

"Oh, it is very good. Don Juan had it prepared and Didjaza explained what should be put in it."

"Eusebio! Not that crazy woman again! What is this gruel?"

"Didjaza is not crazy. She knows more than all your American doctors about what is good or bad for sick people. If you take this atole two or three times, you will be cured of your fever and dysentery."

"Gracious me, this must be quite the cure then! Bring me some."

The young boy went to fetch a bowl in the kitchen and brought it to me filled with a light gruel, that around here is commonly known as *atol*.[B30] I dipped my spoon into it and found it to be not particularly tasty.

"Are you sure," I asked looking up at Eusebio, "that Don Juan recommended giving this to me?"

"Señor, Don Juan told me that you had not eaten anything since morning and that if you were hungry or thirsty, that I should offer you some *atol real*."[78]

"Oh, this atol real! And why is that?"

"That is what we call it in Zapotec, because it is handed down from our former rulers."

"And these are things that you know, Eusebio?"

"Didjaza told me about them, when Don Pancho Portocarrero was sick."

"And this is what cured him?"

"Yes, sir."

With that, I drank down the entire contents of the cup. Almost instantly I felt a great relief. Whatever discomfort I had disappeared and I could feel that I wasn't as feeble as I had thought.

"Eusebio, your atol is quite good," I told him. "You'll give me some more tonight. And after that, if I feel better in a day or two, I

B30. Atol, from the Mexican *atuili*, usually refers to a gruel made of corn or other starches from these regions. [This is also spelled "atole." Brasseur uses both spellings.]

will be able to go to the top of Guiengola," I added looking straight at the young Indian.

"You won't be going to Guiengola," he answered smiling with a shrewd and satisfied look on his face. "I always said that you wouldn't go."

"How's that?"

"You won't be going, I can assure you. In the next few days it will rain quite a bit, but as soon as the weather improves, you will probably leave, just like the Americans."

"The Americans? See here, Eusebio, they certainly are not going to be leaving."

"*Sí señor.* They are getting ready to leave as we speak and this week or next they will all leave together for Chivela . . ."

I was rather astonished. But the young fellow seemed so sure of his facts, that I thought it would be useless to contradict him without any proof. I decided to wait until the next day to confirm the truth of what he was saying. Moreover, I was too content with the effects of the potion he had brought me to badger him anymore with my questions. After the pain that I had experienced, I was now feeling such a sense of well-being thanks to the atole, that I lay back down in a physical and mental state that seemed to bode well. I was too weak to be tempted to chat for any length of time with Eusebio. But, I did ask him for a second bowl, after which I fell gently to sleep, not without thanking God for having restored my good health.

I spent a calm night. When I awoke, the sun was flooding into my room. I felt well rested and serene. I had no more stomach or abdominal pain. As soon as I was dressed, I looked for Avendaño to ask him about the atol he had sent me the previous night. I was told that he had left for Juchitán early in the morning. I later learned that, concerned about an incursion by the Patricios on Tehuantepec, he had decided it was best to protect himself from their brutality, until the governor returned to town. After breakfast, I went to look for Murphy. When I found him, he was busy responding to questions from some of his associates. He seemed uncharacteristically worried and glum.

"Well," he said to me, as he shook my hand, "there will be no excursion. We are leaving for Minatitlán."

"All of you?" I exclaimed, rather surprised and remembering how sure Eusebio had been.

"Yes, all of us. There is nothing more for us to do here. The company is ceasing its operation."

"This is extraordinary! When did this news arrive?"

"The mail arrived last night, after a two-week delay."

Murphy then went into more detail. The negligence and mismanagement of the directors of the Louisiana Tehuantepec Company had compromised everything. As we were already aware, Mr. La Sére, the president of the company, was set to travel on the *Coatzacoalcos* to Minatitlán, two weeks after our departure from New Orleans. Everything was ready. The steamship was ready to sail down the river towards the sea at its usually scheduled departure time. The only thing that was missing was the president. One, two, and then three hours went by. No Mr. La Sére. Everyone knew that he had been in Baton Rouge for several days, involved in his electoral schemes. When he didn't show up, the directors sent him a message via electric telegraph that the steamer was late and was only awaiting his arrival to set off. Mr. La Sére responded with a request that the gentleman grant him another hour explaining that he would be arriving by rail as soon as possible. In general, people thought that this was an arrogant way to act, and that the president was showing great disregard for his customers. They immediately sent another telegraph but this time their message went to New York. They notified the Hargous brothers, the company's main backers and those who had a principle interest in what was happening. They had already received several complaints about the mismanagement of company affairs and the misappropriation of funds by employees, etc. Upon hearing about Mr. La Sére's strange behavior, the Hargous brothers, who had invested more than a million dollars in this enterprise, decided to temporarily suspend payments on the company's bills of exchange that had not yet reached maturity. At the same time, they sent a telegram with orders to stop the mail as well as the departure of the steamer, until they had more information. This was the cause of the delay, which for more than two weeks had thrown the company's representatives on the isthmus into such disarray. In the end, instead of the *Coatzacoalcos*, a much smaller steamer arrived in Minatitlán, carrying two mailbags, but not a single passenger for California. Along with the mail, it also brought the announcement that all employees were being dismissed. They were told that that they could return to New Orleans on the steamship that was waiting in Minatitlán. At the same time, rumor had it that the Hargous brothers' company had gone bankrupt. This was particularly shocking given that they have always had a reputation as one of the most respectable firms in New York. In fact, they had not suspended their payments. They only delayed payment until further notice on bills for the unscrupulous Louisiana Tehuantepec Company. Moreover, we learned that as soon as word spread that payments would be suspended, all the banks in New York unhesitatingly offered to take on their creditors, which the Hargous brothers declined, after explaining the true motives for their actions.

Just imagine the effect that this news produced—especially in the context of the alarming political instability—across the entire isthmus and in the city of Tehuantepec, where the representatives of the Louisiana Tehuantepec Company were universally despised, due to their recklessness, arrogance, and dishonesty. Everyone was united against them. Mr. Sidell, who arrived in Tehuantepec at about this time, did his best to explain that this was just a temporary measure and that the company would pay its debts. The creditors would hear nothing of it. A few days later, acting upon the unanimous demands of those creditors, with the notable exception of Avendaño, the authorities seized all the company's assets from Almoloya to the port of La Ventosa and Tehuantepec.[B31] Murphy and his associates, who were not involved in any of the financial aspects of the company, nonetheless found that they were bearing the brunt of the anger and had no alternative but to return to the United States after having wasted their time with nothing to show for it. Murphy,

---

B31. This seizure was of no use. Less than a month after my departure, a directive was sent to Tehuantepec, signed by the Liberal Party president, Juárez, to lift the sequestration on the company's property.

in particular, seemed quite upset at the prospect of leaving under these circumstances. Nonetheless, he told me that his first order of business was to arrange for his associates' departure. Once that was done, he too would set off with John Hargous.

Young Eusebio had been right. Had his nagual kept him well informed? That is for the reader to decide. There was no doubt about it; the Americans were going to leave the isthmus. And soon, I too would be continuing my travels. In my current state, I was too weak to attempt climbing Guiengola. I would have to wait two or three days. But by the time I was better, the rainy season had resumed its usual course. This was my first obstacle. And then a more serious one emerged. The governor had arrived announcing that he had defeated his enemies after flushing them out of the ravines where they had been lying in wait to ambush his troops. But this had not improved the situation. Both groups were more brazen than ever; the Patricios and the Juchitecos, the victors and the vanquished, were running rampant through the countryside, robbing travelers, pillaging farms and wreaking havoc in villages. The situation was so critical that two American merchants, who had arrived in Tehuantepec from California with the intention of traveling to Mexico City via the Oaxaca road, were afraid of what they might be exposed to, despite being well armed with rifles and revolvers. They decided that it was best to leave with their compatriots for Minatitlán and to make their way to the interior of the country from there. Given the circumstances, there was no hesitation on my part. I had to abandon my trip to Guiengola, much to my dismay and decided instead to head for Guatemala by way of the state of Chiapas.

As soon as I had come to this conclusion, I was eager to leave town at once. My decision coincided with Avendaño's return from Juchitán. He told me that an affable Frenchman in Juchitán, named Alexandre de Gives was eager to make my acquaintance and therefore I had a place to stay. DeGives had been established in Mexico for fifteen years and had made some successful business investments. All the foreigners that I had met on the isthmus and Mexicans of every stripe had spoken to me about him. They praised him for his integrity, kindness, and above all his generous hospitality. With this invitation provided by my host in Tehuantepec, I prepared my departure. With his usual cordiality, Avendaño provided me with a mozo as well as a mount and pack animals for my belongings. I planned to leave for Juchitán on Thursday, June 30.

On the eve of my departure, while I was busy packing, Eusebio came into my room triumphantly. He gave me a small cotton bag with atole flour and told me that it was a gift from Don Juan. Despite my attempts to question him about the composition of this seemingly simple yet mysterious mixture, his constant refrain was quien sabe. It was only much later, while traveling in Chiapas, that I learned the ingredients of this precious porridge. My discussion with Eusebio was interrupted by the arrival of Murphy and Hargous. They had come to say good-bye. They planned on leaving the next day as well. They were making their way to San Geronimo and from there to Suchil. As for their associates, most of them had a taken a head start in company carriages, which Avendaño had persuaded the creditors to temporarily lend out. I was up before five the next morning. After cordially embracing my excellent host to whom I owed so much, I got on my horse, took a left and made my way along the base of the Dani-Guivedchi. Soon I had left behind the high walls of the monastery built by Cocijopij and the beautiful hills of Tehuantepec.

NOTES

Introduction

1. Jorge Skinner Klee was a great bibliophile and collector, whose family has ties with George Ure Skinner (1804–67), a botanist and lepidopterist who was crisscrossing Guatemala at the same time as Brasseur.
2. Michael D. Coe, *Breaking the Maya Code*, rev. ed. (New York: Thames & Hudson, 2012), 101.
3. Coe, *Breaking the Maya Code*, 106.
4. Herbert B. Adams, "Abbé Brasseur de Bourbourg," *Proceedings of the American Antiquarian Society* 6, pt. 3 (1890): 284.
5. Pedro Escalante Arce, *Brasseur de Bourbourg: Esbozo biográfico* (San Salvador: s.n., 1989), 14.
6. Brasseur speaks of Le Vasseur in several insistences, always acknowledging his great debt to him. See for example p. 54 in "From Guatemala City," n. B3. For a portrait of Le Vasseur see Nancy Nichols Barker, *The French Experience in Mexico: 1821–1861: A History of Constant Misunderstanding* (Chapel Hill: University of North Carolina Press, 1979), 118 ff. Barker spells the diplomat's name "Levasseur."
7. Charles Étienne Brasseur de Bourbourg, *Histoire des nations civilisées du Mexique et de l'Amérique-Centrale, durant les siècles antérieurs à Christophe Colomb, écrite sur des documents originaux et entièrement inédits, puisées aux anciennes archives des indigènes* (Paris: Arthus-Bertrand, 1857), 1:x. The Hargous family was heavily involved in the Louisiana Tehuantepec Railway Company that plays a prominent role in Brasseur's *Voyage across the Isthmus of Tehuantepec*. It should be noted that in a later publication Brasseur speaks of having been entrusted with a mission by the Mexican government and the United States envoy, Robert Letcher, regarding the administration of Catholic missions that had formerly been in Mexican territory. Charles Étienne Brasseur de Bourbourg, *Sommaire des voyages scientifiques et des travaux de géographie, d'histoire, d'archéologie et de philologie américaines publiés par M. l'abée Brasseur de Bourbourg* (Saint-Cloud: Imprimerie Mme Veuve Belin, 1862), 4.
8. Charles Étienne Brasseur de Bourbourg, *Lettres pour servir d'introduction à l'histoire primitive des nations civilisées de l'Amérique septentrionale, adressées à Monsieur le duc de Valmy, par l'abbé É.-C. Brasseur de Bourbourg. Cui lus para servir de introducción á la historia primitiva de las naciones civilizadas de la América setentrional, Texte français et traduction espagnole en regard* (Mexico: M. Murguía, 1851).
9. Brasseur, *Histoire des nations* 1:xv. The Bibliothèque nationale in Paris holds a dozen titles, sometimes written under the pseudonym Étienne-Charles de

Ravensberg, with publication dates as early as 1839 and in multiple editions that extend well past the date of his death. Here is a sampling: *Le Sérapéon, épisode de l'histoire du IVe siècle* (Paris: Debécourt, 1839), with another edition in 1853; *La Famille irlandaise, ou les conséquences d'une première faute, ouvrage imité de l'anglais* (Lille: L. Lefort, 1843), this book went through several editions with the latest dated 1888; *Jérusalem, tableau de l'histoire et des vicissitudes de cette ville célèbre depuis son origine la plus reculée jusqu'à nos jours* (Lille: L. Lefort, 1843), the latest edition of which is dated 1860; *Le martyr de la croix, épisode du siège d'Antioche* (Lille: L. Lefort, 1844), the latest edition dated 1883; *Eugénie de Revel, souvenirs des dernières années du XVIIIe siècle* (Lille: L. Lefort, 1845), the latest edition of which is 1885; *Selim, ou le Pacha de Salonique* (Lille: L. Lefort, 1848), the latest edition of which is dated 1883; *Le Khalife de Bagdad, ou l'Exilée, scènes de la vie orientale au IXe siècle* (Paris: Sagnier, et Bray, 1853), the latest edition of which is dated 1894; *Wilhem ou Le pardon du chrétien: histoire du règne de Philippe II* (Lille: L. Lefort, 1849), the latest edition of which is dated 1883; and *Auguste Fauvel* (Lille: L. Lefort, 1843), the latest edition of which is 1869.

10. Unlike his fellow Mayanist, Désiré Charnay, who wrote novels with titles such as *Une princesse indienne avant la conquête* [An Indian Princess Before the Conquest] (Paris: Hachette, 1888), Brasseur never set any of his literary works in the Americas.

11. Brasseur, *Histoire des nations*, 1:xv. In Escalante Arce, *Brasseur de Bourbourg*, 27, the author writes that the vocabulary was sold to John Carter Brown.

12. Brasseur, *Histoire des nations*, 1:xv.

13. Bataillon Marcel, "Mérimée et l'américanisme d'il y a cent ans," *Bulletin Hispanique* 56, no. 4 (1954): 428. Files in the Archives nationales de France in Paris contain documentation from both Brasseur and his supporters making a case for funding his research during the period of the 1854–57 trip. In the end, the responses were a variation on the theme found in a note written in the margin of an official report summarizing Brasseur's request to the Ministre de l'Instruction publique dated July 4, 1855. The handwritten note indicates that the official response was negative. According to the marginalia documenting the final decision, the amount necessary for Brasseur's mission would drain the ministry's entire budget for that year. (Archives Nationales de France, F17/2942.) There is an extremely detailed accounting of Brasseur's letters as well as correspondence from his supporters and official ministry responses related to requests for the funding of his 1854 trip in the extraordinarily well-researched unpublished thesis of Nadia Prévost Urkidi, which Dr. Prévost Urkidi was kind enough to share with me. Nadia Prévost, "Brasseur de Bourbourg et l'émergence de l'Américainisme scientifique en France au XIXe siècle" (Docteur de l'Université diss., Université de Toulouse II, 2007), 421–36.

14. Squier's response was published in French translation in the *Nouvelles annales des voyages, de la géographie, de l'histoire et de l'archéologie*, 148, pt. 4, (1855): 273–85 with the title "Lettre de M. E. G. Squier à propos de la lettre de M. Brasseur de Bourbourg, insérée au cahier des Annales d'août 1855." The text was sent to Alfred Maury in a letter, dated Paris, November 10, 1855. The original letter

in English can be found in the E. G. Squier Papers at the Library of Congress, and I am quoting from that English text.

15. Letter from E. G. Squier to Alfred Maury, dated Paris, November 10, 1855.

16. "From Guatemala City," 62.

17. Carroll Edward Mace, "New Information about Dance-Dramas of Rabinal and the 'Rabinal-Achi'." *Xavier University Studies* 6, no. 1 (1967): 12.

18. Brasseur owed a great deal to Padilla, who gave him a manuscript that Brasseur called at the time Codex Padilla in his honor.

19. The text of this letter and the preceding one were published in Spanish with no mention of translation so it can be assumed that the originals were written in Spanish:

> He descubierto aquí entre los manos de un tío de un criadito mío otro manuscrito; es el texto del diálogo y historia del bayle [sic] antiguo de Rabinal Achi, los héroes de Rabinal y lo poco que he podido averiguar refiere igualmente a los mismos personajes del Ximenes [sic], Padilla, y otros. C'est une bonne trouvaille.

Charles Étienne Brasseur de Bourbourg, "Dos cartas inéditas del Abate Brasseur de Bourbourg, dirigidas al Doctor José Mariano Padilla, fechadas en Rabinal el 23 mayo y 3 de junio de 1855," *Anales de la Sociedad de Geografía e Historia* 16 (1940): 302.

20. Squier later sent Brasseur's letter to the London paper, the *Athenaeum*, after a bit of editing, but the original Brasseur letter, which is written in English, can be found in Squier's papers at the Library of Congress. I am quoting from the original letter and have kept Brasseur's spelling. Squier's edited version was published under the title "A letter from Brasseur de Bourbourg to E. G. Squier, dated Rabinal, August 7, 1855," *Athenaeum*, December 8, 1855, 1435–36.

21. These words are underlined in Brasseur's letter.

22. Brasseur's manuscript letter reads "drive."

23. This is a reference to Karl Ritter von Scherzer (1821–1903), an Austrian scholar who preceded Brasseur in Guatemala by several months. In the seventeenth century, Francisco Ximénez (see "From Guatemala City," n. 13 on p. 254) was given access to the manuscript of the *Popol Vuh* "presumably . . . written by K'iche' lords originally from Utatlán between 1554 and 1558" in Chichicastenango around 1701. Ximénez then translated the original K'iche' text into Spanish, in what Robert Carmack qualifies as a "literal and a paraphrastic version." Robert Carmack, *Quichean Civilization: The Ethnohistoric, Ethnographic and Archeological sources* (Berkeley: University of California Press, 1973), 24–25. In 1857, in Vienna Scherzer is credited with the first translation of the *Popol Vuh* when he published that Spanish translation *Las historias del origen de los Indios de esta provincia de Guatemala, traducidas de la lengua quiché al castellano para mas comodidad de los ministros del S. Evangelio, por el R. P. F. Francisco Ximénez . . . Exactamente segun el texto español del manuscrito original que se halla en la biblioteca de la Universidad de Guatemala, publicado por la primera vez, y aumentado con una introducción y anotaciones, por el D.C. Scherzer* (Vienna: C. Gerold e Hijo, 1857). He also came out with his own travelogue of the region entitled *Wanderungen durch die Mittel-Amerikanischen*

Freistaaten Nicaragua, Honduras und San Salvador, which was published in English translation as *Travels in the free States of Central America: Nicaragua, Honduras, and San Salvador* (London: Longman, Brown, Green, Longmans & Roberts, 1857). Squier omits this mention of Scherzer in his published letter. The history of the transmission of the manuscripts of the *Popol Vuh* as with other Brasseur manuscripts is not exactly crystal clear. In his letter to Squier, Brasseur states that he found the Ximénez manuscript in Guatemala City. In his later publication *Bibliothèque mexico-guatémalienne*, Brasseur provides an inventory of his collection, in which he lists Ximénez manuscripts acquired from Ignacio Coloche in Rabinal. One of these was entitled *Empiezan las historias del origen de los Indios de esta Provinçia de Gvatemala tradvzido de la lengua QUICHE en la Castellana*... which Brasseur explains is a "manuscript in the hand of Father Ximénez" that is the "original *Popol Vuh*" including sections with facing page K'iche'. The last title by Ximénez in his inventory is *Manuscrito Antiguo Kiché, Encontrado á principios del Siglo XVIII entre los Indios del Pueblo de Chichicastenango por el P. F. Francisco Ximenez*..., which the title explains was "faithfully copied by Juan Gavarette" in Guatemala City dated October 23, 1847, and which Brasseur's annotation explains was "copied for the use of Dr. Scherzer and subsequently published in Vienna. This document is a copy of Ximénez's *General History of Guatemala* of which a manuscript copy exists in the library of the university of Guatemala City." Charles Étienne Brasseur de Bourbourg, *Bibliothèque mexico-guatémalienne: précédée d'un coup d'œil sur les études américaines dans leurs rapports avec les études classiques et suivie du tableau par ordre alphabétique des ouvrages de linguistique américaine contenus dans le même volume* (Paris: Maisonneuve, 1871), 156–57. [I have maintained Brasseur's Spanish spelling.]

 24. Brasseur's manuscript letter reads "saw."

 25. "Steady work conquers all," a quotation from Virgil's *Georgics*.

 26. Alain Breton, *Rabinal-Achi: un drame dynastique maya du quinzième siècle* (Nanterre: Société des américanistes & Société d'ethnologie, 1994), 11. When possible, I will cite the English translation of this work, *Rabinal Achi: A Fifteenth-Century Maya Dynastic Drama*, trans. Teresa Lavender Fagan and Robert Schneider (Boulder: University Press of Colorado, 2007); however, this quotation is from a foreword only found in the French edition.

 27. Breton, *Rabinal Achi: Maya Drama*, 1.

 28. René Acuña, *Introducción al estudio del Rabinal Achi* (México: Universidad Nacional Autónoma de México, 1975), xi.

 29. Mace, "New Information," 1.

 30. Charles Étienne Brasseur de Bourbourg, *Gramatica de la lengua quiche: Grammaire de la langue quichée, espagnole-française mise en parallèle avec ses deux dialectes, cakchiquel et tzutuhil, tirée des manuscrits des meilleurs auteurs guatémaliens. Ouvrage accompagné de notes philologiques avec un vocabulaire... et suivi d'un essai sur la poésie, la musique, la danse et l'art servant d'introduction au Rabinal-Achi, drame indigène avec sa musique originale, texte quiché et traduction français en regard* (Paris: Arthus-Bertrand, 1862), 5. Henceforth this work is referred to as Brasseur's *Rabinal Achi*.

31. "From Guatemala City," 92–93. Contemporary ethnographic studies of the dances of the Guatemalan highlands reinforce Brasseur's analysis. Dennis Tedlock writes: "The early missionaries intervened in Mayan theater on a massive scale, substituting Christian hymns for Mayan songs." Dennis Tedlock, *Rabinal Achi: A Mayan Drama of War and Sacrifice* (Oxford: Oxford University Press, 2003), 2. See also Carroll Edward Mace, *Two Spanish-Quiché Dance-Dramas of Rabinal*, Tulane Studies in Romance Languages and Literature, 3 (New Orleans: Tulane University 1970), 9.

32. "From Guatemala City," 94.

33. Carmack, *Quichean Civilization*, 46.

34. "From Guatemala City," 94.

35. Ibid.

36. Brasseur's spelling of this name varies. In Brasseur's *Rabinal Achi* he spells it "Qeché."

37. Breton, *Rabinal Achi: Maya Drama*, 19.

38. Tedlock, *Rabinal Achi*, 16.

39. The rendering of the characters' names varies. Brasseur identifies this character as Ahua Hobtoh in his 1862 publication, but as Goptoh in "From Guatemala" from 1859. Breton identifies him as Job Toj and Tedlock renders his name as Lord Five Thunder.

40. Brasseur also cites him by the name Ahua Galel Rabinal and Tedlock calls him Man of Rabinal.

41. Brasseur also cites him by the name Cavek Queché Achi and identifies him as the prince of the Yaqui people of Cunén and Chajul (which Brasseur spells "Chahul"), and the son of Balam Achi Balam Queché, the king of the K'iche'. Breton calls him Kiché Achi and Tedlock renders his name as Cawek of the Forest People and identifies him as a warrior in the service of the lord of the K'iche'.

42. Breton (*Rabinal Achi: Maya Drama*, 27) says that at least in contemporary stagings these are represented only by an additional two actors.

43. Carmack, *Quichean Civilization*, 45.

44. Mace, "New Information," 18.

45. Carroll Edward Mace, "Charles Etienne Brasseur de Bourbourg, 1814–1874," in *Guide to Ethnohistorical Sources*, ed. Howard Cline, pt. 2 (London: University of Texas Press, 1973), 307.

46. Mace, "New Information," 12.

47. Mace, "New Information," 14.

48. Mace, "New Information," 14.

49. Mace, "New Information," 14, uses both "Ziz" and "Sis."

50. Breton, *Rabinal Achi: Maya Drama*, 11.

51. The emphasis is Brasseur's, the translation is from Breton, *Rabinal Achi: Maya Drama*, 10.

52. Tedlock, *Rabinal Achi*, 6.

53. Tedlock also concludes that Brasseur created the prologue, despite also apparently putting faith in the 1850 date mentioned in it. He maintains that the language of the K'iche' "violates idiomatic usage" and cites as the spelling of Bartolo's name ("Ziz" instead of "Sis") in the prologue as evidence (*Rabinal Achi*, 208).

On the first point, see Carmack in which he analyzes the K'iche' in Sis's prologue. and concludes "This is what one would expect of a Quiche speaker of the 19th century" (*Quichean Civilization*, 46n22). In addition, the examples of Brasseur's idiosyncratic spellings are too numerous to mention, especially for words with *s*, *c*, or *z* sounds. It is also clear that the spelling of many proper names were far from standardized at this time.

54. Breton, *Rabinal Achi: Maya Drama*, 9.
55. Emphasis on "Transcribed for the first time by Bartolo Ziz" is mine.
56. Breton, *Rabinal Achi: Maya Drama*, 11n19.
57. Carmack, *Quichean Civilization*, 229–30.
58. Tedlock, *Rabinal Achi*, 214.
59. "sugar-cane" alcohol.
60. Mace, "New Information," 15.
61. Mace, "New Information," 7.
62. Escalante Arce, *Brasseur de Bourbourg*, 85–88.
63. Brasseur to Léonce Angrand, January 21, 1860, Fonds Angrand, Bibliothèque nationale in Paris.
64. Pierce Butler, *Judah P. Benjamin* (Philadelphia: G. W. Jacobs, 1907), 120.
65. Butler, *Judah P. Benjamin*, 126.
66. *Voyage*, 216.
67. *Voyage*, 216–17.
68. Brasseur, *Bibliothèque mexico-guatémalienne*, xxx–xxxi.
69. Brasseur to Léonce Angrand, January 21, 1860, Fonds Angrand, Bibliothèque nationale in Paris.
70. Charnay wrote about his travels photographing and excavating archaeological sites in his work *Le Mexique, souvenirs et impressions de voyage* (Paris: E. Dentu, 1863).
71. "Excursion de M. l'abbé Brasseur de Bourbourg dans l'Amérique Centrale; son retour à Paris," *Nouvelles Annales des voyages, de la géographie, de l'histoire et de l'archéologie* 168, pt. 4 (1860), 374–75.
72. Coe, *Breaking the Maya Code*, 100.
73. Coe, *Breaking the Maya Code*, 258.
74. Brasseur's translation of Diego de Landa's *Relation des choses de Yucatan de Diego de Landa; texte espagnol et traduction française en regard, comprenant les signes du calendrier et de l'alphabet hiéroglyphique de la langue maya, accompagné de documents divers historiques et chronologiques, avec une grammaire et un vocabulaire abrégés français-maya; précédés d'un essai sur les sources de l'histoire primitive du Mexique et de l'Amèrique Centrale, etc., d'après les monuments égyptiens, et de l'histoire primitive de l'Egypte d'après les monuments américains, par l'abbé Brasseur de Bourbourg* (Paris: A. Durand, 1864), iv. See also Tozzer's English translation: Diego de Landa, *Decipherment: Landa's Relación de las cosas de Yucatán: A Translation*, trans. and ed. Alfred M. Tozzer, Papers of the Peabody Museum of Archaeology and Ethnology 18 (Cambridge: Peabody Museum of Archaeology and Ethnology, 1941).
75. Landa, *Choses De Yucatan*, iv, and Coe, *Breaking the Maya Code*, 101.
76. Later in 1875, "another fragment turned up in Madrid, the so-called *Cortesiano*,

which was soon recognized by Léon de Rosny as part of one and the same codex. Both are now joined in the Museo de América in Madrid, and the entire screen-fold manuscript (with fifty-six leaves painted on both sides, the longest known for the Maya) is known to the scholarly world as the Madrid Codex" (Coe, *Breaking the Maya Code*, 106).

77. While in prison in 1847 for conspiring against King Louis Philippe, the future emperor wrote a pamphlet entitled *Le Canal de Nicaragua, ou projet de junction des Océans Atlantique et Pacifique au moyen d'un canal* (vol. 2, of *Oeuvres de Napoléon III*, Paris: Plon, 1856-59). His wife, Eugènie de Montijo, who was of Spanish birth, longed to see the return of the monarchy to Mexico and had long campaigned for her husband to intervene in that country.

78. Jean-Louis Armand de Quatrefages (1810-92) was a vice-president of the commission. He was a naturalist and the author of works on the emerging field of anthropology.

79. Brasseur to Léonce Angrand, January 20, 1864, revised January 24, 1864, Fonds Angrand, Bibliothèque nationale in Paris.

80. Escalante Arce, *Brasseur de Bourbourg*, 172

81. Coe, *Breaking the Maya Code*, 101.

82. Other contemporary Mayanists, who made important contributions to the field and wrote about the possible communication between the Old World and Mesoamerican civilizations, are Edward H. Thompson, "Atlantis Not a Myth," *Popular Science Monthly* 15 (1879): 759-64; Augustus Le Plongeon, author of *Vestiges of the Mayas, or, Facts tending to prove that communications and intimate relations must have existed, in very remote times, between the inhabitants of Mayab and those of Asia and Africa* (New York: J. Polhemus, 1881); and Léon de Rosny, *L'Atlantide historique: études d'ethnographie et d'archéologie américaines* (Paris: Leroux, 1902).

83. Brasseur, *Bibliothèque mexico-guatémalienne*, xxviii.

84. *Arte de la Lengua Chiapaneca*, cited in Brasseur, *Bibliothèque mexico-guatémalienne*, 5. *Arte* was published in 1875 by August Pinart, who bought Brasseur's library after the abbé's death. See Juan de Alboronz, *Arte de la lengua chiapaneca, compuesto por el M. R. padre fray Juan de Albornoz; y Doctrina cristiana en la misma lengua escrita por el padre mtro fray Luis Barrientos* (Paris: E. Leroux, 1875).

85. Brasseur provides the following information: Cura de Taktic. *Confesionario en lengua Kahchi* (1812), en metodo breve, escrito por un padre cura de la orden de Santo Domingo del pueblo de Taktic, año 1812. Brasseur, *Bibliothèque mexico-guatémalienne*, 52.

86. Alfred P. Maudslay, *Biologia Centrali-Americana, or Contributions to the Knowledge of the Fauna and Flora of Mexico and Central America*, vols. 55-59, *Archaeology*, with appendix by J. T. Goodman (London: R. H. Porter and Dulau, 1889-1902). On Maudslay, see Ian Graham's biography *Alfred Maudslay and the Maya: A Biography* (Norman: Oklahoma University Press, 2002).

87. Joseph T. Goodman, "The Archaic Maya Inscriptions," appendix to Maudslay, *Archeology*, vi.

88. Ibid.

89. Ibid.

"Notes from a Voyage in Central America"

1. Published: "Notes d'un voyage dans l'Amérique Centrale: Lettres à M. Alfred Maury," *Nouvelles annales des voyages, de la géographie, de l'histoire et de l'archéologie* 147, pt. 3 (1855): 129–58.

2. Louis Ferdinand Alfred Maury (1817–92) was a librarian at the Institut de France starting in 1844 and a scholar of archeology as well as ancient and modern languages. In 1862 he became a professor at the Collège de France and was a cofounder of the École des Hautes Études.

3. Joseph Marius Alexis Aubin (1802–91). From 1830 to 1840 Aubin was in Mexico as part of a scientific expedition when his interest in the ancient civilization of the country was sparked. He began to collect rare documents. His most notable acquisition was a vast collection that had once belonged to Lorenzo Boturini. This trove of documents, which the Italian had been forced to abandon in Mexico after his arrest in 1743, had been left more or less untouched "like Sleeping Beauty" until Aubin acquired it. After returning to France in 1840 Aubin devoted the rest of his life to the publication of rare documents as well as studies on the languages and figurative writing of ancient Mexico. In 1857 he was, along with Brasseur, one of the founders of the Société Américaine de France, and later he was a member of the Scientific Mission to Mexico (1864–67), but by that time he had become increasingly withdrawn and paranoid. His collection was bought by Eugène Goupil, who also eventually acquired Brasseur's collection from Alphonse Pinart. Today, Goupil's collection constitutes the majority of the *fonds américains* of the Bibliothèque nationale in Paris. Albert Réville, "Antiquités mexicaines: les aventures de la collection Aubin-Goupil," *Revue des bibliothèques* 8 (1896): 122–27. See also Michael W. Swanton and Jacqueline de Durand-Forest, "Un regard historique sur les fonds mexicains de la Bibliothèque nationale de France," *Journal de la Société des Américanistes* 84, no. 2 (1998): 9–19.

4. Brasseur is referring to the bombardment and destruction of Greytown by the USS *Cyane*, a United States Navy sloop, in July 1854.

5. Brasseur is referring to Cornelius Vanderbilt's Accessory Transit Company, which established a route through Greytown that brought passengers from New York to California. Like the Isthmus of Tehuantepec, which Brasseur traveled across in 1859, this area was the focus of speculation for those looking for a quick transit route between California and the East Coast of the United States, and there were several attempts to build a canal across Nicaragua.

6. Fruto Chamorro (1804–55) served as the first president of Nicaragua from 1853 to 1855, thus coinciding with Brasseur's arrival in the country.

7. Francisco Castellón (1815–55) was named president of Nicaragua on June 11, 1854, by the liberal faction and served until 1855, during the period when Brasseur traveled through the area.

8. Brasseur's text misspells this as "Foro" and later as "Poro."

9. According to the 1870s map "Panoramic View of the Nicaragua Canal," Lake Nicaragua was 56.5 miles long, with an average width of 40 miles, and the canal was 110 feet above sea level. "Panoramic View of the Nicaragua Canal" (New York:

Julius Bien & Co., 187-), available at the Library of Congress Geography and Map Division online, https://www.loc.gov/item/ (accessed July 5, 2016).

10. Today known as Ometepe.

11. Today known as Maderas.

12. According to William Scroggs the distance from San Juan del Sur to Virgin Bay was twelve miles. *Filibusters and Financiers: The Story of William Walker and His Associates* (New York: Russell & Russell, 1916), 80.

13. Scroggs describes the road from La Virgen to San Juan del Sur:

> at first [the ride] was made on mules over a bridle path through very rugged country, and the discomforts were serious especially for women and children. In 1854, however, the macadamized road was completed, and comfortable carriages were placed upon it. Each of these were painted in the national colours of Nicaragua, white and blue, and was drawn by four mules. The vehicles would move in a line of twenty-five at a time, carrying the passengers of the latest ship to arrive and being followed by the many wagons conveying freight and baggage. *Filibusters and Financiers*, 80.

14. John Hill Wheeler (1806–82) was the United States minister to Nicaragua from 1855 to 1856.

15. The term translates as the "highroad," "Royal Highway," or "King's Highway."

16. When the city was founded in the seventeenth century, it was given the name Purísima Concepción de Rivas de Nicaragua. Brasseur is perhaps referring to Patricio Rivas, who, in October 1855, was selected by William Walker to serve as president of Nicaragua. William Walker (1824–60) was the American filibuster who led an invasion of Nicaragua in 1856 and eventually usurped that country's presidency.

17. Today known as Mombacho.

18. Brasseur is no doubt referring to E. G. Squier (see "Introduction," 8), *Nicaragua: Its People, Scenery, Monuments and the Proposed Interoceanic Canal* (New York: D. Appleton, 1852).

19. Émile-Jean Horace Vernet (1789–1863). Vernet was known for his paintings depicting great military scenes and Orientalist subjects as well as religious themes.

20.

> The face of the rock upon the left side was comparatively smooth and literally covered with figures rudely cut in outline. A few were still distinct, but most were so much obliterated that they could not be made out with any degree of satisfaction. Many were covered with the fallen debris, and the earth which the rains had brought down; and still others were carved so high up on the precipitous rocks, that their character could not be ascertained. They covered the face of the cliffs for more than a hundred yards, and consisted chiefly of rude representations of animals and men, with some ornamented and perhaps arbitrary figures, the significance of which is now unknown.... [In one section] there seems to have been an attempt at delineating the sun in two

places, and perhaps also to record some event, for it is a plausible supposition that the straight marks [seen in one area] were intended for numerals. The principal right hand figure of this section seems to have been designed to represent a shield, arrows, or spears and the *xiuatlatli*, or aboriginal instrument for throwing spears, which are frequently grouped in similar manner in the Mexican paintings. The principal figure in the inferior section is evidently intended to represent a monkey. Squier, *Nicaragua*, 2:23–24.

21. Today known as Cerro Asososca.
22. Today known as Volcán Rota.
23. Brasseur's text spells this "Felica," but this is no doubt a typographical error.
24. Also called Volcán San Cristóbal.
25. Brasseur discusses the early history of Nicaragua and this place name in his *Histoire des nations* 2:chap. 3 (see in particular 111nn5, 7). He cites both Juan de Torquemada and Fernández de Oviedo as his sources. Torquemada writes: "El Sitio, donde està sentada esta Cuidad de Leon, se llama, en Lengua de los Naturales, Nagarando." *Primera[-tercera] parte de los veinte i vn libros rituales i monarchia indiana: con el origen y guerras, de los indios ocidentales, de sus poblaçones: descubrimiento, conquista, conuersion, y otras cosas marauillosas de la mesma tierra* (Madrid: En la oficina y acosta de Nicolas Rodriguez Franco, 1723) 1:330. Oviedo's *Histoire du Nicaragua* uses the place name León de Nagarando throughout the text. Fernández de Oviedo y Gonzalo Valdés, *Histoire du Nicaragua* (Paris: Arthus-Bertrand, 1840).
26. Narciso López (1797–1851), who was born in Venezuela, advocated annexation of Cuba by the United States. After leading a failed uprising in Cuba, he fled to the United States, from where he led a failed expedition to liberate Cuba from Spain in 1851.
27. The Mangue Indians are also known as the Chorotega Indians. Torquemada, *Monarchia Indiana*, 1:330.
28. Trique, Chiapanec, and Subtiaba are now considered extinct languages of the Oto-Manguean family.
29. Francisco Hernández de Toledo (1514–87). Hernández's work, which had a complicated editorial history, was published by Antonio Nardo Recchi under one of its several titles as *Noua plantarum, animalium et mineralium Mexicanorum historia* (Rome: sumptibus B. Deuersini, & Z. Masotti, typis V. Mascardi, 1651). For more on the story of the publication of this manuscript see Silvia de Renzi, "Writing and Talking of Exotic Animals," in *Books and the Sciences in History*, ed. Marina Frasca-Spada and Nick Jardine (Cambridge: Cambridge University Press, 2000), 151–70.
30. Brasseur refers to this language and those who spoke it as Tzendal here and elsewhere. I have used modern spelling for languages throughout.
31. Odin and his son Thor are major gods in Germanic and especially Norse mythology.
32. José Mariano Padilla (1810–69), a Guatemalan doctor who was instrumental in putting several important manuscripts in Brasseur's hands, was the

owner of a "collection of books and papers which may be considered the most complete library of Americana in Central America" [according to Brasseur and was a] generous and disinterested person, and a friend of other students working in this field.... In the case of Brasseur de Bourbourg, Padilla's generosity went so far as to present him with some of the documents from his valuable collection. Adrián Recinos and Delia Goetz, *Annals of the Cakchiquels* (Norman: University of Oklahoma Press, 1953), 5–6.

In Arce's biography of Brasseur he writes that what Brasseur called the Padilla Codex is not mentioned again after 1855 nor does it appear under that name in Brasseur's *Bibliothèque mexico-guatémalienne* (1871): "it was lost or was given a different name." Arce suggests that perhaps the Padilla Codex was the same text as a Kaqchikel manuscript found by Juan Gavrette in 1845, which later became known as the *Annals of the Cakchiquels*. Escalante Arce, *Brasseur de Bourbourg*, 62–63. See also Horacio Figueroa Marroquín, *Biografía del doctor José Mariano Padilla* (Guatemala: Editorial Cultura, 1998).

33. Brasseur is referring to Tullan, a lake in Sweden. In Allen Christenson's *Popol Vuh: The Sacred Book of the Maya, The Great Classic of Central American Spirituality Translated from the Original Maya Text* he writes:

> According to the *Popol Vuh*, the founders of the various Quichean lineages traveled a great distance eastward "across the sea" to an epi-Toltec city called Tulan Zuyva where they received their titular gods and tokens of kingship. ... Tulan is a Nahua word meaning "place of reeds," or more broadly "city," in the same sense that it is filled with a great multitude of people as reeds crowd the shores of a lake or river. Many major Toltec-influenced ceremonial and administrative centers were therefore called Tulan. As a result, it is difficult to identify precisely which Tulan the Quiché progenitors saw as the origin of their power, although it was likely located somewhere on the Yucatán Peninsula.... Chichén Itzá, or its successor Mayapan, are good possibilities for this Tulan. (Norman: University of Oklahoma Press, 2007), 29.

34. Responding to this section of Brasseur's letter E. G. Squier addressed his own letter to Alfred Maury, in which he reacted strongly to Brasseur's theory:

> There are no earnest investigators in any department of science, who have not had frequent occasion to regret the too rapid and sweeping generalizations of men engaged in kindred pursuits. The temptation to create startling effects by startling enunciations and deductions often overcomes that cautious reserve which the true student is always most anxious to maintain; and however much we may admire scientific zeal it degenerates into something worse than ignorance when it carries its possessor beyond the domain of rigid criticism or seduces him into a careless statement of fact.
>
> Without intending these remarks to apply to your correspondent [Brasseur] I nevertheless cannot help thinking that he is compromising the dignity of his subject, and needlessly imperiling the value which would otherwise attach to his investigations and conclusions, in throwing out even interrogatively, the

hypothesis of a Northern European or possible Scandinavian origin for the Indians of Central America. The field of positive investigation is wide enough for the exercise of the great zeal both in the accumulation and combination of facts, and there can be no excuse for mere speculations and points, which if they shall ever be reached, lie in the distant development of the subject. Unfortunately, for American Archeology, its study has seldom been pursued on those sound inductive principles, to which we are indebted for whatever real progress the world has made in the various departments of human knowledge.... Instead of studying the American nations, their languages, religions, organizations, monuments and relations *per se* these legitimate subjects of investigation have been neglected for crude speculations on the subject of the origin, in which only such facts and even those loosely collected as favored the foregone conclusions of the writer have been presented to the consideration of the reader. Europe, Asia, Africa, and the Islands of the sea, Jew and Gentile, Scandinavian, Phoenician and Hindou [*sic*], have been alternately assigned the honor of spreading themselves over the American continent and of originating a race, which if we may accept the conclusions of Physiological science, differs equally from them all, as they differ from each other! They have been led by long and circuitous routes from Tartarian deserts, over an ocean bridged with ice, and through regions of darkness and eternal snow from one Aleutian island to another in bark canoes, drifted across the broad Pacific in open boats and unwieldy junks, and finally it would seem, are to be carried across the stormy northern Atlantic to Greenland past the dreary wastes of Labrador, through the vast forest and over the arid plains and volcanic regions of North America, to people the plateaus of Guatemala! If any possible wandering, exposures, changes of climate or amount of suffering could be supposed capable of changing the fair skinned, light-haired, blue-eyed Northman into the Central American Indian, with his dark skin, black eyes and long coarse black hair, certainly this hypothetical journey must have been adequate to produce the startling result!

... It may well be doubted if this question of origins be one capable of satisfactory solution, it is certainly one which should not be approached rashly so far as the American Indians are concerned in the present state of American Archaeology. And I am sure that true students throughout the world will accept with more gratitude a well-digested series of facts on the languages, manners, organizations, religions and monuments of Central America, than any number of hypotheses however startling or supported by speculations however plausible, or however agreeable to foregone conclusions and vulgar prejudices.

I can only say that after a residence of upwards of two years and a half in Central America, after having traversed its territories for thousands of miles in various directions, studied its people, their language, monuments and traditions, I have failed to discover a single fact, in any of these departments of research, which would necessarily indicate an extra-American and least of all a Scandinavian origin for the aboriginal inhabitants of that country.

I am ready to admit, at the same time, that many resemblances, in some cases, perhaps amounting to absolute identities, exist between the aboriginal families of America, and those of the continent which we are accustomed to distinguish as the "Old World." But the philosophical mind will hesitate in deducing descent or even relationship from the fact, before enquiring how far similar conditions and like constitutions, mental, moral and physical may serve to approximate institutions, religions and monuments to a common or cognate type. In the departments of physiology and philology, it may be said with scarcely any qualification, that nothing has been discovered, which would identify any of the American nations (with the probable exception of the Esquimaux [sic]) with any of those of the old world. In their cosmogony, some of their religious superstitions, symbols and structures and in their astronomical computations and signs, we find, as I have said many resemblances. But if these be admitted to indicate communication, they indicate that the latter must have taken place at the remotest assignable period.... In their general institutions and habits, as well as in their arts the coincidences which the American nations exhibit with those of the Old World, are apparently founded in the necessities of human life.

This was published in French translation in *Nouvelles annales des voyages, de la géographie, de l'histoire et de l'archéologie*, 148, pt. 4 (1855): 273–85, under the title "Lettre de M. Squier à propos de la letter de M. Brasseur de Bourbourg, insérée au cahier des *Annales* d'août 1855," credited to Alfred Maury. The text was sent to Maury in a letter, written in English, which is in the E. G. Squier Papers at the Library of Congress. I am quoting from this English original and maintaining the original spelling and usage.

"From Guatemala City to Rabinal"

1. Originally published: Charles Étienne Brasseur de Bourbourg, "De Guatemala à Rabinal: Episode d'un séjour dans l'Amerique Centrale pendant les années 1855 et 1856," *Revue Européenne: Lettres, sciences, arts, voyages, politiques* 1 (1859):46–74, 275–301.
2. Tax collector.
3. Muleteer. Brasseur spells this "moço" throughout (see *Voyage*, p. 187, n. B24).
4. Brasseur is referring to his first trip to the region in 1848.
5. The Siege of Sevastopol, the final and determining battle of the Crimean War, was being fought while Brasseur was traveling in Guatemala from 1854 to 1855. Sevastopol was taken in September 1855.
6. José Rafael Carrera Turcios (1814–65) dominated Central American and Guatemalan politics for three decades. In 1854, the year before Brasseur arrived in Guatemala, Carrera was made president for life. By 1855, the conservative Carrera had acted to reverse key elements of the liberal agenda such as allowing for the return of monastic orders and the archbishop to the country.
7. Alexander von Humboldt's (1769–1859) work on Mexico and South America ushered in an era of European interest in Mexico and South America, which had

been cut off from travelers and scholars until the start of the nineteenth century. He traveled throughout the region from 1799 to 1804 and produced his widely admired works which include *Vues des Cordillères et monuments des peuples indigènes de l'Amérique*, which was originally published in French (Paris: F. Schoell, 1810). See also Alexander von Humbolt, *Views of the Cordilleras and Monuments of the Indigenous Peoples of the Americas*, trans. J. Ryan Poynter, ed. Vera M. Kutzinski and Ottmar Ette (Chicago: University of Chicago Press, 2012).

8. Brasseur consistently spells this "Utlatlan."

9. In Brasseur's translation of the *Popol Vuh* he explains: "Oxib Quieh and Belheb Tzi [sic], from the twelfth generation of kings. They reigned when Donadiu arrived and were hung by the Castellans." In a footnote Brasseur adds:

> Oxib Quieh (Three Deer), Beleheb Tzy (Nine Dogs), were named based on the signs of the calendar. Donadiu is *Tonatiuh*, "the Brillance," which is the name of the sun, and was the name that the Mexicans gave Alvarado... Oxib Quieh and Beleheb Tzi, Ahpop and Ahpop Camha, the last of the true K'iche' kings, were drawn into a trap by Alvarado, and sentenced to be burned alive. According to certain sources this sentence was executed, whereas according to others, they were strangled or hung first and then burnt. Charles Étienne Brasseur de Bourbourg, *Popol Vuh. Le Livre Sacré Et Les Mythes De L'antiquité Américaine: Avec Les Livres Héroïques Et Historiques Des Quichés. Ouvrage Original Des Indigènes De Guatémala, Texte Quiché Et Traduction Française En Regard* (Paris: Arthus-Bertrand, 1861), 339.

In Brasseur's *Histoire des nations* he describes the summary trial and execution:

> History hasn't provided us the details of this terrible tragedy, in which Alvarado, who was nothing more than Cortés's lieutenant, designated himself as the supreme judge of the sovereigns of a powerful independent kingdom.... We don't know how the court, who had been taken prisoner with their sovereigns... reacted to this extraordinary sentence. We do know that as they were marched towards their execution, Oxib Queh and Beleheb Tzy confessed, apparently overwhelmed by horror...." Brasseur, *Histoire des nations*, 4:646.

As a point of comparison with contemporary scholarship, in Allen Christenson's translation of the *Popol Vuh* he explains that

> Donadiu (or Tonatiu) was the name given to Don Pedro Alvarado, the Spanish captain of Hernán Cortés who conquered the highland Maya region of what is today Guatemala. [Donadiu] is the Quiché Maya version of Tonatiuh (Nahua for "sun, heat"), the name by which Alvarado was known to the Aztecs and his Tlaxcalan mercenaries. He likely received this nickname because of his blonde hair, a physical trait unknown in the Precolumbian New World (other than albinos, which are still called "children of the sun" in many Quiché communities). The name may have had further significance for the Quichés, however. Earlier in the *Popol Vuh* text, the appearance of a

Note to Page 61

new sun represented the death of the old world and the establishment of new, divinely sanctioned political power. Alvarado as the new "sun" destroys the old world and its gods inaugurating a new age.

Christenson continues:

> Following a brief and disastrous defensive campaign . . . the Quiché lords Oxib Quieh and Beleheb Tzi invited Pedro Alvarado and his conquering army to enter their capital city of Cumarcah without resistance on March 7, 1524. Once inside the city, Alvarado suspected treachery and ordered the arrest, torture and execution of the lords. The following is taken from his report to Hernán Cortés: "And I saw that by occupying their land and burning it I could bring them into the service of His Majesty. Thus I decided to burn the lords.". . . The Cakchiquel version of this incident, as recorded in the *Annals of the Cakchiquels*, confirms that the Quiché lords were burned: "Then [the Spaniards] went forth to the city of Gumarcaah, where they were received by the kings, the Ahpop and the Ahpop Qamahay, and the Quichés paid them tribute. Soon the kings were tortured by Tunatiuh. On the day 4 Qat [March 7, 1524] the kings Ahpop and Ahpop Qamahay were burned by Tunatiuh. The heart of Tunatiuh was without compassion for the people during the war. . . ." Fray Bartolomé de las Casas believed that the Quiché lords were executed for failing to satisfy Alvarado's demand for gold, which is rare in Guatemala: "Guiltless of other fault and without trial or sentence, he immediately ordered them to be burned alive. . . ." The "hanging" mentioned in this passage of the *Popol Vuh* likely refers not to the execution of the lords, which was by flame, but rather to the torture and elicitation of confessions mentioned by both Alvarado and the Cakchiquel document. [Dennis] Tedlock [in his notes to his translation of the *Popol Vuh* explains] that the method for obtaining such confessions, according to the Spanish methods of the time, was to hang a prisoner by the wrists while inflicting various types of torture. Undoubtedly this must have been done in a very public way to have impressed the authors of the text writing decades after the events. Christenson, *Popol Vuh*, 294–96nn855–58, citing Recinos and Goetz, *Annals of the Cakchiquels* and Dennis Tedlock, *Popol Vuh: The Mayan Book of the Dawn of Life*, rev. ed. (New York: Simon and Schuster, 1996). [I have kept the variations in spelling for proper names as written in the cited material.]

10. Santo Tomás de Castillo was settled by Belgium, starting in 1843. The territory was administered by the Compagnie belge de colonisation, a private Belgian company under the protection of King Leopold I of Belgium. The living conditions were extremely difficult for the settlers, who lacked food and soon fell victim to disease. In 1854, the year prior to Brasseur's arrival in Guatemala, the Belgian company withdrew from the unprofitable concession. See Belgium Consulate, *Santo-Tomas. Rapport de M. Cloquet, consul de Belgique à Guatemala, sur la situation de la colonie de Santo-Tomas, au 1er janvier, 1850* (Bruxelles: Imprimerie de Deltombe, 1851).

11. Francisco Morazán (1792–1842) was the last president of the Federal Republic of Central America from 1830–39. Rafael Carrera's forces in Guatemala overthrew Morazán's supporters by March 1840.

12. Francisco Castellón (see "Notes from a Voyage," n. 7 on p. 246).

13. Brasseur is referring to the *Popol Vuh*. Carmack calls Francisco Ximénez (1666–ca. 1729) "the foremost linguist and ethnographer of Quichean culture during the colonial period." *Quichean Civilization*, 189. Ximénez was the Dominican priest who made the only surviving copy of the K'iche' text of the *Popol Vuh* and translated it into Spanish, while serving as the parish priest in Chichicastenango between 1701 and 1703. The K'iche' text was most likely written down by "Quiche lords originally from Utatlán (who may have moved [to Chichicastenango] shortly after the conquest), between 1554 and 1558." Carmack, *Quichean Civilization*, 25. Ximénez would later serve as the priest of Rabinal from 1704 to 1714. The story of how the Ximénez manuscript came into being is quite instructive in the context of Brasseur's transcription of *Rabinal Achi*. In his translation of the *Popol Vuh*, Christenson explains:

> The text of the *Popol Vuh* was kept hidden by indigenous elders for centuries in the town of Chichicastenango in Guatemala. So successful were these efforts to preserve early Colonial texts that two hundred years after the Conquest, . . . Ximénez wrote that the people of that town possessed many ancient books, including the manuscript of the *Popol Vuh*. Ximénez wrote that these books were kept in secret so that local Christian authorities would not learn of them. Far from being forgotten tales, he found that these texts were "the doctrine which they first imbibed with their mother's milk, and that all of them know it almost by heart." Ximénez was able to convince the elders who kept the *Popol Vuh* manuscript to allow him to borrow it for the purpose of making a copy. *Popol Vuh*, 22

Since that time, that original manuscript has not been seen. Carmack states: "From my experience in modern Quiche Indian communities, I would suggest that the original manuscript is still in the possession of the *principales* of Chichicastenango, though this is denied by officials of the *municipio*." *Quichean Civilization*, 25.

14. A reduction, from Spanish *reducción*, is a village or colony of South American Indians converted and governed by the Jesuits.

15. Municipal officer with administrative and judicial functions.

16. This is the Latin word for the female headdress of Egyptians. Alexander von Humboldt makes the same comparison in his *Views of the Cordilleras*, 17–20, when describing the bust of an Aztec Priestess.

17. Brasseur uses the Spanish term *fiscal* throughout his text. This term may refer to a layperson who assists the pastor and plays a role in managing the functions of a church. The term could also refer to a church constable or *alguacil eclesiástico*.

18. A mestizo, according to the *Compilation of Colonial Spanish Terms* (s.v. "Mestizo/a") is a "mixture of Spaniard and Indian. Person of mixed European and Indian blood."

19. From Nahuatl, the tlamama were Indian porters who carried loads on their backs (whether people or goods).

20. The Plátanos River seems too far east and given the route that Brasseur describes it is not clear that he would have to cross this river to get to Rabinal.

21. Elsewhere this is *ru qux huyu*. In the translation of the *Annals of the Cakchiquels* by a contemporary of Brasseur, Daniel Garrison Brinton:

> The ambiguity of the word *huyu* here as often offers difficulty in ascertaining the precise sense of the original. It means mountain or hill, woods, or forest or simply place or locality. While *qux* means literally "heart" it also has the sense "soul, spirit." Hence the phrase may be translated "the Spirit of the Forest" or "of the Mountain." Brasseur prefers the latter, while I lean to the former. Daniel Garrison Brinton, Francisco Díaz Gebuta Quej, and Francisco Hernández Arana Xajilá, *The Annals of the Cakchiquels: the Original Text, With a Translation, Notes And Introduction* (Philadelphia: s.n., 1885), 200.

22. "Sir, there is the capital."

23. In Brasseur's 1862 publication of *Rabinal Achi* he writes that this is a mountain range that extends to north of the Rabinal plain and where the ruins of Cakyug are located. In Tedlock's *Rabinal Achi* (177, 345), Chi Tikiram is the place he calls "Pitted and Planted," three kilometers from B'alamwak (Standing Jaguar), near the northeast corner of the lands of the town of Joyabaj.

24. From Nahuatl, a teocalli is an ancient Mexican or Central American place of worship, usually consisting of a truncated pyramid surmounted by a temple.

25. Adrián Recinos (and Goetz, *Annals*, 66) writes that this place name means "the Great Pokom," and that "it was in ancient times an important center of population and today is an archeological site a short distance from the modern town of Rabinal."

26. Perhaps Brasseur is referring to the ruins of Xokoc.

27. I have kept Brasseur's spelling, alternatives are "Tzamaneb" and "Zamaneb." This is where the Rabinaleb settled on the ridge separating the current basins of Cubulco, Rabinal, and Joyabaj, according to Alain Breton (*Rabinal Achi*, 20–21). According to Recinos (and Goetz, *Annals*, 80), "in the Zamaneb Mountain came the dawn for the Rabinals."

28. Also spelled "Meauan." This is mentioned in the *Popol Vuh* as the mountain beneath which Hunahpú and Xbalanque defeat Zipacna. In Brasseur's translation of the *Popol Vuh* (39) he writes: "this is a tall mountain, with the Chixoy or Lacandon River—a branch of the Usumacinta River—flowing to its south and east." Dennis Tedlock suggests that it is "possibly located within the great bend of the Río Negro or Chixoy north of Rabinal." *Popol Vuh*, 347. Allen Christenson writes that "Meauan . . . is likely the mountain known today as Miagua, located some 20 KM northwest of Rabinal and bordering the Chixoy River." *Popol Vuh*, 105.

29. Although Brasseur writes "Chirun," he is most likely is referring to the locality outside Rabinal called Chirrum.

30. "The Land of War," whereas Vera Paz translates as "True Peace."

31. Brasseur spells this "aguazil," which is, according to the *Compilation of Colonial Spanish Terms* (s.v. "alguacils"), a constable or peace officer and a title used by both civil and ecclesiastical officers. Again, I would like to thank Allen

Christenson (e-mail communication, November 16, 2015) for his comments to me on this passage. He points out that the alguacils are the "symbolic guardians and protectors of the cofradía officials." The weapons they carry are not the "vestiges of sovereign power" that Brasseur might interpret them as, rather they aid the alguacil in crowd control.

32. "And we, the children of this city of Rabinal, all hope that Your Worship will reign over us for a long time!"

33. "French priest."

34. This is a Spanish official in charge of a province or district; a local magistrate and administrator with jurisdiction over an Indian polity.

35. "Our mother."

36. Brasseur spells this "bayle."

37. This translates as "kissing of the hand." Brasseur is most likely using it here to refer to the act of hand kissing that occurs after a priest has celebrated his first mass.

38. This is a dance mentioned in the *Popol Vuh*. In Brasseur's translation of that text he writes of this dance: "[This] is a very curious ballet that is still performed today in Guatemala amongst the Indians. They perform it during certain yearly festivals, wearing extremely well-made wooden masks, representing the different characters as well as corresponding costumes. Each one of these ballets or plays has its own masks, costumes and music." *Popol Vuh*, 112–13n1.

39. Xtzul is a "centipede." This dance is mentioned in the *Popol Vuh*. In Christenson's *Popol Vuh* (180), in the section entitled "The Resurrection of Hunahpú and Xbalanque," Hunahpú and Xbalanque

> appeared again as two poor orphans. They wore rags in front and rags on their backs. Rags were thus all they had to cover themselves. But they did not act according to their appearance when they were seen by the Xibalbans. They danced the Armadillo and the Whippoorwill and the Dance of the Weasel. They danced the Armadillo and the Centipede.

In a footnote the translator describes the form that this ceremonial dance took, citing two seventeenth-century vocabularies:

> The Varea dictionary lists *xts'ul* as "a dance with small masks and macaw tail feathers." During this dance, participants put sticks down their throats (like sword swallowers), bones in their noses, and give themselves hard blows on their chests with a large stone. Basseta also defines this as a dance, in which masked performers with tortoiseshell rattles put sticks or daggers in their mouths (like sword swallowers). A variant name for centipede is *Q'uq'kumatz* (Feathered Serpent), indicating this may be a dance in honor of that creator deity. Christenson, *Popol Vuh*, 180n416.

In a note in Brasseur's *Popol Vuh* (176n3), he writes of the dances mentioned in the text: "These are the names of staged entertainment that are sometimes only mimicry, but sometimes have elements of dance, dialogue, or music. Most of them are still practiced in the Indian population."

40. Domingo Juarros (1752–1820) was the author of a history of Guatemala entitled *Compendio de la historia de la ciudad de Guatemala* (Guatemala: I Beteta, 1808–10).

41. In his introductory remarks to the *Popol Vuh*, in which Brasseur ironically enough dismisses Ordoñez for his association with fringe theories of the origins of the Mesoamerican people, Brasseur writes that Roman de Ordoñez y Aguiar, the late eighteenth-century Canon of San Cristóbal de Chiapas, Mexico,

> seems to have been the first person with knowledge of the historic works of Ximénez and the first to have used the translation of his Quiché manuscript [the *Popol Vuh*]. He copied that document, altering it completely, in order to incorporate it into his indigestible *Historia del cielo y de la tierra*, in which he attempts to establish that Votan, ... was the descendant of ... the Canaanites, who had been chased from Palestine by Joshua, and who emigrated to the Canary Islands and then purportedly continued on to the West Indies. His primary objective was to prove that Quetzalcoatl was none other than Thomas the Apostle, who had supposedly been miraculously carried from India to America to preach the Gospel. Ordoñez's work ... was lost with the pillaging of the Library of Guatemala. But drafts of the first volume, with a few fragments of the second, ... were placed in the archives of the National Museum in Mexico City, which is where I transcribed them in 1849. This is how I learned of Ximénez, whose name, along with Ordoñez's, was revealed for the first time to the public in the biography that I wrote of them in the first of my [*Lettres pour servir d'introduction à l'histoire primitive de nations civilisées de l'Amérique septentrionale*] published in Mexico in 1851. Brasseur, *Popol Vuh*, xiv.

42. Brasseur spells his name "Ciz" in this 1859 text. In his 1862 publication of *Rabinal Achi* (18) he spells the name "Ziz." But according to Pedro Escalante Arce, documents in the archives of Rabinal record his name as "Sis." *Brasseur de Bourbourg*, 91n78.

43. This is one of Brasseur's several accounts of this moment, which has been analyzed in detail by later scholars. For some the very integrity of Brasseur's *Rabinal Achi* rests on these few words. In this 1859 account Brasseur writes: "Il termina en me proposant de l'écrire sous sa dictée." (He concluded by suggesting that he could dictate it to me.) "De Guatemala à Rabinal," 288. However, in his published translation of *Rabinal Achi* from 1862, his turn of phrase is slightly different: "Il termina en me proposant de le transcrire à mon tour sous sa dictée." (He concluded by suggesting that he could dictate it to me so that I *in turn* could transcribe it.) 18, emphasis mine. Alain Breton makes the case that the use of the phrase *à mon tour* suggests that Sis had previously written the text down, perhaps in 1850 as is suggested by the wording in Brasseur's *Rabinal Achi* prologue, and was proposing that the Frenchman make his own transcription (*Rabinal Achi*, 9). For more on the controversies surrounding Brasseur's *Rabinal Achi*, see "Introduction," 8–20.

44. The Feast of the Conversion of Saint Paul is January 25.

45. See "From Guatemala City," n. 5 on p. 251.

46. Christenson's *Popol Vuh* refers to "Cucumatz," with an alternative of "Q'ukumatz" (Quetzal Serpent). In a note the translator explains that this was likely

> the son of Co Tuha, who acceded upon the death of his father at the hands of the Ilocab. The manuscript always spells the name of this lord as Cucumatz, whereas the creator deity with the same, or similar, name is spelled Qucumatz. The variant spellings may be the result of multiple scribes working on the same manuscript, each with his/her own creative ways of spelling. Alternatively, it may simply be a means of distinguishing between the deity and this lord. With Cucumatz, who reigned (ca. 1400–1425), we are entering into a period of Quiché history in which historical details are better known. Under the direction of Cucumatz the power of the Quichés expanded northward to the area of present-day Sacapulas in a series of campaigns aided by allied Cakchiquel warriors. Christenson, *Popol Vuh*, 267n733.

Brasseur is referring to the following passage in the *Popol Vuh*:

> Cucumatz became a truly enchanted lord. In one transformation he would rise up into the sky and in another transformation he would go down to Xibalba.... Tales about him were quickly spread abroad and all the lords of the nations heard of the nature of this enchanted lord. This, then, was the beginning of the increase of the Quichés. Lord Cucumatz founded the grandeur of his descendants. Christenson, *Popol Vuh*, 275–76.

47. In Christenson: "Xib'alb'a (Place of Fear) is the Quiché name for the underworld, ruled by lords of death and disease. Modern Quichés still use the word to describe an underground hell inhabited by demons who cause sickness." *Popol Vuh*, 114n231. In Brasseur's *Popol Vuh* (315), he states his belief that Ximénez, clouded by his religious beliefs in his interpretation of this place name Xibalba, thought that it referred to hell. In Recinos's *Popol Vuh: The Sacred Book of the Ancient Queché Maya*, trans. Delia Goetz and Sylvanus Morley (Norman: University of Oklahoma Press, 1950), 54, he explains that it is debatable whether this refers to an actual place name as Brasseur believes, as is indicated by the parenthetical "Palenque" that follows it in the text, or if it is a mythologized place in the lower regions "inhabited by evil spirits who are tormentors of men." In Recinos's *Annals* he notes that

> the Cakchiquel manuscript mentions Xibalbay as one of the places endowed with riches and beauty and the cradle of the sacred stone, *Chay Abah*. The implication that the obsidian stone, which, like all minerals, was produced in the interior of the earth, came from the precious Xibalbay shows that the Cakchiquels imagined this place a subterranean kingdom of great power and magnificence, an idea which coincides in part with the Quiché conception of this place, which is elaborately described in the *Popol Vuh*. Recinos and Goetz, *Annals*, 45–46n10.

48. In Christenson's *Popol Vuh* (277n775): "Quicab or K'iq'ab' (many hands), the son of Cucumatz, reigned... from ca. 1425–1474. The name of this lord suggests

his power to accomplish what would be impossible for someone with only two hands. It may also suggest the number of vassals and servants he possessed."

49. Aimable Jean Jacques Pélissier, first duc de Malakoff (1794–1864).

50. Brasseur is referring to the opera *Fernand Cortez ou la conquête du Mexique* by Gaspare Spontini with a libretto by Joseph-Alphonse d'Esmenard and Etienne de Jouy. First performed in 1809 and later in 1817. According to the entry on Gasparo Spontini in Grove's *Dictionary of Music and Musicians* (London: Macmillan, 1889), 668, "Napoleon took an interest in the production . . . from an idea that it might influence public opinion in favor of his plans for the Spanish war, then in progress." The librettist Jouy was asked "specially to strengthen the contrast between the humane views of Cortés and the fanaticism of the Mexicans and thus suggest a comparison between the liberal-minded French and the bigoted Spaniards of the day." Since Jouy was not keen on altering his work, a more compliant Esménard was found to replace him. Unfortunately, "Spontini had thrown so much life into the character of the Spaniards and had made them so bold, patriotic and fearless of death, that the sympathies of the audience were enlisted in behalf of Spaniards." The opera was revived and completely revised in 1817. Again, according to the Grove's *Dictionary*, the opera opened with the execution of Spanish prisoners by the Aztecs, "thus showing the Mexican people in all their savage barbarity" and therefore disposing the audience more favorably towards the Spaniards. "But . . . the sympathies of the audience still wavered between the heroism of the conquerors and the misfortunes of the conquered." Grove, *Dictionary*, 669.

51. George Catlin (1769–1872) specialized in portraits of Native Americans, especially of the Plains Indians. In 1837 he created the Indian Gallery, which opened in New York. He later took the gallery on a European tour with stops in London in 1840.

52. This is Brasseur's parenthetical explanation.

53. Brasseur's published version of *Rabinal Achi* differs in many ways from the translation that he gives in this earlier publication.

54. In Brasseur's *Rabinal Achi*, this seems to be pronounced by Rabinal Achi, and he is quoting his father.

55. No single passage seems to correspond exactly to this in Brasseur's *Rabinal Achi*, although each element appears in speeches by Qeché Achi, listing his requests.

56. François-Auguste Gevaërt (1828–1908) was the director of the Brussels Conservatory. *Quentin Durward* is an opera based on a novel by Walter Scott from 1858.

Voyage across the Isthmus of Tehuantepec in the State of Chiapas and the Republic of Guatemala in 1859 and 1860

1. This text was published in *Nouvelles annales des voyages, de la géographie, de l'histoire et de l'archéologie* as "Voyage sur l'isthme de Tehuantepec dans l'état de Chiapas et la République de Guatemala dans les années 1859 et 1860" [Voyage across the Isthmus of Tehuantepec in the State of Chiapas and the Republic of Guatemala in 1859 and 1860], 172, pt. 4 (1861): 129–96, 274–370; 173, pt. 1 (1862): 47–89. It was

also published as a book under the same title, *Voyage sur l'isthme de Tehuantepec dans l'état de Chiapas et la République de Guatemala dans les années 1859 et 1860* (Paris: Arthus-Bertrand, 1861). The latter is the source for this translation. *Voyage* was to be the first of a two-part travelogue. A year before the publication of *Voyage*, a piece entitled "Voyage de Brasseur de Bourbourg à Tehuantepec, dans l'Etat de Chiapas et son arrive à Guatemala" [Brasseur de Bourbourg's Voyage to Tehuantepec, in the state of Chiapas and his Arrival in Guatemala City] was published in the *Nouvelles Annales des Voyages, de la géographie, de l'histoire et de l'archéologie* 166, pt. 2 (1860): 5–13. It is a third-person report of the rest of Brasseur's travels through Chiapas to Guatemala City but is not fully developed. An unpublished letter sent to Léonce Angrand, dated January 1860, in which Brasseur recounts the rest of his trip after leaving Tehuantepec does survive and is part of the Fonds Angrand at the Bibliothèque nationale in Paris. In that letter, Brasseur recounts traveling across the Gineta Pass to Tuxtla, San Cristóbal, and Ocosingo, where he visited the ruins of Toniná, which he writes were "like those of Palenque, with powerful archways, a host of rooms and galleries, as well as sculptures, statues and bas-reliefs that are unquestionably just as beautiful as the Babylonian vestiges on display in the Louvre Museum." From there he traveled on to Comitán, where he reports that he was "almost arrested by an imbecile of an alcade who had a government decree against priests in the region." This led Brasseur to flee for the Guatemalan border. In the same letter Brasseur reports meeting Désiré Charnay:

> While I was in Zanatepec (on the road between Tehuantepec and the Gineta Pass) two Frenchmen arrived from Palenque on their way to Mexico City. One of them, Désiré Charnay, is a photographic artist.... He had spent several months in Yucatán taking photos of Uxmal, Chichén Itzá, etc. and had also been to Palenque. The photographs are one meter long and are magnificent. He planned to go to Paris at the end of this year and mount a public exhibition, which I hope will convince Parisians that America has antiquities that are worthy of exploration.

2. François-René de Chateaubriand (1768–1848). Chateaubriand's bestselling novels *Atala* (1801) and *René* (1802), with their vivid (and mostly fanciful) descriptions of the natural landscape along the Mississippi, were set among the Natchez Indians.

3. Lake La Biche the French translation for Lake Itasca or Elk Lake, the source of the Mississippi River.

4. Hernán Cortés, *Hernán Cortés: Letters from Mexico*, trans. and ed. Anthony Pagden (New Haven: Yale University Press, 1986).

5. His name is also sometimes spelled "Gaetano Moro."

6. Author of *L'Isthme de Panama, examen historique et géographique des différentes directions suivant lesquelles on pourrait le percer et des moyens à y employer, suivi d'un aperçu sur l'isthme de Suez* (Paris: C. Gosselin, 1844).

7. Peter and Eugene Hargous founded Hargous Brothers, a banking and shipping concern in New York. They later formed the Louisiana Tehuantepec Railroad Company, a joint-venture company.

8. The McLane-Ocampo Treaty was signed between the United States and Mexico in 1859. As part of this transit treaty, the United States paid $4 million for the rights to create and control routes, including one along the Isthmus of Tehuantepec. "In the meantime, the Louisiana Tehuantepec Company obtained a new concession to construct first a stagecoach road and then a railroad across the isthmus and with lobbying assistance from Louisiana's John Slidell, . . . a US senator, the company obtained a Post Office subsidy to carry the mail between New Orleans and San Francisco." Lars Schoultz, *Beneath the United States: A History of US Policy Towards Latin America* (Cambridge: Harvard University Press, 2009), 45.

9. Miguel Gregorio de la Luz Atenógenes Miramón y Tarelo, 1832–67.

10. The *Appleton Biographical Dictionary* writes the following in its entry on John McLeod Murphy, a civil engineer (1827–71):

He entered the US navy as midshipman, 18 February, 1841, was promoted passed [sic] midshipman . . . and resigned, 10 May 1852. He served in the war with Mexico, and in 1851 was detailed as hydrographic assistant on Major John G. Barnard's survey of the Isthmus of Tehuantepec. . . . In 1860–1 [he] was a member of the New York state senate. In the latter year he was commissioned colonel of New York engineers, and took part in the campaigns of the Army of the Potomac until the close of 1862, when he returned to the navy as acting lieutenant and was in command of the Carondelet during the Vicksburg campaign." Wilson et al., eds., *Appleton's Cyclopedia of American Biography* (New York: D. Appleton, 1887–89), 4:466–67.

11. In a book first published in 1849, John Murphy mentions being in the Mediterranean on the sloop-of-war USS *Fairfield* in 1841. *Spars and Rigging from Nautical Routine, 1849* (New York: Dover Publications, 2003), 25.

12. *The Biographical Directory of the United States Congress* (accessed April 1, 2015, http://bioguide.congress.gov/biosearch/biosearch.asp) spells this name "Emile La Sére." His name is also sometimes spelled "La Sere" or "Lasère," including in the original French text, which uses the latter spelling. La Sére (1802–82) was a representative from Louisiana from 1845 to 1850, replacing John Slidell. He was also the president of the Louisiana Tehuantepec Railroad Company.

13. Brasseur's emphasis.

14. Brasseur's emphasis. Brasseur provides the following footnote: "*Carta segunda de Relacion*, apud Lorenzana, p. 91, 92." He is apparently referring to *Historia de Nueva-España escrita por su esclarecido conquistador Hernan Cortes; aumentada con otros documentos, y notas, por el ilustrissimo Señor Don Francisco Antonio Lorenzana, Arzobispo de Mexico* (Mexico: La Imprenta del Superior Gobierno, del Br. D. Joseph Antonio de Hogal, 1770). In English translation, Cortés's letter can be found in Cortés, *Letters from Mexico*, with the passage referred to by Brasseur on pp. 94–95.

15. Also spelled "Diego de Ordaz" (1480–1532).

16. Francisco Burgoa (ca. 1600–1681) was born in Oaxaca and entered the Dominican Order in 1629. His knowledge of the Zapotec and Mixtec languages was extensive. In his career he served as procurator of his province to the Holy See,

officer of the Inquisition in New Spain, inspector of libraries, and finally provincial of Oaxaca in 1662. He retired to the convent of Zaachila and wrote *Palestra historial de virtudes, y exemplares apostólicos* (1674; facsimile, Mexico: Talleres gráficos de la nación, 1934) and *Geográfica descripción de la parte septentrional, del polo ártico de la América, nueva iglesia de las Indias Occidentales y sitio astronómico de esta provincia de predicadores de Antequera Valle de Oaxaca* (1670; facsimile, Mexico: Talleres gráficos de la nación, 1934). The latter text was an important source for Brasseur regarding the history of the region and indigenous traditions. In Brasseur's *Bibliothèque mexico-guatémalienne* (33) he writes of *Geográfica*: "This book is full of very interesting details on the history . . . of the state of Oaxaca, its princes, priests, temples, palaces, sepulchral caves, as well as the ancient religion and idolatrous rites of this area. Burgoa was very fond of the landscape and its picturesque charms and this comes across clearly when reading this book." Both Burgoa's *Palestra historial* and *Geográfica* were published in reproductions of the original editions (Mexico: Talleres gráficos de la nación, 1934).

17. According to maps from Brasseur's period, Paso Nuevo is downstream from the Uspanapa River, at the confluence of the Coatzacoalcos and the San Antonio River.

18. Brasseur spells both the town and the ship "Xuchil," although maps from the period spell the town name "Suchil."

19. McLane was appointed envoy extraordinary and minister plenipotentiary to Mexico on March 7, 1859, and was charged to determine whether or not to recognize the government of Benito Juárez. As the US ambassador, he later negotiated the McLane-Ocampo Treaty, which granted the transit rights across the Isthmus of Tehuantepec to the United States.

20. These words are in English in the text and the emphasis is Brasseur's.
21. These words are in English in the text and the emphasis is Brasseur's.
22. These words are in English in the text and the emphasis is Brasseur's.
23. These words are in English in the text and the emphasis is Brasseur's.
24. These words are in English in the text and the emphasis is Brasseur's.
25. In Spanish in the original; this is a customs house collector.
26. Brasseur's emphasis.
27. In English in the original text.
28. In Spanish in the original text.
29. In Spanish in the original text: "an American wedding."
30. In English in the original.
31. In Spanish in the original: "gentlemen."
32. In English in the original.
33. In Spanish in original.
34. William Henry Sidell (1810–73).
35. In English in the original.
36. This first paragraph follows almost exactly the text from Williams's *Isthmus of Tehuantepec*, 13–14.
37. Currently this town is known as Ixhuatlán.
38. Most of the information in this section can be found in Williams's *Isthmus*

of Tehuantepec; this section on ixtle is a direct translation of that text (184).

39. Brasseur is perhaps referring to Santa María Chimalapa.

40. Most of the information in this section follows Williams's *Isthmus of Tehuantepec*, 16.

41. Brasseur seems to have been mistaken here. I have found no such river names on nineteenth-century maps. Moreover, the path of the river that Brasseur is describing seems to correspond to the Tehuantepec River. The corresponding section of Williams's *Isthmus of Tehuantepec* (17), on which Brasseur relies heavily for this passage, describes the Tehuantepec's path in terms similar to those used by Brasseur.

42. Antonio Fraconi (1737–1836) was an Italian equestrian who founded a riding school and later an equestrian theater called the Cirque Olympique in Paris.

43. Eugène Joseph Marie Sue (1804–57) wrote successful, popular novels such as *Les Mystères de Paris* (The Mysteries of Paris; 1842–43) and *Le Juif errant* (The Wandering Jew; 1844–45), which championed his socialist beliefs.

44. The emphasis is Brasseur's.

45. These words are in English in the text.

46. Armida, a character in Tasso's *Jerusalem Delivered* (1581), was also the protagonist in Jean-Baptiste Lully's opera *Armide* (1686) and later Christoph Willibald Gluck's opera (1777) of the same name.

47. Brasseur is referring to William Walker (see "Notes from a Voyage," n. 16 on p. 247).

48. Brasseur spells this "Xochiapa," like the plains in this area. However, the stream in question is spelled "Xuchiapa" on contemporary maps and in Williams's *Isthmus of Tehuantepec*. There is also a Xochiapa River (alternatively spelled "Sochiapa") in Veracruz that flows towards Acayucan.

49. In his *Histoire des nations* (3:48), Brasseur writes: "Legend has it—and all legends have an element of the fantastic to them—that [Condoy] had neither father nor mother and emerged one day from the cave of Atitlán, the burial ground for the lords of this area." Brasseur notes that this Atitlán should not to be confused with place of the same name in Guatemala and says that Condoy's birthplace is reputed to be near the Zempoaltepec Mountains. He cites Burgoa's *Geográfica* as his source.

50. Don José Eustaquio Manzano and his brother Apolonio Manzano both fought for the Liberal cause.

51. See "From Guatemala City," n. 15 on p. 254.

52. See "From Guatemala City," n. B20 on p. 89.

53. Brasseur's text says "Pinopinaa," however this appears to be a misspelling. Brasseur's source is Burgoa's *Geográfica*, 2:330. Aside from Burgoa, there are references to Pinopiaa in Juan Bautista Carriedo, *Estudios historicos, y estadisticos del Estado Oaxaqueño* (Oaxaca: Imprenta del autor, 1847–49) 1:8, 39–40, a text with which Brasseur was clearly familiar and Pinopiaa is cited in Daniel G. Brinton, *Nagualism: A study in native American folk-lore and history* (Philadelphia: MacCalla, 1894), 55. Brinton writes the following, citing Carriedo: "We find a record of an *auto de fé* held in 1609, in the province of Tehuantepec, in which eight full-blood natives were punished for worshiping the goddess Pinopiaa."

54. John Lloyd Stephens writes of this discovery in Uxmal in *Incidents of Travel* (177):

> Over the cavity left in the mortar by the removal of the stone [that was removed in order to make a breach through the wall of the Casa del Gobernador] were two conspicuous marks, which afterward stared us in the face in all the ruined buildings of the country. They were the prints of a red hand with the thumb and fingers extended, not drawn or painted, but stamped by the living hand, the pressure of the palm upon the stone.

55. Williams's *Isthmus of Tehuantepec* (243–44) includes the following description:

> The chief attractive features of [the vicinity of Santo Domingo] are the mountain caves, which merit some attention, from their connection with the past history of the indigenous people. The entrance to the principal cave, called that of Santo Domingo, is elevated about 700 feet above the base of a limestone mountain, a mile north from the village, and is accessible only by a steep path. The mouth to this cave has an arch spanning 80 by 20 feet in height, and the plane of its floor cuts the horizon at an angle of thirty degrees, until reaching a depth of 100 feet below the entrance. At the foot of this slope is a magnificent apartment some 300 feet in diameter and 50 in height, with its sides ornamented with stalactites and stalagmites of every conceivable form and variety. The floor is quite level; and at one extremity is a sparking pool of clear, cold water. Beyond this antechamber, the cave extends into the mountain for a distance of more than 2000 feet, sometimes expanding into large halls, or forming regular arched passage-ways several hundred feet in length, alternately ascending and descending into ridges and valleys. On the walls, at the extreme end of the cave, are several circular paintings, rudely executed with red ochre, and probably intended to represent the sun and moon. There are also several representations of the human hand, done in black. Immediately fronting these drawings, in the floor of the cave, is a small aperture through which, by means of ropes, access is obtained to an apartment beneath. In this are fragments of arrow-heads, human bones, and antique pottery.

56. In English in the original.

57. Williams, in *Isthmus of Tehuantepec* (244), identifies him as Don Estavan Maqueo.

58. In *Isthmus of Tehuantepec*, Williams predicts that the springs of Chivela, whose curative properties he does not discuss, "are doubtless destined to become places of frequent resort. Indeed, it is not unlikely that the Spring of Chivela may become in the course of time, as well known and as fashionably frequented as those of Saratoga and White Sulfur," 249.

59. This place name varies in spelling in documents from Brasseur's time; it can also be found spelled "Itztlaltepec."

60. Brasseur does not explain this, however, in Williams, *Isthmus of Tehuantepec* (249–50), we read that the town's name means "Hill of Salt" in the Zapotec language.

61. Alcalde mayor was an official appointed by the provincial governor to administer a district composed of one or more towns and their countryside, the equivalent of a corregidor (see "From Guatemala City," n. 34 on p. 256) or deputy governor. He had judicial responsibility on a local or district level.

62. A visitador is an inspector appointed by the king and royal council to assess and act for them in colonial lands, like New Spain.

63. Burgoa writes of the discovery of the clandestine religious practices of Cocijopij in his *Geográfica*, 2:338–59, in chap. 72: "De la Provincia de Tehuantepeque de su Ministerio y Doctrina."

64. Thomas Gage, *Travels in the New World*, ed. J. Eric S. Thompson (Westport: Greenwood Press, 1958), 115–16.

65. Juan Nepomuceno Álvarez Hurtado de Luna (1790–1867) served as interim president of Mexico for a short period in 1855.

66. Guatimozín was the youngest son of Ahuitzotl, cousin of Montezuma II and the last Aztec ruler, ca. 1495–1525. There are many alternative spellings of his name including in Brasseur's *Histoire des nations* where it is given as "Quahtemotzin."

67. Brasseur calls this Guidji-Lieza.

68. Brasseur's emphasis. According to Burgoa, Cocijopij and his people worshiped a deity known as "Corazón del Reino," whose effigy was found on an island in the lagoon of San Dionisio (*Geográfica*, 2:351). In Orozco y Berra's telling of the story of Cocijopij, he mentions Monopostiac as a mountain in the lagoon, which was the location of an ancient temple used by the people of Tehuantepec. Manuel Orozco y Berra, *Diccionario universal de historia y de geografía* (Mexico: Imp. de F. Escalente, 1853–56), 8:704.

69. See "From Guatemala City," n. 16 on p. 254.

70. "Who knows?"

71. In his *Bibliothèque mexico-guatémalienne* Brasseur writes of Bernardino de Sahagún (1499–1590), who was born in Spain and arrived in Mexico in 1529 as a Franciscan friar: "he possessed the most admirable mastery of the Mexican language, whose history he studied with the scholarly elite of this vanquished race and he wrote a great many works in this language. He was often persecuted [by the his fellow priests] who claimed that he was encouraging idolatry by writing the history of the ancient religious ceremonies of Mexico." 132. Brasseur cites the Sahagún's *Historia general de las cosas de Nueva España*, a three-volume edition published in Mexico in 1829 by Carlos Maria de Bustamente (Mexico: Impr. del ciudadano A. Valdés, 1829–30). Brasseur does not appear to have been aware of the manuscript version of Sahagún's work, know commonly as *The Florentine Codex*, in the collection of the Medicea Laurenziana Library in Florence. This manuscript was not widely known until a description was first published in 1879, which was after Brasseur's death. Sahagún is seen today as an important protoethnologist who "attempted to fix Indian tradition at the moment that it was interrupted by the conquest." Luis Nicolau D'Olwer and Howard F. Cline, "Bernardino de Sahagún," in *Guide to Ethnohistorical Sources*, ed. Howard F. Cline and John B. Glass, pt. 2 (Austin: University of Texas Press, 1973), 189.

72. Juan de Torquemada (1564–1624) was the author of another important colonial work of ethnohistory, *La Monarquia Indiana* (1615). In an inventory of his collection of books and manuscripts in his *Histoire des nations* (1:xc), Brasseur lists the 1723 edition of Torquemada's *Monarchia Indiana*.

73. In the first section of Sahagún's *Historia general de las cosas*, where he provides examples of the "gods that the natives of New Spain worship," the author has a chapter entitled "About the goddess of water, that they call Chalchiuhtlicue [whose name he also spells 'Chiuhtliycue'] or another Juno." He explains that she is depicted as a woman and is said to have been the sister of the rain gods, known as *Tlaloques*. She was said to control the sea and rivers and had the power to create stormy or turbulent waters. 1:9.

74. In his *Histoire des nations* (4:823) where we find this same sentence, Brasseur cites *Informe del teniente general don Jacobo de Barba Figueroa, Corregidor de la provincial de Suchitepeque* as his source.

75. In the bibliography of his collection printed in *Bibliothèque mexico-guatémalienne*, Brasseur lists Nuñez de la Vega's *Constituciones diaecesanas del obispado de Chiappa* [sic] . . . from 1702. Brasseur notes that the book contained many details relating to the ancient history of Chiapas, with a section devoted to the myth of Votan as well as a "pastoral letter regarding the errors of the idolatrous sect of Nagualism." (110) Brasseur writes that Nuñez de la Vega (1634–1703) became the bishop of Chiapas in 1683. He continues: "Boturini accuses the priest of having burnt vestiges of indigenous antiquity that had come into his possession." (110) Brasseur also lists a copy that he made of a letter by Nuñez regarding Nagualism (111), which Brasseur found in the Episcopal Archives of San Cristóbal (formerly Ciudad Real) in Chiapas in September 1859, thus, right after he left Tehuantepec.

76. Hubert Howe Bancroft writes about this rebellion in his *History of Central America*: "In 1712 the Tzendal formed an alliance with numerous kindred nations, and grafting some Christian rites upon their paganism, followed the lead of an Indian girl, who claimed inspiration from the virgin Mary." (San Francisco: History Company, 1882–86), 2:696. He continues:

> At Cancuc [the Tzendal] had erected 24 whipping-posts, and the Spaniards were given 50 blows at each post, provided they held out so long against death. . . . Such as had been friendly to Spaniards were suspended over a slow fire until their feet were roasted. The fiscal of Oxchuc and friars Jorge and Marcos, together with other Spaniards, were thrown by the Indians into pits and stoned to death. 698n5

Bancroft's source is *Informe sobre la Sublevación de los Zendales, escrito par el Padre W Pedro Marselino García de la orden de Predicadores, Pred^{or} general calificado des Santo Oficio, y Vicario provincial de San Vicente de Chiapa, dirigida al Ilmo Señor Obispo deste diócesis, y fecho en 5 junio 1716*. This manuscript once belonged to Brasseur and is listed in the inventory of his library. The manuscript describes the investigation into

> the death of four clergymen at the hands of rebelling Tzendal Indians. . . . This document contains extremely important information. It presents the

ramifications of the actions of the idolatrous parties that attempted in 1713 to free the Indians of Chiapas as well as a great deal of information about the celebrated Indian, María Candelaria, who was worshiped as the Mother of the Gods in churches, as she sat on the altar, etc. This revolution was hatched in Cancuc, and almost led to the Spanish losing Chiapas. In order to quell the rebellion, they had to bring their entire colonial might to bear. This manuscript can be considered one of the most extraordinary expressions of Nagualism, which was founded on the ruins of the ancient idolatrous religion of both Chiapas and Guatemala. Brasseur, *Bibliothèque mexico-guatémalienne*, 68–69.

77. A downpour or rain shower. In Spanish in original text.
78. Royal atole.

SELECTED WORKS BY CHARLES ÉTIENNE BRASSEUR DE BOURBOURG

Selected Works Related to Mexico and Central America

"Aperçus d'un voyage dans les États de San-Salvador et de Guatemala, par M. l'abbé Brasseur de Bourbourg. Lu dans la séance publique annuelle du 17 avril 1857," *Bulletin de la Société de Géographie de Paris* 13 (1857): 272–93. [This article contains many elements found in the three texts in this volume, with added details about the author's travels in the State of San Salvador.]

"A letter from Brasseur de Bourbourg to E.G. Squier, dated Rabinal, August 7, 1855," *Athenaeum*, December 8, 1855, 1435–36.

Bibliothèque mexico-guatémalienne: précédée d'un coup d'œil sur les études américaines dans leurs rapports avec les études classiques et suivie du tableau par ordre alphabétique des ouvrages de linguistique américaine contenus dans le même volume. Paris: Maisonneuve, 1871.

"De Guatemala à Rabinal: Episode d'un séjour dans l'Amerique Centrale pendant les années 1855 et 1856," *Revue Européenne: Lettres, sciences, arts, voyages, politiques* 1 (1859): 46–74, 275–301.

"De Guatemala a Rabinal," *Anales de la Sociedad de Geografía e Historia* 20 (1945): 113–18, 232–35, 296–99.

"Dos cartas inéditas del Abate Brasseur de Bourbourg, dirigidas al Doctor José Mariano Padilla, fechadas en Rabinal el 23 mayo y 3 de junio de 1855," *Anales de la Sociedad de Geografía e Historia* 16 (1940): 298–303.

Gramatica de la lengua quiche: Grammaire de la langue quichée, espagnole-française mise en parallèle avec ses deux dialectes, cakchiquel et tzutuhil, tirée des manuscrits des meilleurs auteurs guatémaliens. Ouvrage accompagné de notes philologiques avec un vocabulaire . . . et suivi d'un essai sur la poésie, la musique, la danse et l'art servant d'introduction au Rabinal-Achi, drame indigène avec sa musique originale, texte quiché et traduction français en regard. Paris: Arthus-Bertrand, 1862.

Histoire des nations civilisées du Mexique et de l'Amérique-Centrale, durant les siècles antérieurs à Christophe Colomb, écrite sur des documents originaux et entièrement inédits, puisées aux anciennes archives des indigènes. 4 vols. Paris: Arthus-Bertrand, 1857.

Lettre à M. Léon de Rosny sur la découverte de documents relatifs à la haute antiquité américaine, et sur le déchiffrement et l'interprétation de l'écriture phonétique et figurative de la langue maya. Paris: Amyot, 1869.

Lettres pour servir d'introduction à l'histoire primitive des nations civilisées de l'Amérique septentrionale, adressées à Monsieur le duc de Valmy, par l'abbé É.-C. Brasseur de Bourbourg. Cartas para servir de introducción á la historia primitiva de las naciones civilizadas de la América setentrional, Texte français et traduction espagnole en regard. Mexico: M. Murguía, 1851.

Manuscrit troano: études sur le système graphique et la langue des Mayas. Paris: Imprimerie impériale, 1869-70.

"Notes d'un voyage dans l'Amérique Centrale: Lettres à M. Alfred Maury," *Nouvelles annales des voyages, de la géographie, de l'histoire et de l'archéologie* 147, pt. 3 (1855): 129-58.

Popol Vuh. Le Livre Sacré Et Les Mythes De L'antiquité Américaine: Avec Les Livres Héroïques Et Historiques Des Quichés. Ouvrage Original Des Indigènes De Guatémala, Texte Quiché Et Traduction Française En Regard. Paris: Arthus-Bertrand, 1861.

Relation des choses de Yucatan de Diego de Landa; texte espagnol et traduction française en regard, comprenant les signes du calendrier et de l'alphabet hiéroglyphique de la langue maya, accompagné de documents divers historiques et chronologiques, avec une grammaire et un vocabulaire abrégés français-maya; précédés d'un essai sur les sources de l'histoire primitive du Mexique et de l'Amèrique Centrale, etc., d'après les monuments égyptiens, et de l'histoire primitive de l'Egypte d'après les monuments américains, par l'abbé Brasseur de Bourbourg. Translated and edited by Charles Étienne Brasseur de Bourbourg. Paris: A. Durand, 1864.

Sommaire des voyages scientifiques et des travaux de géographie, d'histoire, d'archéologie et de philologie américaines publiés par M. l'abée Brasseur de Bourbourg. Saint-Cloud: Imprimerie Mme Veuve Belin, 1862.

Voyage sur l'isthme de Tehuantepec dans l'état de Chiapas et la République de Guatemala, exécuté dans les années 1859 et 1860. Paris: Arthus-Bertrand, 1861.

"Voyage sur l'isthme de Tehuantepec dans l'état de Chiapas et la République de Guatemala, exécuté dans les années 1859 et 1860," *Nouvelles annales des voyages, de la géographie, de l'histoire et de l'archéologie* 172, pt. 4 (1861): 129-96, 274-370; 173, pt. 1 (1862): 47-89.

Selected Literary and Religious Works

Auguste Fauvel. Lille: L. Lefort, 1843.

Eugénie de Revel, souvenirs des dernières années du XVIIIe siècle. Lille: L. Lefort, 1845.

La Famille irlandaise, ou les conséquences d'une première faute, ouvrage imité de l'anglais. Lille: L. Lefort, 1843.

Jérusalem, tableau de l'histoire et des vicissitudes de cette ville célèbre depuis son origine la plus reculée jusqu'à nos jours. Lille: L. Lefort, 1843.

Le Khalife de Bagdad, ou l'Exilée, scènes de la vie orientale au IXe siècle. Paris: Sagnier, et Bray, 1853.

Le martyr de la croix, épisode du siège d'Antioche. Lille: L. Lefort, 1844.

Selim, ou le Pacha de Salonique. Lille: L. Lefort, 1848.

Le Sérapéon, épisode de l'histoire du IVe siècle. Paris: Debécourt, 1839.

Wilhem ou Le pardon du chrétien: histoire du règne de Philippe II. Lille: L. Lefort, 1849.

BIBLIOGRAPHY

Archival Sources

ARCHIVES NATIONALES DE FRANCE *(Paris, France)*
F17 2942 (Brasseur de Bourbourg File)
F17 2909, F17 2910, F17 2911, F17 2912, F17 2913, F17 2914A, F17 2914B, F17 2914/3 (Commission scientifique du Mexique).

BIBLIOTHÈQUE NATIONALE DE FRANCE *(Paris, France)*
Fond Angrand

LIBRARY OF CONGRESS *(Washington, D.C.)*
E. G. Squier papers

Books, Articles, and Dissertations

Acuña, René. *Introducción al estudio del Rabinal Achi*. México: Universidad Nacional Autónoma de México, 1975.

Adams, Herbert B. "Abbé Brasseur de Bourbourg," *Proceedings of the American Antiquarian Society* 6, pt. 3 (1890): 274–90.

Alboronz, Juan de. *Arte de la lengua chiapaneca, compuesto por el M. R. padre fray Juan de Albornoz; y Doctrina cristiana en la misma lengua escrita por el padre mtro fray Luis Barrientos*. Paris: E. Leroux, 1875.

Bancroft, Hubert Howe. *History of Central America*. 3 vols. San Francisco: History Company, 1882–86.

Barker, Nancy Nichols. *The French Experience in Mexico: 1821–1861: A History of Constant Misunderstanding*. Chapel Hill: University of North Carolina Press, 1979.

Bataillon Marcel. "Mérimée et l'américanisme d'il y a cent ans," *Bulletin Hispanique* 56, no. 4 (1954): 424–30.

Belgium Consulate. *Santo-Tomas. Rapport de M. Cloquet, consul de Belgique à Guatemala, sur la situation de la colonie de Santo-Tomas, au 1er janvier, 1850*. Bruxelles: Imprimerie de Deltombe, 1851.

Breton, Alain. *Rabinal Achi: A Fifteenth-Century Maya Dynastic Drama*. Translated by Teresa Lavender Fagan and Robert Schneider. Boulder: University Press of Colorado, 2007.

———. *Rabinal-Achi: un drame dynastique maya du quinzième siècle*. Nanterre: Société des américanistes & Société d'ethnologie, 1994.

Brinton, Daniel Garrison. *Nagualism: A study in native American folk-lore and history*. Philadelphia: MacCalla, 1894.

Brinton, Daniel Garrison, Francisco Díaz Gebuta Quej, and Francisco Hernández Arana Xajilá. *The Annals of the Cakchiquels: the Original Text, with a Translation, Notes and Introduction*. Philadelphia: s.n., 1885.

Burgoa, Francisco. *Geográfica descripción de la parte septentrional, del polo ártico de la América, nueva iglesia de las Indias Occidentales y sitio astronómico de esta provincia de predicadores de Antequera Valle de Oaxaca*. Mexico: Talleres gráficos de la nación, 1934. Facsimile of the first edition, 1674.

———. *Palestra historial de virtudes, y exemplares apostólicos. Fundada del zelo de insignes héroes de la sagrada Orden de predicadores en este nuevo mundo de América en las Indias Occidentales*. Mexico: Talleres gráficos de la nación, 1934. Facsimile of the first edition, 1670.

Butler, Pierce. *Judah P. Benjamin*. Philadelphia: G.W. Jacobs, 1907.

Carmack, Robert. *Quichean Civilization: The Ethnohistoric, Ethnographic and Archeological sources*. Berkeley: University of California Press, 1973.

Carriedo, Juan Bautista. *Estudios historicos, y estadisticos del Estado Oaxaqueño*. 2 vols. Oaxaca: Imprenta del autor, 1847–49.

Charnay, Désiré. *Le Mexique, souvenirs et impressions de voyage*. Paris: E. Dentu, 1863.

———. *Une princesse indienne avant la conquête*. Paris: Hachette, 1888.

Charpenne, Pierre. *Mon voyage au Mexique, ou Le colon du Guazacoalco*. Paris: Roux, 1836.

Chevalier, Michel. *L'Isthme de Panama, examen historique et géographique des différentes directions suivant lesquelles on pourrait le percer et des moyens à y employer, suivi d'un aperçu sur l'isthme de Suez*. Paris: C. Gosselin, 1844.

Christenson, Allen. *Popol Vuh: The Sacred Book of the Maya, the Great Classic of Central American Spirituality Translated from the Original Maya Text*. Norman: University of Oklahoma Press, 2007.

Coe, Michael D. *Breaking the Maya Code*, rev. ed. London: Thames & Hudson, 2012.

Cortés, Hernán. *Hernán Cortés: Letters from Mexico*. Translated and edited by Anthony Pagden. New Haven: Yale University Press, 1986.

D'Olwer, Luis Nicolau and Howard F. Cline. "Bernardino de Sahagún," In *Guide to Ethnohistorical Sources*, edited by Howard F. Cline and John B. Glass, pt. 2:186–207. Handbook of Middle American Indians, edited by Robert Wauchope, vol. 13. Austin: University of Texas Press, 1973.

Escalante Arce, Pedro. *Brasseur de Bourbourg: Esbozo biográfico*. San Salvador: s.n., 1989.

"Excursion de M. l'abbé Brasseur de Bourbourg dans l'Amérique Centrale; son retour à Paris," *Nouvelles Annales des voyages, de la géographie, de l'histoire et de l'archéologie* 168, pt. 4 (1860): 372–76.

Figueroa Marroquín, Horacio. *Biografía del doctor José Mariano Padilla*. Guatemala: Editorial Cultura, 1998.

Gage, Thomas. *Travels in the New World*. Edited by J. Eric S. Thompson. Westport: Greenwood Press, 1958.

Goodman, Joseph T. "The Archaic Maya Inscriptions." Appendix to *Biologia Centrali-Americana, or Contributions to the Knowledge of the Fauna and Flora of Mexico and Central America, Archaeology* by Alfred P. Maudslay. London: R. H. Porter and Dulau, 1889–1902.

Graham, Ian. *Alfred Maudslay and the Maya: A Biography.* Norman: Oklahoma University Press, 2002.

Gransagne, J. B. François-Étienne Ajasson de and Valentin Parisot. *Nouveau discours sur les révolutions du globe.* Paris: tous les libraires, 1839–40.

Grove, George, ed. *Dictionary of Music and Musicians.* London: Macmillan, 1889.

Hernández de Toledo, Francisco. *Noua plantarum, animalium et mineralium Mexicanorum historia.* Rome: sumptibus B. Deuersini, & Z. Masotti, typis V. Mascardi, 1651.

Humboldt, Alexander von. *Views of the Cordilleras and Monuments of the Indigenous Peoples of the Americas.* Translated by J. Ryan Poynter. Edited by Vera M. Kutzinski and Ottmar Ette. Chicago: University of Chicago Press, 2012.

Juarros, Domingo. *Compendio de la historia de la ciudad de Guatemala.* Guatemala: I Beteta, 1808–10.

Le Plongeon, Augustus. *Vestiges of the Mayas, or, Facts tending to prove that communications and intimate relations must have existed, in very remote times, between the inhabitants of Mayab and those of Asia and Africa.* New York: J. Polhemus, 1881.

Lorenzana, Francisco Antonio. *Historia de Nueva-España escrita por su esclarecido conquistador Hernan Cortes; aumentada con otros documentos, y notas, por el ilustrissimo Señor Don Francisco Antonio Lorenzana, Arzobispo de Mexico.* Mexico: La Imprenta del Superior Gobierno, del Br. D. Joseph Antonio de Hogal, 1770.

Mace, Carroll Edward. "Charles Etienne Brasseur de Bourbourg, 1814–1874." In *Guide to Ethnohistorical Sources,* edited by Howard Cline, pt. 2:298–325. Handbook of Middle American Indians, edited by Robert Wauchope, vol. 13. London: University of Texas Press, 1973.

———. "New Information about Dance-Dramas of Rabinal and the 'Rabinal-Achi.'" *Xavier University Studies* 6, no. 1 (1967): 1–19.

———. *Two Spanish-Quiché Dance-Dramas of Rabinal.* Tulane Studies in Romance Languages and Literature 3. New Orleans: Tulane University, 1970.

Marquez, Ophelia and Lillian Ramos Navarro Wold, eds. *The Compilation of Colonial Spanish Terms and Document Related Phrases.* Midway City, CA: Shhar Press, 1998.

Murphy, John McLeod. *Spars and Rigging from Nautical Routine, 1849.* New York: Dover Publications, 2003.

Maudslay, Alfred P. *Biologia Centrali-Americana, or Contributions to the Knowledge of the Faunu and Flora of Mexico and Central America,* vols. 55–59, *Archaeology,* with appendix by J. T. Goodman. London: R. H. Porter and Dulau, 1889–1902.

Napoléon III. *Le Canal de Nicaragua, ou projet de junction des Océans Atlantique et Pacifique au moyen d'un canal.* Vol. 2, of *Oeuvres de Napoléon III.* Paris: Plon, 1856–59.

Orozco y Berra, Manuel. *Diccionario universal de historia y de geografía*. 10 vols. Mexico: Imp. de F. Escalente, 1853–56.

Oviedo y Gonzalo Valdés, Fernández de. *Histoire du Nicaragua*. Paris: Arthus-Bertrand, 1840.

Peláez, Francisco de Paula García. *Memorias para la historia del antiguo reyno de Guatemala*. Guatemala City: Tipografico de L. Luna, 1851.

Prévost Urkidi, Nadia. "Brasseur de Bourbourg et l'émergence de l'Américainisme scientifique en France au XIXe siècle." Unpublished Docteur de l'Université diss., Université de Toulouse II, 2007.

Recinos, Adrián. *Popol Vuh: The Sacred Book of the Ancient Quiché Maya*. Translated by Delia Goetz and Sylvanus Morley. Norman: University of Oklahoma Press, 1950.

Recinos, Adrián and Delia Goetz. *Annals of the Cakchiquels*. Norman: University of Oklahoma Press, 1953.

Renzi, Silvia de. "Writing and Talking of Exotic Animals." In *Books and the Sciences in History*, edited by Marina Frasca-Spada and Nick Jardine, 151–70. Cambridge: Cambridge University Press, 2000.

Réville, Albert. "Antiquités mexicaines: les aventures de la collection Aubin-Goupil," *Revue des bibliothèques* 8 (1896): 122–27.

Rosny, Léon de. *L'Atlantide historique: études d'ethnographie et d'archéologie américaines*. Paris: Leroux, 1902.

Sahagún, Bernardino de. *Historia de la cosas de Nueva España*. 3 vols. México: Impr. del ciudadano A. Valdés, 1829–30.

Scherzer, Karl Ritter von. *Las historias del origen de los Indios de esta provincia de Guatemala, traducidas de la lengua quiché al castellano para mas comodidad de los ministros del S. Evangelio, por el R. P. F. Francisco Ximénez... Exactamente según el texto español del manuscrito original que se halla en la biblioteca de la Universidad de Guatemala, publicado por la primera vez, y aumentado con una introducción y anotaciones, por el D.C. Scherzer*. Vienna: C. Gerold e Hijo, 1857.

———. *Travels in the Free States of Central America: Nicaragua, Honduras, and San Salvador*. London: Longman, Brown, Green, Longmans & Roberts, 1857. Translated from the original *Wanderungen durch die mittel-amerikanischen Freistaaten*. Braunschweig: G. Westermann, 1857.

Schoultz, Lars. *Beneath the United States: A History of US Policy Towards Latin America*. Cambridge: Harvard University Press, 2009.

Scroggs, William. *Filibusters and Financiers: The Story of William Walker and His Associates*. New York: Russell & Russell, 1916.

Squier, Ephraim George. "Lettre de M. E. G. Squier à propos de la lettre de M. Brasseur de Bourbourg, insérée au cahier des Annales d'août 1855," *Nouvelles annales des voyages, de la géographie, de l'histoire et de l'archéologie* 148, pt. 4 (1855): 273–85.

———. *Nicaragua: Its People, Scenery, Monuments and the Proposed Interoceanic Canal*. 2 vols. New York: D. Appleton, 1852.

Stephens, John Lloyd. *Incidents of Travel in Central America, Chiapas and Yucatan*. 2 vols. New York: Harper & Bro., 1852.

Bibliography

Swanton, Michael W. and Jacqueline de Durand-Forest. "Un regard historique sur les fonds mexicains de la Bibliothèque nationale de France," *Journal de la Société des Américanistes* 84, no. 2 (1998): 9–19.

Tedlock, Dennis. *Popol Vuh: The Mayan Book of the Dawn of Life*. New York: Simon and Schuster, 1996.

———. *Rabinal Achi: A Mayan Drama of War and Sacrifice*. rev. ed. Oxford: Oxford University Press, 2003.

Torquemada, Juan de. *Primera[-tercera] parte de los veinte i vn libros rituales i monarchia indiana: con el origen y guerras, de los indios ocidentales, de sus poblaçones: descubrimiento, conquista, conuersion, y otras cosas marauillosas de la mesma tierra*. 3 vols. Madrid: En la oficina y acosta de Nicolas Rodriguez Franco, 1723.

Thompson, Edward H. "Atlantis Not a Myth," *Popular Science Monthly* 15 (1879): 759–64.

"Voyage de Brasseur de Bourbourg à Tehuantepec, dans l'Etat de Chiapas et son arrive à Guatemala," *Nouvelles annales des voyages, de la géographie, de l'histoire et de l'archéologie* 166, pt. 2 (1860): 5–13.

Williams, John J. *The Isthmus of Tehuantepec: Being the results of a survey for a railroad to connect the Atlantic and Pacific Oceans, Made by the Scientific Commission Under the Direction of Major J. G. Barnard, etc. Arranged and prepared for the Tehuantepec railroad company of New Orleans, by J. J. Williams, principal assistant engineer*. New York: D. Appleton, 1852.

Wilson, James Grant, John Fiske, and Stanley L. Klos, eds. *Appleton's Cyclopedia of American Biography*. 6 vols. New York: D. Appleton, 1887–89.

GENERAL INDEX

A separate index of geographical places mentioned in Brasseur's writings follows this general index.

Acuña, René, 12
Ahuitzotl (Aztec ruler), 194, 206, 265n66
Alvarado, Pedro de, 45–46, 57, 58, 81, 194, 252–53n9
Angrand, Léonce, 20, 23, 25, 259–60n1
Aubin, Joseph Marius Alexis, 29
Ayer, Edward, 27

Bancroft, Hubert Howe, 27, 266n76
Barnard, John Gross, 109, 114, 116, 214, 261n10
Benjamin, Judah, 20, 21
Brasseur de Bourbourg, Charles Étienne: *Bibliothèque Mexico-guatémalienne*, 11, 22–23, 26, 241n23, 261n16, 265n71, 266nn75–76; *Gramatica de la lengua quiche* (see *Rabinal Achi*); *Popol Vuh*, 3, 9, 11, 12, 24, 25, 26, 27, 249n33, 252n9, 254n13, 255n28, 256nn38–39, 257n41, 258nn46–48
Breton, Alain, 17, 18, 85n, 242nn26–27, 243n39, 243nn41–42, 243n51, 255n27, 257n43
Burgoa, Francisco, 21, 118, 215, 263n49, 263n53, 265n63, 265n68

Carmack, Robert, 18, 241n23, 243n33, 243n43, 243–44n53, 244n57, 254n13
Carrera Turcios, José Rafael, 9, 55, 62, 88, 251n6, 254n11
Casaus y Torres, Francisco Ramón Valentín de (archbishop of Guatemala), 39
Castellón, Francisco, 33, 34, 37, 40, 62
Catlin, George, 100
Chamorro, Fruto, 33, 34, 35, 37, 38, 40
Charnay, Désiré, 4, 23, 240n10, 244n70, 259–60n1
Chateaubriand, François-René de, 112
Chevalier, Michel, 114
Cocijoeza (Zapotec king), 194, 206
Cocijopij (last Zapotec king) (Juan Cortés de Montezuma), 22, 194–98, 203–6, 216, 218, 230, 238
Codex Padilla, 48
Cogolludo, Diego López de, 12
Comonfort, Ignacio, 176, 201

General Index

Condoy (Mixe king), 173–74, 224, 226
Cortés, Hernán, 13, 45–46, 57, 93, 94, 109n, 113, 117–18, 122, 140, 144, 194, 198, 209, 252–53n9, 259n50, 261n14
Cramer, Agustín, 113
Cueva, Beatriz de la, 58

Dias del Castillo, Bernal, 10, 109n
Díaz, Porfirio, 21, 201, 204–5
Didjaza (Zapotec woman), 21, 209–11, 214–15, 221, 223–25, 233
Drivon, Dr. (Brasseur's host in Sonsonate), 55
Durán, Diego, 12

Escalante Arce, Pedro, 5, 240n11, 244n62, 245n80, 248–49n32, 257n42

Gage, Thomas, 199
Garay, José de, 21, 113–14, 119, 142
García Peláez, Francisco de Paula (archbishop of Guatemala), 56, 63
Gevaërt, François-Auguste, 105
Goodman, Joseph T., 27–28

Hargous, John (son of Louis), 115, 124, 148–51, 156–58, 160, 165, 167, 168, 172, 175, 237, 238
Hargous, Louis S., 6, 115
Hargous, Peter and Eugene (founders of Hargous Brothers), 114, 235–36
Hernández de Toledo, Francisco, 46
Humboldt, Alexander von, 56, 254n16

Juárez, Benito, 21, 115, 123, 131–33, 136, 154, 176–77, 186, 205, 207, 236n
Juarros, Domingo, 94

Laîné de Villévêque. *See* Laîsné de La-Ville-l'Évêque
Laîsné de La-Ville-l'Évêque, 121n, 145
Landa, Diego de, 3, 12, 24–25, 26
Las Casas, Bartolomé de, 10, 81, 252–53n9
La Sére, Emile (president, Louisiana Tehuantepec Railroad Company), 115, 131–34, 154, 189, 235
Le Vasseur, André Nicolas, 6, 54
López, Narciso, 44
Louisiana Tehuantepec Company, 20–21, 109, 113, 122–23, 130, 133, 138–51, 153, 172, 180, 186, 188, 189, 227, 235–38. *See also* Hargous, Peter and Eugene (founders of Hargous Brothers); Hargous, John (son of Louis); La Sére, Emile (president, Louisiana Tehuantepec Railroad Company); Murphy, John McLeod

Mace, Carroll Edward, 15–16, 18, 19, 241n17, 242n29, 243n31, 243n44
Marroquín, Francisco (first bishop of Guatemala), 58

General Index

Mathé, Joaquim, 40
Maudslay, Alfred, 4, 27–28
Maudslay, Anne, 4
Maury, Alfred 7, 29, 240n14, 241n15, 246n2, 249n34
McLane, Robert, 123–34, 137–38, 261n8
Meléndez, José Gregorio, 199–200
Mellinet, Alexandre (French Interim Consul in Guatemala), 55, 56, 97, 98, 99
Mérimée, Prosper, 6, 7, 9
Miramón y Tarelo, Miguel Gregorio de la Luz Atenógenes, 115, 123, 132, 176, 176, 179n, 186, 201, 207
Montezuma II, 13, 45, 67, 94, 117, 194, 198, 265n66
Morazán, Francisco, 61, 62, 84
Moro, Cayetano, 114
Murphy, John McLeod, 115–16, 123–24, 127–29, 131, 133, 135, 137, 138, 145, 147, 148–49, 151–52, 156–58, 160, 162–68, 170–72, 175, 179–81, 211–12, 231, 234–36, 238

Nagualism, 21, 210–27, 232, 237, 263n53
Nahuatl, 6, 45–47, 119n
Napoleon III (emperor of France), 5, 24, 25, 98, 99
North American Louisiana Tehuantepec Company. *See* Louisiana Tehuantepec Company

Orbegozo, Juan, 113
Ordás, Diego de, 118, 122
Ordoñez y Aguiar, Roman de (Canon of San Cristóbal de Chiapas, Mexico), 94
Ortiz, Tadeo, 113
Oxib Queh (king of K'iche'), 57

Padilla, José Mariano, 9, 10, 12, 15, 56–57, 62, 67–69
Pinart, Alphonse, 27, 245n84, 246n3
Pinopiaa, 184
Prescott, William, 5

Quatrefages, Jean-Louis Armand de, 25

Rabinal Achi, 3, 9, 10, 12, 13–19, 24, 79n, 85n, 93–108
Ravensberg, Charles Étienne de (Brasseur pseudonym). *See* Brasseur de Bourbourg, Charles Étienne
Recchi, Nardo Antonio, 46

Sahagún, Bernardino de, 21–23, 216
Scherzer, Karl Ritter, 11
Sidell, William Henry, 133, 153, 180, 189, 236
Sis, Bartolo, 15–19, 94–96, 108
Squier, Ephraim George, 8, 10, 12, 15–16, 31, 41–42, 241–42n23, 249–51n34

General Index

Stephens, John Lloyd, 4, 55n, 184

Tedlock, Dennis, 17, 18, 19, 85n, 243n31, 243nn38–41, 243nn52–53, 244n58, 253n9, 255n23, 255n28
Torquemada, Juan de, 45, 216, 248n25
Trastour, Pierre E., 112

Vanderbilt, Cornelius, 7
Vernet, Émile-Jean Horace, 42

Walker, William, 7, 88n, 146, 167, 169, 247n16

Ximénez, Francisco, 9–11, 62, 241–42n23, 257n41, 258n47. *See also* Brasseur de Bourbourg, Charles Étienne: *Popol Vuh*

GEOGRAPHICAL INDEX

This geographical index is divided into four sections: Guatemala, Mexico, Nicaragua, and San Salvador. Entries are for place names mentioned by Brasseur in his writings about his travels in Mexico and Central America from 1854 to 1859. Page numbers in italic *type refer to places found on maps in this volume.*

GUATEMALA

Agua Volcano, 57, 58, 60, 75
Antigua Guatemala (also Hunahpú), 58–59, 68, 218

Cakyug (ancient city), *53*, 80, 81, 82, 101, 106, 255n23
Carchag (ancient city), 101, 104
Chinauta, *53*, 69, 71
Chinauta River (aka Río de las Vacas), *53*, 69, 71
Chirrum, 80
Chirrum River, 84
Chi Tikiram, "Pitted and Planted," 80, 98
Chol, *53*, 76–77
Ciudad de Santiago de los Caballeros de Guatemala (aka Cuidad Vieja), 58
Coaxiniquilapa, 51

El Rodeo, 76

Fuego (volcano), 60, 75

Guatemala City, 8, 9, 10, 20, 23, 42, 46, 51, *53*, 54–63, 78, 86, 87, 97, 98, 99, 108, 241–42n23

Hunahpú. *See* Agua Volcano

Los Órganos, 68

Mixco, 59
Mopán River, 77

Motagua, Río Grande de, 53, 72–75

Nimpokom (ancient city), 80, 90n

Pacaya (volcano), 60
Petén Itzá, Lake, 77

Q'umarkaj. *See* Utatlán (ancient city) (also Q'umarkaj)

Rabinal, 9–19, 23, 53, 63–65, 68–69, 77, 79–108, 141n
Retalhuleu, 105

Salamá, 53, 63, 88
San Antonio, 70
San Juan Sacatepéquez, 19, 89

Tikiram (mountain range), 80, 98

Utatlán (ancient city) (also Q'umarkaj), 14, 57, 98, 254n13

Vacas, Río de las. *See* Chinauta River (aka Río de las Vacas)

Geographical Index

MEXICO

Abasolo-titlán, 147
Acapulco, 6, 119, 186, 211
Acayucan, *111*, 125, 128, 130, 135, 136, 140, 263n48
Almoloya Mountain, *111*, 171, 182, 185
Almoloya River, 143, 190
Amate Creek, 158
Apotzongo (branch of Coatzacoalcos River), 144
Atravesado Mountain, *111*, 187, 190

Bacalar, 219
Banderilla Mountain, 171, 182
Barrio de la Soledad (also Barrio), *111*, 153, 154, 156, 165, 170–75, 179–81, 186–87, 211
Boca del Monte. *See* San Gabriel Boca del Monte (also Boca del Monte)

Campeche, 141
Chalchijapa River, *111*, 143, 148
Chichihua River, 143
Chimalapa *See* Santa María Chimalapa (also Chimalapa)
Chinameca, 128, 135, 136, 139
Chivela, *111*, 143, 154, 156, 180, 183, 186, 187–90, 193, 225, 234, 264n58
Coachapa River, *111*, 144
Coahuapa River, *111*, 144
Coatzacoalcos River, 109n, 110, *111*, 113–22, 138–40, 143–48, 150, 161, 162, 173, 174, 179
Cosoleacaque, 128, 135, 139

Dani-Guivedchi Mountain, *111*, 205, 238
Dani-Lieza Mountain, *111*, 206, 208, 229

Encantada Mountain, *111*, 139
Espíritu-Santo, 118, 122, 140

Fabrica, 119

Gineta Pass, 188, 259–60n1
Guacamaya Mountain, *111*, 143, 170, 190, 225–27
Guadalcázar. *See* Tehuantepec (city) (also Guadalcázar)
Guichicovi. *See* San Juan Guichicovi
Guichilona (ancient city), *111*, 173, 226
Guiengola Mountain (and site of ancient fortress), 191, 206–7, 211–15, 221, 223, 224, 231, 234, 237
Guie-vixia Mountain, *111*, 169, 173
Guie-xila Mountain, *111*, 169–73, 183

Geographical Index · Mexico

Guivedchi Mountain (also Dani-Guivedchi Mountain), *111*, 205, 207, 208, 223, 225, 238

Hidalgotitlán (also Los Almagres), *111*, 144
Huatulco, 133, 211–12

Iztáltepec, *111*, 192, 200

Jaltepec River, *111*, 114, 139, 142, 150, 158
Juchitán, *111*, 179n, 180, 185, 199–203, 234, 237–38
Jumuapá River, *111*, 161, 162

La Barrilla, *111*, 139
La Ventosa, 114, 115, 138, 143, 147, 153, 156, 186, 194, 236
Los Almagres. *See* Hidalgotitlán (also Los Almagres)

Macuilapa Mountain, 173, 187, 190
Malatengo River, 143, 165–67, 169, 171, 181, 190
Mal Paso, 147, 161
Masahua Mountain, *111*, 143, 170
Mexico City, 6, 23, 47, 52, 54, 110, 114, 115, 118, 123, 134, 186, 194, 197–98, 214, 237, 254n41, 259–60n1
Mictlan. *See* Mitla (also Mictlan)
Minatitlán, 110, *111*, 114, 115, 119, 122–40, 144, 155, 156, 164, 167, 186, 189, 235–37
Mistan (branch of Coatzacoalcos River), *111*, 144
Mitla (also Mictlan), 195, 218
Mogañe River, *111*, 165
Monopostiac Island, *111*, 206

Nejapa, 198
Niza-Conejo, 171

Ocosingo, 219, 259–60n1

Pachiñe River, 166, 169
Palenque (ancient city), 23, 24, 47, 98, 219, 259–60n1
Paso Nuevo, *111*, 122, 139
Paso Puerta, *111*, 161–62
Pechugui (ancient city), 118, 122
Pelón Mountain, *111*, 116, 139
Petapa. *See* Santa María de Petapa

Rayudeja Mountain, 210, 215, 224, 226

San Cristóbal Ishuatlán, 139
San Gabriel Boca del Monte (also Boca del Monte), *111*, 147, 157–58, 161, 165
San Gerónimo, *111*, 200, 238
San Juan de Ulúa, 113, 176
San Juan Guichicovi, *111*, 142, 144, 147, 161, 162, 164, 166, 170, 173, 174, 175, 185, 191
San Martín Mountain, 116, 117n, 139
Santa María Chimalapa (also Chimalapa), 142, 147, 150, 159, 183
Santa María de Petapa (also Petapa), *111*, 154, 169–73, 181, 183, 185, 187
Santiago Moloacán, 139
Santo Domingo, 172, 181; caves, 181–86
Sarabia River, *111*, 147, 161–62, 165
Soconusco, 46, 107, 218
Suchil, *111*, 114–16, 124, 137, 147–48, 150–57, 159–61, 164, 167, 238

Tacamichapa (island), 138, 144–46
Tehuantepec (city) (also Guadalcázar), 20, 21, 23, *111*, 191–211, 227–38
Tehuantepec (isthmus), 7, 21, 24, 109–238, *111*
Texistepec, 140
Tonalá, 194
Tortuguero Creek, *111*, 161
Tuxtla, 139, 150, 259–60n1

Uspanapa River, *111*, 122, 190, 262n17
Uxmal (ancient city), 23, 185, 260n1, 264n54

Vera Cruz, 20, 54

Xaltepec, 174
Xochiapa Mountain, 143, 169
Xochiapa Plain, 170, 174

Yopaa. *See* Mitla (also Mictlan)

Zanatepec, 173, 259–60n1
Zempoaltepec Mountain, 173, 174

Geographical Index

NICARAGUA

Axuzco (volcano) (also Cerro Asososca), *30*, 42

Castillo Viejo, 33–34, 36–37
Castillo Viejo Rapids, *30*, 33
Cerro Asososca. *See* Axuzco (volcano) (also Cerro Asososca)
Chinandega, 40, 44

El Realejo, 43, 44
El Viejo (volcano) (also Volcán San Cristóbal), *30*, 42

Granada, *30*, 32–35, 38, 40–41, 42, 44, 88n
Greytown. *See* San Juan de Nicaragua (also Greytown)

Lake Nicaragua, 7, *30–31*, 32, 34–35, 38, 41–42
Las Pilas (volcano), *30*, 42
La Virgen. *See* Virgin Bay (also La Virgen)
León, *30*, 33, 40, 42–45, 62
Los Valos Rapids, *30*, 33

Machuca Rapids, *30*, 33
Madeira Volcano, *30*, 35
Maderas Volcano. *See* Madeira Volcano
Managua (city), 7, *30*, 42
Managua (lake), *30*, 42, 43
Masaya (city), 7, *30*, 40, 41, 42
Masaya (volcano), *30*, 41, 42
Mombacho (volcano). *See* Momobacho (volcano)
Momobacho (volcano), *30*, 41
Momotombo Island, 42–43

Nandaime, 40
Nicaragua (city). *See* Rivas (also Nicaragua)
Nicaragua Lake, 7, *30*, 32, 34, 38, 40–42
Nindirí, *30*, 41–42

Ometepe (volcano). *See* Ometepec (volcano) (also Ometepe)
Ometepec (volcano) (also Ometepe), *30*, 35
Orota (volcano) (also Volcán Rota), *30*, 42

Panaloya River, *30*, 42
Punta Arenas, 29

Rivas (also Nicaragua), *30*, 35, 39–40

San Juan, River 7, *30–31*, 32–34, 36
San Juan del Sur, 34, 36, 37
San Juan de Nicaragua (also Greytown), 7, 29, 32, 34, 36
Santa Clara (volcano). *See* El Viejo (volcano) (also Volcán San Cristóbal)
Serapiquí River, *31*, 32
Subtiaba, 45

Telica (volcano), *30*, 42
Toro Rapids, *30*, 34

Virgin Bay (also La Virgen), *30*, 35–38
Volcán Rota. *See* Orota (volcano) (also Volcán Rota)
Volcán San Cristóbal. *See* El Viejo (volcano) (also Volcán San Cristóbal)

Geographical Index

STATE OF SAN SALVADOR

La Union, 55

Santa Ana la Grande, 51
Sonsonate, 51, 55n